RAGE

RAGE

Gilbert Moore

With a new Introduction and
Afterword by
Ekwueme Michael Thelwell

Carroll & Graf Publishers, Inc.
New York

Grateful acknowledgment is made for permission to reprint the following:

From *Eldridge Cleaver: Post-Prison Writings and Speeches,* edited by Robert Scheer. Copyright © 1967, 1968, 1969 by Eldridge Cleaver. Reprinted by permission of Random House, Inc.

Lines from "Black Panther," on page 256, and "Warning," on page 267, from *The Panther and the Lash* by Langston Hughes. Copyright © 1967 by Arna Bontemps and George Houston Bass. Reprinted by permission of Alfred A. Knopf, Inc.

Published by arrangement with the author.

Originally published as *A Special Rage* in 1971 by Harper & Row, Publishers.

First Carroll & Graf edition 1993

Carroll & Graf Publishers, Inc.
260 Fifth Avenue
New York, NY 10001

Library of Congress Cataloging-in-Publication Data

Moore, Gilbert (Gilbert Stuart)
    [Special rage]
    Rage / Gilbert Moore; with a new introduction and afterword by
  Michael Thelwell.—1st Carroll & Graf ed.
    p.   cm.
    Originally published: A special rage. [1st ed.]. New York :
  Harper & Row, [1971].
    Includes index.
    ISBN 0-88184-973-1 : $10.95
    1. Newton, Huey P.—Trials, litigation, etc.   2. Trials (Murder)—
  California—Oakland.   3. Police murders—California—Oakland.
  4. Black Panther Party.   I. Title.
  KF224.N4M65   1993
  345.794'02523—dc20
  [347.94052523]   93-18034
                                                        CIP

Manufactured in the United States of America

For Marjorie
and my mother and father

To create today is to create dangerously. Any publication is an act, and that act exposes one to the passions of an age that forgives nothing, hence the question is not to find out if this is or is not prejudicial to art. The question, for all those who cannot live without art and what it signifies, is merely to find out how, among the police forces of so many ideologies, the strange liberty of creation is possible.

—ALBERT CAMUS

Some people have read a few Marxist books and think themselves quite learned, but what they have read has not penetrated, has not struck root in their minds, so that they do not know how to use it and their class feelings remain as of old. Others are very conceited and having learned some book phrases think themselves terrific and are very cocky; but whenever a storm blows up, they take a stand very different from that of the workers. . . .

—MAO TSE-TUNG

All we want is a cool, clear, fresh drink of water. But we can't get a cool, clear fresh drink of water 'cause there's a hog in the stream, so we're gonna have to get the hog out the stream, or die trying.

—BOBBY SEALE

Introduction

"TO DIE FOR THE PEOPLE?"
by Ekwueme Michael Thelwell

■────────────────────────────────────

In 1972, the *Los Angeles Times* called Gilbert Moore's account of the 1968 political high drama that was the trial of Huey P. Newton in for the alleged murder of an Oakland policeman "a classic document in the literature of the black-white experience in the 20th century."

Read today, the immediacy and perceptiveness of Moore's report speaks across the years with an alarming contemporary relevance to the deteriorating social conditions in our large cities. Indeed, there is a dismaying, timeless exactness in Moore's reportage of the extent to which the trial, where "conditioned by history, both sides blinded by myth and images, moved by rage and fear . . . each in their own blind way incapable of seeing each other as human beings . . . was a tragedy in the making." That applies as much to the fatal meeting between Newton and the cops as to the confrontation at the trial, between the police and their partisans and the Panthers and theirs.

Unfortunately, in places like South Central L.A. or

Bensonhurst, Brooklyn, that description applies today not only to organized political entities but to individuals, to neighborhoods, to entire communities of American citizens, which is but another reason for this book's continuing and increased importance.

Writing in 1969, Moore is able to preserve for us, with a graphic immediacy and intelligence, the political ambiance of the trial and its times. And, as a *New York Times* reviewer observed in 1972, his final chapter was "the most eloquent and sensitive analysis of the Panther phenomenon I have yet read." Even so, the passage of twenty-five years affords us an added perspective, which can only complement the particularity of Moore's account while enhancing our appreciation of the book's achievement, and the continued presence and increased gravity of the issues he investigates. It is this perspective of historical hindsight which we have tried to provide.

Late June 1968 . . . New York

When, the editors of *Life* magazine assigned a writer to a story either "on Eldridge Cleaver, the Panthers in general, or on Oakland: a tinderbox about to explode" (because of the highly politicized and publicized trial of a black man accused of killing a white policeman) all three—the decision, the subject, and the reporter—were equal reflections or products of the times.

Gilbert Moore, the reporter, was an ambitious, sharply intelligent and gifted young black man who had been hired by Time/Life as a research trainee in 1966, at approximately the same time, a continent away and worlds apart, that two part-time employees in an Oakland antipoverty program were launching the Black Panther Party for Self-Defense.

Both—the career and the Party—in their quite different

ways consequences of the Civil Rights Movement, had in the interim prospered, though in very different ways. By mid-1968, Moore had, by dint of industry and talent, worked his way from the anonymity of the research library into the high visibility, relatively speaking, of *Life*'s editorial staff, where he would be the second of only two black men. And, during that time, the Party had done more than enough to thrust itself vigorously into the attention of Moore's employers.

The other black pioneer at *Life*—the novelist Richard Hall— would himself soon depart to write an excellent novel set during the Civil Rights struggle in Mississippi, while the Panther assignment would be Moore's last, ending a promising career at Time/Life and result in the book you are holding.

The similar fates of *Life*'s two black pioneers reflected yet another aspect of those changing times: the poignant division of loyalties experienced by the best of that black generation torn between the illusion of a suddenly available upward mobility within the white corporate establishment and the obligation to the struggle of the kinfolk outside, in the streets, which had created the openings through which they had slipped. This is obviously a tension by which the next generation would remain blissfully untouched. Witness the Hill-Thomas hearings.

Early on, Moore did not seem consumed by this particular ambivalence, either. Indeed, he had sought the job precisely because he craved association with an organization that was "big and powerful." And, once on the editorial staff, "if you were unaccustomed to luxury as I was, you became giddy in the whirlpool of cocktail parties, first class air travel, and expensive hotels." He "enjoyed the spectacle of power and influence at work," of being able to announce himself as Gil Moore "from *Life* magazine," and seeing previously closed doors magically open. (On this assignment, a dawning realization that "neither Huey, Bobby Seale, nor Eldridge Cleaver [the Panther leadership] essentially gave a rat's ass whether *Life* magazine did a story or not" may or may not have somewhat deflated that professional hubris.)

In any event, the assignment was accepted, albeit with some misgivings on Moore's part. While he welcomed assignments to racially sensitive stories, he was as a "first" black, vigilant against the notion that *only* black reporters could cover those issues fairly and absolutely hostile to its illogical extension: that they could cover *only* that subject. But in this instance, his misgivings were of a different order. Of the Black Panthers, he like most Americans at that time, had only a meager awareness "a very fleeting impression of a bizarre bunch of California niggers talking bad and occasionally shooting someone. I was not anxious to get my head blown off."

He worried also that the Panthers would prove "a California version" of Chicago's notorious Blackstone Rangers, a large federation of youthful hustler/criminals about which, earlier on, he had found it impossible to do a story suitable for *Life*. With the Panthers he feared that "I would not be able to communicate with them" or worse, though this seemed hardly probable, "that we would communicate only too well."

One fascinating aspect of Moore's account is precisely the effect of this growing communication—often subliminal—between the respectable, well-adjusted young professional and the pull of revolutionary black defiance presented by the Panther's battle-hardened cadres, "in their own way forcing him to confront his blackness," as the *Los Angeles Times* reported. "It is precisely this tension between his making it, and the others who did not, or more accurately, made it another way, that gives the book its excitement and insights."

October 1966 . . . Oakland

That in 1968 the subject even arose in *Life's* editorial councils was evidence of the spectacular "progress" of the Party from rather modest and improbable beginnings in 1966.

By any rationally objective criteria, the infant should have been stillborn. Why should this one, the brainchild of a couple of obscure young black men—occasional students and part-time organizers in an antipoverty program—have had any greater a life expectancy than the countless other "revolutionary" initiatives of the time? How was it different from the other formulations for struggle spawned in the imaginations of disinherited black youth everywhere, in equal parts of desperation, idealism, bravery and fantasy?

The founders—twenty-five-year-old Huey Pierce Newton and Bobby George Seale, five years his senior—were not atypical. They were first generation urban, their parents having, in the early fifties, emigrated out of the Jim Crow South to the Oakland ghetto in search of California's egalitarian promise. Neither family was what has since come to be known as "underclass." No welfare "addicts" here, but people representative of "emigrant energy" and hope. Hard-working enterprising, respectable, traditional southern folk, the families brought with them their oral traditions and southern values of family, community, and church as they sought out a fairer chance for their children in California's promised land.

Huey's father, for example, was archetypal. A man of physical courage and moral strength, he was a Christian minister who supported his family working for the City of Oakland. He is remembered in the family as a stern disciplinarian and for his "heroic" and constant resistance to the day-to-day racism in his native Louisiana. Evidence of his political consciousness can be seen in the naming of his last child and seventh son after the

populist governor, the legendary Huey P. Long, who was remembered in the lore of black Louisiana as "the onliest cracker
politician ever to look out for pore folk an' give the colored a
fair shake."

Their parents' southern heritage is seen by David Hilliard,
Panther Chief of Staff and Huey's childhood friend, as having a
real effect on the party their children created: "When I think of
the influences that inspired the spirit and work of the Party
. . . this culture figures large. Many of the most important
members—John and Bobby Seale, Geronimo Pratt, Bobby
Rush, Fred Hampton—were imbued with the spiritual and
moral values of their parents. The hard work of the Party; our
dignity as independent people; the communal ideal and practice . . . all stem from that civilization of which my mother
and father were so representative."

This traditional southern element, though largely overlooked, is indisputably present in the Panthers. It is overlooked
because this high-minded rural community orientation con-
tended in uneasy tension with another incompatible current:
the *in-yo-face, up-against-the-wall-motherfuckah,* quasi-crimi-
nality and macho violence of the urban street-gang culture.
This is merely the first—and not necessarily even the most
fundamental—of the unresolved contradictions warring in the
personalities of the founders (especially Huey) and in the organization they created.

Yet another of the abounding ironies: had these two striving,
upwardly mobile southern families not "escaped north to freedom," the energetic, self-respecting parents and children almost certainly would have been very early and present in the
kinder, gentler more "acceptable" movement inspired by the
precepts of the black church and led by Dr. King. The fate of
their sons—and the nation's—might then have been very different.

But by October 1966, the time of the Party's formation, that movement, having accomplished all it could in the South was a spent force, effectively over. Dr. King had already deployed his nonviolent, direct-action strategies into a northern urban situation, and Chicago's oppressive racial conditions and the Daly machine had brutally and finally exposed its severe limitations. SNCC's young militants, recognizing a more fundamental limitation in that posture, had themselves turned from integration to a variously defined "black power," saying in effect that blacks, rather than continuing to seek to "escape" the ghetto and by implication black culture, should instead seek to transform the one and to celebrate the other.

Malcolm X, himself a living metaphor of personal transformation, had preached a peoples' self-redemption, inspired a militant racial pride, self-respect and the goal of self-determination . . . and been murdered. Behind penitentiary walls, black prisoners—then as now, some 50 percent of the nation's inmate population—inspired by Malcolm's prison transfiguration, had begun a prisoner rights movement.

Outside, a series of urban insurrections—the media's "riots" —had given northern black youth an entirely different political baptism from that of their southern cousins. Many of these urban eruptions had been community reaction to police misconduct. In 1964, in Harlem, an off-duty lieutenant shoots a fifteen year old youth; in 1965, the brutal arrest of a young man for speeding (sound familiar?) triggers the Watts riot in Los Angeles; and in 1966, across the bay in San Francisco, another fifteen-year-old black is shot in the back and killed, causing another insurrection. (In Detroit, six months later, two of the Panthers' major issues would clang together in ironic dissonance to produce the most lethal and destructive of the urban conflagrations. It happened after the cops raided a "blind Pig" where an after-hours party celebrating the safe return of two young black men from the Vietnamese jungles had been in progress.)

Add to this explosive equation the fact that the baby boomers, a generation of relatively affluent white youth—the putative beneficiaries of the system—conditioned by nightly television images of anti-civil rights violence and Southeast Asian firefights, are now moving into revolt against the war. Perhaps because of the American class dynamic which ensured that the brunt of the killing and dying in Vietnam would be borne by the sons of the nation's poor, disproportionately Black, Hispanic and Native American, these disaffiliated middle class kids would become the Panthers most vociferous cheerleaders.

By that October evening in the Oakland Community Center when the founders sat down to formulate the Party's platform —Huey rapping in a veritable ecstasy of political free association with Bobby furiously taking notes—every single one of these disparate elements and issues would find expression, however inchoate.*

Bobby's rough notes were taken to an older Newton brother, Melvin, an instructor in sociology at Merrit College, for literary shaping, and the document that emerged was the Ten Point Manifesto of the Black Panther Party for Self-Defense. Modeled after the Nation of Islam's credo "What We Believe," which appeared weekly in their newspaper *Mohammed Speaks*, the Panther Ten Point Program was, in its final form, a remarkable political document.

It was, depending on one's perspective, either very naive, "an ill-digested mishmash of half-baked political ideas" or a monument to Huey's synthesizing and eclectic genius, a radical

---

* For the day-to-day chronology of the party, I have relied on the excellent doctoral dissertation of Kit Kim Holder (University of Massachusetts, 1990), who had become at age thirteen the youngest official member of the Black Panther Party.

expression of grass roots grievance addressing explicitly every area of community exploitation: the courts, police, prisons, the war, education, housing, and jobs.

The Ten Points: What We Want, What We Believe*

1. We want freedom. We want power to determine the destiny of our Black Community . . .
2. We want full employment for our people . . .
3. We want an end to the robbery by the capitalists of our Black Community . . .
4. We want decent housing, fit for shelter of human beings . . .
5. We want education for our people that exposes the true nature of this decadent American society. We want education that teaches us our true history and our role in present-day society . . .
6. We want all Black men to be exempt from military service . . .
7. We want an immediate end to POLICE BRUTALITY and MURDER of Black people . . .
8. We want freedom for all Black men held in federal, state, county, and city prisons and jails . . .
9. We want all Black people when brought to trial to be tried in court by a jury of their peer group or people from their Black communities, as defined by the Constitution of the United States . . .
10. We want land, bread, housing, education, clothing, justice and peace. And as our major political objective, a United Nations-supervised plebiscite to be held throughout the Black colony in which only Black colonial subjects will be allowed to participate, for the purpose of determining the will of Black people as to their national destiny . . .

* See Appendix for complete text.

It is with their Tenth Point that an often overlooked quality of youthful earnestness emerges. First we get nine rigidly non-negotiable demands united only by an underlying logic of revolutionary nationalist certitude. Then suddenly, almost as an afterthought: "But, just in case we could be mistaken—unlikely as that is—maybe we'll just let the people vote on it." And what is to be so democratically determined? Nothing less than the national black community's future relationship to the white racist polity called America. The notion of United Nations supervision of the plebiscite coming, of course, from the program of Malcolm's Organization of Afro-American Unity.

But it was in the commentaries, the explanatory paragraph or two that amplified each demand that the exuberantly eclectic variety of the sources became clear.

The language and ideas of these commentaries borrowed freely across centuries and cultures. They ranged from: classic liberalism (full employment with the federal government as the employer of last resort); hardline Marxism (an end to the exploitation of the community by capitalist businessmen from whom the means of production should be wrested); an international black consciousness (we should not fight and kill other people of color in the world to defend a racist government . . .); a vague gentle Fabian socialism (the land and housing to be organized into cooperatives . . . to the evocations of documents of classic Americanism: the Fourteenth Amendment to the Constitution and culminating appropriately enough on the Tenth Point with the Declaration of Independence: *"When in the course of human events . . ."*

That its various elements were intellectually incompatible (forget political anathema to American power) would have mattered little were the organization merely yet another "study group" of graduate school intellectuals aspiring to be radicals. In that case the document would long since have disappeared without trace or effect, and I should hardly be writing this, nor you reading it.

But its intellectual provenance is important precisely because it wasn't a study group but an activist grass roots organization of ghetto youth such as this nation had never seen. And the Ten Points became their basic text for political education, the central item of political faith to be published, studied, and hotly debated in circles both friendly and hostile in this country and around the world. Because serious political actions would be based on its prescriptions, its intellectual inconsistencies would come back to haunt them in practice, and bear some further examination here.

The rhetoric (and ultimately the practice) would juxtapose elements of Elijah Mohammed and Malcolm with Marx and Jefferson, and disastrously conflate Chairman Mao's maxim about power and the barrels of guns** with a *literal* acceptance of Franz Fanon's supremely abstract theoretical speculations on the liberating psychological effect on the wretched of the earth from revolutionary violence.

At the heart of this analytical thrust was one central metaphor: the black community as a territory under colonial occupation. A startling image, but neither so fanciful or so new, this insight had been preached in certain circles of radical thought for some time. Six years earlier I had first encountered the idea from that exemplar of intellectually respectable radicalism, Bayard Rustin, who used it to describe Harlem.

"Why, just look," he explained: "The laws governing it are imposed from outside; the armed forces which enforce them come from outside its borders; the people making the laws, forget live there, never even visit; the land and housing is largely owned by absentees and the economy is controlled in

** "All power grows out of the barrel of a gun."
—Mao Tse-Tung, The Great Helmsman

the interest of people who would never think of living there: a classic colonial situation."

With Rustin this was a clever intellectual formulation, a mere debater's flourish, but for the Panthers it became literal truth, with real implications for action. In this, their models and inspiration were Third World anticolonial struggles, primarily the Cuban, Chinese, Algerian and most especially the National Front for the Liberation of Vietnam—the Viet Cong. In this latter case, the argument by analogy proceeded with a grim literalness, a pure logic that couldn't be bothered by details of history, culture or geography, to predictable results:

Since the Vietnamese people and the Afro-American community were equally victims of colonial occupation, then their struggle (and their enemy) were the same. Therefore, the same spirit of courage and sacrifice and the same techniques of guerrilla warfare that seemed to work for the Viet Cong, should apply with equal success far in the belly of the beast. Consequently what the Panthers had to do was . . .

But that takes us beyond the story at this point. First, they had to build the party. The initial step was to reproduce for community consumption one thousand copies of the spanking-new manifesto, presumably using the resources of President Johnson's war on poverty. Then the manifesto had to be translated into action, and those activities had to be funded. This initial problem was solved by old-fashioned, all-American entrepreneurship, creative revolutionary merchandising. In this case the product was particularly appropriate: copies of the Red Book, *Quotations of Chairman Mao,* and Fanon's widely misread psychological treatise, *The Wretched of the Earth,* were procured for sale to white radical students across the bay at Berkeley, the profits to be invested in literature and guns. It is possible to detect in this initial enterprise an early pattern that the Panthers would never be able to transcend fully—the purveying of revolutionary inspiration to more affluent whites for a fair profit, a reasonable mark-up.

By November, the two founders, with their first recruit, fifteen-year-old Li'l Bobby Hutton, were ready to undertake the Party's first public political activity. They elected to address dramatically point #7, "an immediate end to police brutality and the murder of black people."

Thus, police attempting arrests in the Oakland community suddenly found themselves under close and critical observation by a trio of young black men, one of whom carried and quoted from a legal manual and all of whom casually and openly displayed firearms.

"What the fuck? Just who the hell you think . . . ?"

"Citizens, Officer. Citizens observing police behavior as we have a legal right to do. The legal code of the State of California states. . . ."

"You better put those goddamn guns down."

"Are we under arrest?"

"Not yet, but . . ."

"Then we have the right to carry these weapons so long as they are openly displayed. The legal code states . . . So if you want our weapons you are gonna have to take them. Which you have no legal right to do."

"Listen, you better stand back. Move on now."

"Nobody move! As long as we maintain a reasonable distance we have a legal right to advise your prisoner. We are approximately twenty feet away. Brother, are you under arrest? Do you have a lawyer?"

Newton remembers.

"At first the patrols were a total success. Frightened and confused, the police did not know how to respond because they had never encountered this before . . . There were community alert patrols in other cities, but never before had guns been an integral part . . . with weapons in our hands we were no longer their subjects, but their equals . . ."

The operative words there, of course, were *"at first."* His last insight, "With weapons in our hands we were no longer subjects," was Mao Tse-Tung and Franz Fanon at their purest. It set another precedent that, try as they might, the Panthers would never successfully transcend in the public mind: the omnipresence of the gun.

And again, there is that grand, abstract literalness, this time in respect to the sanctity of law, for even the type of weapon they each used reflected this literal strict constructionism. Newton carried the now legendary pump-action shotgun because being on probation he could not *legally* carry a handgun. And Bobby Hutton's M3 Carbine? The same, being underaged he could not legally have a handgun, either. But Bobby Seale, having neither constraint, boasted a 45 automatic, worn, in full compliance with the law, in a shoulder harness *outside* his leather jacket, in full view.

As if this hair-splitting observance of the full letter of the law was likely to make any difference to cops who felt their territory being invaded, and at gunpoint even! "Only respect the law, my son, and the law shall be as a shield and armor unto thee?" It could fairly be said that initially these young revolutionaries displayed a greater respect for, and faith in, American law than do the law's true owners.

Now things begin to move very quickly.

By January 1967, the Party is able to open a storefront office in the heart of the ghetto in which political education classes are held. The texts: The Ten Points and Mao's Red Book. During the initial week the first converts are signed up. After studying, understanding, and memorizing the Ten Point Program and being introduced to Mao-thought, Mark Johnson, Sherman Forte, John Sloan, and Warren Tucker, reincarnate as

defenders of the community, qualified to bear arms and participate in community patrols. Under Party discipline they must
not use or carry drugs, commit crimes or take "as much as a
needle from the people" without payment.

The patrols and confrontations with the police worked won-
derfully well for recruitment.

As Newton remembered: "I did a lot of recruiting in bars
and pool halls . . . working twelve to sixteen hours a day . . .
passing out the Ten Point Program, explaining each point to all
who would listen . . . An interesting ramification, I tried to
transform many of the so-called criminal activities of the streets
into something political, although this had to be done gradually. Instead of trying to completely eliminate these activities at
first—numbers, hot goods, drugs, I tried to channel them into
significant community action. Many of the brothers who were
burglars still had to sell their loot to survive, but they began to
contribute weapon and materials to community defense.

By showing the people how to defend themselves, we provided a needed example of strength and dignity. . . . Since
we lived among them, they could see every day, that with us,
the people came first."

Now, in fairly rapid succession, three events would indelibly
inscribe the young organization's image in the local community
and, for better or worse, its identity in the perceptions of the
national media and within the ranks of the welter of radical
political formations of the times.

The leadership of the Oakland police had responded to the
patrols with a call for restraint from the ranks. This, too, they
reasoned, would pass. Besides, legislation was being prepared
in the California legislature that would render the patrols illegal. In the meantime, the troops were instructed to treat the
public, especially "minorities" with greater tact and respect.

For example, the use of terms like "nigger," "spick," "coon," and "spade" was to be avoided.

It is not possible to determine the extent to which the demeanor and diction of the Oakland police was sensitized, but clearly their behavior wasn't: that April, police buckshot riddles the body of young Denzil Dowell, whom they allege was trying to escape an attempted burglary. The Panthers—and many in the community—called it simply murder, a police lynching. George Dowell, the victim's brother, enlists in the Party and the Panthers seize on the issue, making it the centerpiece of their first "Community Newsletter," later to become the Black Panther newspaper. Enlistment by the community's youth picks up sharply and the attention of the national press is increased. This "serious" attention exposes a troubling dissonance in the Panther rhetoric and raises serious questions about their media strategy and judgment.

A *New York Times* magazine story of August 6, foreshadows this eerily. The reporter, Sol Stern, is quite naturally interested in *the gun* question. Newton explains that the guns were mostly symbolic and educational. "Ninety percent of the reason we carried guns in the first place," he answers, "was educational. To set an example . . . to establish that we had the right."

At the same time, he allows the journalist to accompany them to recruiting rallies—one at the Dowell family home—where he hears and reports Bobby Seale describe how a "couple of bloods could ambush cops on their coffee breaks. . . . They march up and they shoot him down—voom, voom—with a twelve-gauge shotgun . . . an example of 'righteous power,'" and Newton affirming that "every time you execute a white racist gestapo cop, you are defending yourselves."

Like Gilbert Moore and any number of journalists after him, Stern is unsure just how to take the rhetoric. He reports the following conversation in the Sunday Times: "Asked whether the talk at the rallies about killing cops is serious, Newton replies that it is very serious. Then he is asked, why stake everything, including Panthers' lives, on the killing of a few cops?

'It won't be just a couple of cops,' he says. 'When the time comes it will be part of a whole national coordinated effort.' Is he willing to kill a cop? Yes, he answers, and when the time comes he is willing to die. What does he think will happen to him?

'I am going to be killed,' he says with a smile on his face." The reporter thinks that in that moment, "he looked very young."

I can still clearly recall the cold tremor that passed through me when I first read that, seeing clearly in my imagination that section being red-lined and prominently displayed on a thousand notice boards in a thousand urban precinct houses around the nation.

This would be a recurring problem for the Panther leadership, giving a new 1960's media spin to Dr. Du Bois's famous dictum on divided consciousness. On the contradiction of black life in America at the turn of the century, the Doctor had written: "One ever feels his twoness—an American, a Negro; two souls, two thoughs, two unreconciled strivings; two warring ideals in one dark body, whose dogged strength alone keeps it from being torn asunder." With the Panther leadership, the 1960's version of this divided consciousness, "the unreconciled striving," would become and continue to be how to negotiate " 'the warring ideals' of black revolution and media celebrity in the same dark body."

Two events a few months earlier were almost certainly what had attracted the sudden attention from the national media. Soon to become major items in the Panther legend and mystique, these events had in common the style and flair that would become the group's signature: both were bold, media-compatible capers with elements of high drama, bravado and guerrilla theatre; the display of paramilitary discipline and guns, and an inevitable edge of danger and risk.

That February, the recently widowed Betty Shabazz, relict of the martyred Malcolm X, had made the Bay Area the venue for her first public appearance since the assassination. The sponsoring organizations—and most blacks—were justifiably apprehensive. No one knew at the time how far beyond the Muslim triggermen the web of complicity in the murder might extend (state, local, federal?), so the matter of Ms. Shabazz's security was a cause of serious concern.

Enter the Panthers, armed, with a flat-out guarantee of complete security. Period. And sho nuff, a phalanx of uniformed Panthers in tight formation, weapons at the port, materialized at the San Francisco airport. They marched past cops and airport security alike to greet and surround the sister at the gate. Later there is a second tense stand off with the police before the offices of *Ramparts* magazine.

In the long run this would prove the most consequential—one could say disastrous—single early action by the young organization. Because, far outweighing the short-term effect of the instant publicity, was the long-term consequences of an association with one Eldridge Leroy Cleaver, his employers at *Ramparts,* and through them, with the most impressionable and erratic elements of the white, essentially middle-class based "New Left."

The other spectacular media event was the May second "invasion under arms" of the California State House in Sacramento. The protest was called ostensibly to protest the passage of legislation limiting the right to transport and display arms, and to present the Party's executive mandate #1. This document denounced the pending legislation as genocidal, in effect being aimed at blacks. It called on "black people to arm themselves" to "rise up as one man" against "the escalating repression" of "the racist American government" or face "a trend that leads inevitably to our total destruction."

Not surprisingly after this, the Mulford Act outlawing the carrying of loaded firearms on the person or in vehicles passed overwhelmingly. Obedient to the law, the Party had "officially" suspended their police patrols in anticipation of the law's passage.

The ground being thus prepared, we can move ahead to October 26, 1967, approximately one year to the day after the Party's formation. Huey P. Newton and friends are out celebrating not the anniversary, but the *end* of his police probation. In the wee small hours of the morning, he and a companion are stopped by the police. The result: one officer is killed, the other wounded, and a gut-shot, seriously wounded Newton is charged with murder.

In the nine months between the shooting incident and the trial's opening in July of 1968, which had brought Moore across the country, much of significance had taken place within the Party. With Newton wounded and imprisoned and Seale for much of the time also in jail, the public representation of the organization had largely devolved to a parolee named Eldridge Cleaver, a party member of only four months' standing.

This instant political association which was to prove controversial, brief, and, at the same time, of great—some say disastrous—importance in defining the Party's political direction and ultimately its fate, was a most revealing one.

Paroled in December 1966, and invited to edit the second issue of the embryonic *Black Panther* in May 1967, Cleaver, having spent one-third of his life in the toils of the California penal system, had been back on the street a mere six months. Consequently he had absolutely no political history or experience in any accepted sense of that term. What he brought instead was a fleeting "literary" celebrity and some dubious political associations.

His parole had resulted from the publication of *Soul on Ice,* a best-selling collection of his prison writings and on the patronage and advocacy of a group of influential white literateurs who had convinced themselves that in Cleaver they had discovered an American Jean Genet, in black face.

A volatile, unstable personality, Cleaver was an admitted sexual predator (racist oppression, he wrote, had made him a rapist) and a career criminal in a way that the inexperienced Panther leadership was not. At least not yet. He had been paroled to a job as a staff writer of a born-again New Left journal called *Ramparts,* which would play a great role in the Panthers rapid ascendance.

With a past as improbable as that of its newest staffer, *Ramparts* had always been something of an intellectual anomaly. Beginning as a sedate vehicle of "progressive" Catholic opinion, the magazine had labored for years in well-earned obscurity, floundered, been refinanced by a posse of wealthy young "radicals," and been born again as the stridently ideological, hard-line "Maoist" voice of the New Left. Help us, Jesus! The magazine developed instant influence in those radical chic circles of the sentimental New Left that claimed to read. For *Ramparts'* affluent white radicals—and apparently for Cleaver —the *Ramparts*/Panther connection was a marriage made in revolutionary heaven, a consummation devoutly to be wished with each side supplying the others' lacks.

The Panthers got exposure, ideological legitimation on the white left and, best of all, access to the philanthropy of rich radicals. For the oppression-deprived *Ramparts* theoreticians, the Panthers were heaven-sent. They appeared as if on cue out of America's Third World, home-grown surrogates for the Viet

Cong. They seemed made to order for anointment as the vanguard party of the American revolution. And why not?

They had real grievance, raw courage, and great black style. An expression of ghetto youth culture in their leather jackets and berets—the political approximation of gang colors—with firearms visible or implied, and a well-developed sense of theater, the Panthers were the embodiment of white American revolutionary fantasy. These hip, black, virile, menacing urban guerrillas were instant gratification for all the vicarious and voyeuristic revolutionary impulses of the *Ramparts* editors and their readers.

With Huey off the scene, Cleaver and *Ramparts* undertook, almost certainly in good faith, the campaign for the projection of the Party and the freeing of Huey, to quite remarkable if unintended effect. The fevered excitement reported by Moore is largely a consequence of their success in this effort, as is the open-ended vagueness of Moore's instructions to do a story "either on Eldridge Cleaver, the Panthers or Oakland itself."

Whether or not the mercurial Mr. Cleaver, "El Rage" as he was admiringly christened by his supporters, was ever an agent of the government, has long been a subject of speculation in political circles. No evidence has ever emerged that he was. Indeed, quite the contrary: those FBI documents which I have seen reveal strategies to frame Newton, Hilliard, Carmichael, and numerous others with rumors and planted "evidence" to the effect that they were in government employ.* However, none of the voluminous documentation I have examined suggests that Cleaver should be so targeted, even though he would have been an obvious and vulnerable target. It should be pointed out, however, that massive though it be, the file I have

* For this and all subsequent information on government activities, I am indebted to the generosity of Professor C. E. "Bud" Schultz of Trinity College, Hartford, Connecticut, who graciously and spontaneously shared his files with me.

been able to see is nothing but the tip of the government's dirty tricks iceberg. And, by the time these attempts to discredit the leadership were being advanced, he may already have been in exile outside the country.

This should not suggest that Cleaver was exempt from all destabilizing operations. One agent seems to have been quite taken with Kathleen Cleaver. In his report of August 15, 1968, he observes that there appeared to be a "natural rivalry between Cleaver and Seale for leadership." In this Cleaver is aided and abetted by his dynamic, attractive wife Kathleen, who lacks patience with the more lethargic elements . . ." This agent finds that "the Cleavers are people of more education and a degree of class compared to the average Black Panther . . ." So far as operations currently being affected in this area, he had to report that there was none. So two weeks later he came up with a proposal that seems curiously wishful.

"Kathleen," he writes, "appears to have genuine feelings for Eldridge, and if it could be shown that he is intersted in another female (sic) a split might ensue."

There is, unfortunately, no record of the Director's response. Given his distaste for "black immorality," it would have been interesting to see his response to a suggestion to destabilize one of the few apparently intact black "radical" marriages.

So . . . was he or wasn't he? Clearly, in the absence of evidence to the contrary, Brother Cleaver deserves the benefit of the doubt. Thus, I'm quite prepared to believe that the brother was never actually on the government payroll. But that being said, I would also say that in simple justice and on the basis of his actions and their consequences, certain of the more unsavory federal agencies would appear to owe him some very long bread indeed. There may indeed be a case to be made retroactively, and like most of us after twelve years of Reaganomics, the brother is rumored to need the money.

In any event, by the time Mr. Moore arrived in Oakland, the entire Free Huey Campaign and the public political image of the Party bore the distinctive signature of Cleaver, *Ramparts* magazine, and the white New Left.

I
Ripples on the Lake

War hath no fury like a noncombatant.

—C. E. MONTAGUE

I HAVE DECIDED that my emotional involvement with that peculiar movement America has come to know as the Black Panther Party is a matter of more than casual significance. That this involvement should have ever come about is readily suggested by very little in our respective pasts.

The Panthers are American and black; I am American and black. That, for a start, is a bond of enormous proportions. But aside from considerations of nationality and race, there are no obvious links between me and them.

Give or take a few months, I am about the same age as Eldridge Cleaver, but there are very few experiences we share. I have seen the inside of a prison cell only in the process of interviewing someone. Although I have not the slightest doubt that there are any number of American law officers who are far more accurately described as pigs, there is nothing in my own experience that could reasonably lead me to call them that.

Eldridge Cleaver has been consumed by rage almost every hour of his life. I haven't lost my temper (so that you would notice) in three years.

And yet Eldridge Cleaver and I are not so emotionally distant from each other as you (and perhaps also he) might suppose.

It occurs to me lately that at no time in my life have I joined anything—no clubs, no fraternities, no gangs, no political parties. I did briefly belong to the Cub Scouts of America, but my association with them was forced upon me.

I have been driven to physical violence three times in my life. I was in grade school when it happened last. A classmate insulted me about my new haircut; I took offense and beat her up.

A million years ago, in 1942, six Moores moved from the one-room squalor of an East Harlem apartment to the five-room lesser squalor of a West Harlem apartment. One Hundred and Forty-sixth Street between Amsterdam Avenue and Broadway did not then qualify as a slum block. There were still white families there (indeed, I'm told we were the first black family to encroach upon the working-class comfort of 514 West 146th Street). Landlords had not yet begun to let their buildings slide into the full flower of decay that would come a decade or so later. "514" was a six-floor walkup. In time the Fitzgeralds, the O'Haras, the Anzalones moved out; in time the Jacksons, the Johnsons, the Browns moved in. In time 514's dumbwaiter developed defects that went unrepaired. Mice and an occasional rat took up residence. The platoon of roaches in our fourth-floor apartment gradually became a battalion.

But worry about who's moving out and who's moving in and what color they are, are adult concerns. And what to grownups is squalor, to children are playthings: dumbwaiters that won't work, toilets that won't flush and rats that refuse to die.

As far as my childhood sensibilities were concerned, it was a good spot to live. Nothing was more important to me then than the movies, and I was surrounded by movie houses. The Washington Theatre was less than two blocks away. The Dorset, the Lido and the RKO Hamilton were all less than half a block away. On Saturday afternoons at twelve o'clock sharp we would line up outside the Washington by the hundreds, to be admitted for six solid hours of escape. Price of admission in those ancient times? Fourteen cents. And then up on the screen came two main features, one or two short Westerns, two serials and half a dozen cartoons—Dana Andrews in *The Purple Heart,* Johnny Weissmuller as Tarzan, Sydney Greenstreet and Peter Lorre in *The Verdict,* Dracula, Bela Lugosi, Boris Karloff, Roy Rogers, Dale Evans, Gabby Hayes, Tyrone Power as Zorro, Lash LaRue, Hopalong Cassidy, the Dead End Kids, Abbott and Costello, Captain America, the Purple Monster, Bugs Bunny.

But all of that is fodder for the Late Show now. Television was then some remote dream. The only kid I knew whose folks owned one of these marvelous toys was an intense, skinny little guy by the name of Bernard Strumpf. Bernard lived around the corner on 147th Street, and every day after school I weaseled my way into the Strumpf household to watch the Yankees whip everybody in the American League. The elder Mr. Strumpf was an electronic technician and had built that fabulous gadget with his own hands. The set was crude, but it brought us within six inches of people like Joe DiMaggio, Charlie Keller and Yogi Berra, and that's all that mattered.

It seemed a grand neighborhood to me because so many important places were nearby. Woolworth's, a very important institution in my life with its ocean of potato chips and things for ten cents, was just down the street. Riverside Drive—a narrow strip of sanity in a town driven mad by concrete—was within running distance. On Riverside Drive you could play softball on living, breathing grass; you could climb trees and get sick on green crab apples; you could dig up worms and kiss ten-year-old girls in the bushes.

In between my house and Woolworth's there was school —Public School 186, stretching for a whole block to 145th Street. I remember the little containers of milk gone warm and the chocolate cookies. I remember kindergarten where they were always trying to get us to take naps. Broad daylight and those teachers wanted us to go to sleep! Miss Thornton would look at her watch, see that it was two o'clock and time for us kids to take naps. She would spread those great rolls of brown paper on the floor and down we all would go. No one ever went to sleep of course. Certainly, I never did. I spent a whole year in kindergarten, drinking warm milk, lying on the floor and looking up Miss Thornton's dress when she went by.

I remember some of the kids who were in the fifth grade with me: They had names like Herman Weingartner, Roger Darby, Albert Sablovsky, Marcella Parrot, Roberta Metzl, James Sato and Bernard Strumpf. I suppose now that Miss Banks—stern, priggish Miss Banks—presiding over the fifth grade, may have thought of me or Roger (who was also black) as being lesser mortals than say Herman, who was German, or Albert, who was Russian. If she did feel that way, she never mentioned it to Roger or me. Nor was it of any immediate concern to us.

Public School 186 was then what would now be called an "integrated" school. It seems to me now that it stopped being an "integrated" school about the same time that the slogan was born. I remember posters in those hallways speaking of "discrimination" and what a terrible thing it was. Teachers were always tossing the words "race, color and creed" around, but to us all these were abstractions. In a world cushioned by potato chips, crab apples and Lash LaRue, racism never got off the posters.

I got to be twelve years old and the world became broader (or narrower, depending on which way you look at it). If you graduated from P.S. 186, the districting rules required that you thereafter go to the infamous Edward Stitt Junior High School, unless of course your address changed in the interim or your parents falsified your address so that you could go to a safer school. I went to Stitt.

Stitt thought it was a school. It had a principal and teachers and classrooms and most of the things that schools have. But it really wasn't a school at all. It was a playground for a half-dozen gangs with swashbuckling names like the Sabers, the Royalistics, the Buccaneers. *They* ran the school. *They* decided what classes would be broken up in midstream. *They* decided whose ass was going to be kicked—and on what day and in which hallway. Mostly one got one's ass kicked over money. Before you could get to the school gate each morning a couple of Sabers might approach you and say, "Hey, boy—loan me a nickel," which is to say, "Turn your pockets inside out and turn over whatever you have on you." If you said you didn't have any money and they searched you and found that you were lying, you got your ass kicked. Those of us who stayed at Stitt long enough to become familiar with the daily routine did not wait to be asked for money when we saw the Sabers or the Royalistics approaching. As we saw them coming, we would simply hold our hands up in the air and say, "All you find."

There were kids going to Stitt, however, who could not

come to grips with this "nickel-lending" system. Mostly these latter were white boys. "Paddy boys" were constantly "getting their heads whipped" for saying something stupid and square like "My mother told me not to lend money to strangers." Quite often, of course, the paddy boys would get their asses kicked for no other reason than that they were paddy boys. That was thought plenty reason enough.

The *raison d'être* of the Sabers, however, was not fundamentally racial. Essentially, each gang was collective security against attack from another gang. Sometimes the attack came from a white gang, but more often than not black gangs went to war with each other.

The Buccaneers, the Sabers, the Royalistics had in them the same human elements that now constitute the Black Panthers. They were the urban black poor stripped down to their nerve endings. They were the people society remembered only when property rights were violated. In their total alienation they were America's tumor—gradually becoming malignant. Like the Panthers, they were armed, but their weapons were far less sophisticated.

The 1940's when the Buccaneers flourished in Harlem was not a period that could have produced a Black Panther Party. These times, after all, were pretelevision, pre-Korea, pre-Vietnam, prerevolutionary Cuba, pre-Black Power. The Black Panthers are intensely political. The Sabers, the Royalistics, had no politics. The Black Panthers think collectively. Each Saber had his own individual hustle. The Black Panthers think of themselves as intimately linked with struggles in Latin America and Asia and Africa. The Sabers', the Royalistics', the Buccaneers' "struggles" were confined to ten square blocks. Introduce a Royalistic to someone from Nigeria and he would laugh raucously at you and your "funny-talkin'" African friend. Call a Buccaneer "black" and he'd "smack the piss outa you." It was, indeed, too soon for the Black Panthers.

Political or no, these Harlem street gangs did not have very much to do with my existence. Sure, they regularly "borrowed" nickels from us in the Stitt school yard. Sure, they regularly broke up Chinese handball and stickball games, relieving us of bats and gloves and whatever else we happened to have on us at the time. And sure, they were the ones who periodically swooped down on our marble games as we played in the gutter or on manhole covers. They would yell "Cockscramble!" which meant that a marble raid was about to ensue. But to have any intimate connection with the Sabers one had to be on the street at night. I never was. It just wasn't allowed. Not that I wanted to argue the matter with my parents. Nothing the Sabers had to offer on the street could match the outpourings of a buxom Philco radio we had: "The Lux Radio Theatre," "The Lone Ranger," "The FBI in Peace and War," "The Shadow," "Ellery Queen," "Tracer of Lost Persons," "The Thin Man," "Boston Blackie."

Abruptly in April, 1948, the whole fabric of my life changed. My parents had always said that we might someday go to Jamaica, but I always doubted that so delicious a dream could come true. Yet on that not-to-be-believed day in spring six Moores got on a train and went to Miami, Florida. Two of them—my parents—made the return trip to New York; the rest of us boarded a plane and flew on to Paradise—my sister Carol, age nine, another sister Joyce, seven, my brother Keith, six, and big-brother me, twelve.

Jamaica! Land of wood and water! We went past the grand old Myrtle Bank Hotel, past the luxurious North Shore which Hugh Hefner and Conrad Hilton would soon desecrate with multimillion-dollar squalor, past tourists romping in the sand at Montego Bay, past Round Hill where in another decade John F. Kennedy would come to rest after a campaign.

We ended up in a tiny village called Maryland on the western side of the island. My mother had grown up there and we had come to live with her sister, who had a home and a prodigious family of her own. We four were welcomed grandly by Aunt Lil and by a hundred "cousins" we had never seen or heard of before. It was marvelous for us to be there; it was marvelous for them to have us among them.

We had, after all, just come from that distant land of plenty they thought America to be. We spoke in a strangely nasal though quaintly charming tone, they thought, and it was a joy to hear words flow from our mouths. There were many other curious things about our behavior.

We were inclined to be brazenly disrespectful of established authority, particularly at school. What right had a pupil to omit saying "sir" in addressing his teacher or indeed any adult? What right did I, at the age of twelve, have to wear long pants? Wasn't it strange that we had heard nothing of David and Bathsheba, of Joshua and Jericho, of the Miracle of the Loaves and Fishes?

The Maryland school was a tiny, wooden, zinc-covered building, maximum capacity 125. The headmaster, Mr. King, was very much like his predecessors and those who would come after him—a strict disciplinarian who could not abide lapses in mental arithmetic, English grammar and general deportment in the classroom.

Maryland was (and still is) what a creature of a technological society would call "primitive." There was no running water, hot or cold, no electricity, no sewer system. Drinking water came from tiny mountain springs and from the straightforward act of putting buckets and barrels out-doors when it rained.

We took our baths and women washed our clothes in rivers, of which Maryland has a plentiful supply. The bath-rooms were outhouses; the kitchens were little thatched huts a few yards away from the house in which some of the best meals I've eaten in my life were cooked in giant kettles over wood fires.

My aunt's husband was a man whom circumstances had forced to learn to do everything for himself. He was an elder and choirmaster at the local Presbyterian church. He was farmer, beekeeper, shoemaker and master carpenter. He built his own house, cut his son's hair, raised chickens, goats and pigs. And for many years he was a first-rate spin bowler for the Maryland Cricket Team.

Nothing was more impressive to our young sensibilities than the fact that this new place to live had so many fruits to devour. And they were all free for the picking. There were the familiar ones like oranges, grapefruits, tangerines, man-goes. But there were so many delicious others that we had never heard of: star apples, jackfruit, naseberries, soursop, sweetsop, guavas, rose apples. The list was endless.

Maryland and environs was a 100 percent black com-munity. To be sure, there were in Maryland, as elsewhere on the island, those with light skins, straight noses and hair, who were just tickled to be so endowed. There were those who were visibly part-Chinese, part-Indian, part-white who took every available opportunity to suggest that God in His mercy had seen fit to temper their blackness with a dash of whiteness. But in those years race as a corrosive preoccupa-tion, race as the albatross, did not exist. For that I would have to return to New York six years later.

In 1952 I left the splendid provincialism of Maryland to take up residence with another aunt in Kingston on the other side of the island. Here, as in Maryland, I discovered that the simple announcement that "I was born in the States" generated endless wonderment and admiration among my classmates—this despite the clear fact that whatever "American" life style I brought to the island with me, I now, four years later, no longer had.

There were, however, unpleasant stereotypes about America which forced me into the position of "defending my country." Young Jamaicans were under the distinct impression that all Americans, black, white or whatever, had bad penmanship, unnaturally large feet and an intellectual capacity much inferior to any produced under the exalted British system of education.

Excelsior, my high school in Kingston, took pride in being "progressive" in its approach to secondary education. It experimented with what were then new directions in curricula, but principal among its explorations was coeducation. Somehow, though, the headmaster and faculty never became fully at ease with the perils of having teen-age sexual opposites on the same campus grounds. Having brought boys and girls together, the staff went to extraordinary lengths to keep them apart. The headmaster called a general assembly one day to report what he considered to be one of the most shameful, one of the most shocking episodes in the history of the school: he was riding his bicycle home from school last evening, he said, when there before his eyes—in broad daylight, in full public display—were an Excelsior boy and an Excelsior girl, both in school uniform, walking along the street, *holding hands!* The faculty gasped in horror and disbelief, and we students wondered which among us could have been so brazen.

At Excelsior, as at Maryland school, race as a preoccupation did not exist. The school was about 90 percent black. The other 10 percent was made up of the white sons and daughters of resident Englishmen, of Jews, of Chinese, of Indians. But as far as I could tell, we blacks did not think of ourselves as being "in control." Nor were the 10 percent preoccupied with their status as a minority, oppressed or otherwise.

After an accelerated two-year course ending in January, 1954, I was considered sufficiently steeped in algebra, plane geometry, religious knowledge, the rigors of English grammar and the glories of the British Empire to sit for the all-important examination, the Cambridge School Certificate. Once I had passed this exam, it was time to think of returning to New York. I looked forward to this with much the same excitement I had felt six years before about coming to Jamaica.

It was as though I were a West Indian going to America for the first time, and there is no human being so happy as a West Indian about to embark upon his maiden voyage to "the States." He is a man who has been completely seduced by tales of that wondrous land to the north with its limitless opportunity and excitement.

On April 10, 1954, I was back in town! A few things were different, but 146th Street looked very much the same to me. The block, the sky above it, the buildings, the people on it, all seemed to be painted a melancholy shade of gray. Hallways were dirtier, candy bars and radios were smaller, automobiles were longer. After six years of looking at tiny English Fords and Morris Minors, I couldn't imagine why anyone would want a car as large and as clumsy-looking as a Buick.

I had very little success at re-establishing contact with old friends. I found that several had traded the pain of this world for what they deemed was the lesser pain of the world of drugs. And whereas an occasional reefer might have done the trick in the old days, nothing less than heroin would now provide adequate escape.

There were other friends still on the block with whom communication might have been possible, but they found me hopelessly square. Several things were wrong with me, I discovered. I didn't dress properly, I didn't know how "to talk to chicks." I couldn't dance. On top of this it was said that I was trying to act "sadiddy"—I thought I was superior; I thought I was "hot shit" because I was about to go to college. Worst of all was my speech. I hadn't realized it, but my whole way of speaking had been West-Indianized to a point indistinguishable from that of the native West Indian. And there was nothing funnier to black Americans than hearing a West Indian speak. The simplest phrase generated orgies of laughter. The consequence was that for two years I said practically nothing. At home, at school, on the street, at parties, I literally shut up from 1954 to 1956.

Bernard Strumpf and his marvelous TV set had moved, but we had our own now. It seemed to me that the chance to see television in one's own living room was by itself worth coming back to America. In those first few weeks I sat before the screen with endless fascination, indiscriminately devouring everything it served up: commercials, cartoons, wrestling, soap opera and the Army-McCarthy hearings. I had never heard of this Senator Joseph McCarthy; I had not the faintest idea what the hearings were all about; but the televised proceedings became prominent in my daily TV watching. It struck me that the Senator was something of a bully and that the frail-looking guy who always tagged along with him looked a little too shifty to be trusted. And so I started to root for the "good guys" on the other end of the table.

That spring, I exercised my Hobson's choice and decided to go to the City College of New York, known to intimates as .just plain "City." It was within walking distance from where I lived and it was free. But the registrars shook their heads at me and said that I could not be admitted until I got some background in American history. I signed up for evening courses at a high school in the Bronx, where one classmate advised me, "The British Empire ain't hittin' on shit. The cats who have the world by the nuts are Americans."

The ensuing years at City were largely spent in discomfort. In classroom and cafeteria, the races, black and white, by mutual unspoken consent, very carefully separated themselves from each other. Alternating between fits of superiority and inadequacy, I excluded myself from both camps. Though on separate tracks, they both seemed headed in the same direction: money-making—lots and lots of it. And since it went without saying that one could not make money without an education, here they were going to school. Every course in the catalogue was carefully tabulated according to its future dollar-gathering worth. The white boys were going to take over the empires left to them by their daddies, and the black boys had their sights fixed on outstripping their low-level daddies by becoming the "first Negro" to inch his wormy way into this or that heretofore closed white empire. And so the race was on.

The raucous activities of the fraternities I found ridiculous and so never had an inclination to join them. Social clod that I was, I don't suppose I would have been welcome anyway. The only extracurricular activity that I did get involved in was reporting for one of the college papers, where I managed to make a few friends. Together we grappled editorially with the burning campus issue of the day—"student apathy."

In looking for part-time jobs after school, I quickly discovered that the more I de-emphasized the American side of my background and built up the West Indian end of it, the better were my chances of being hired. Somehow, black people were more palatable with a little exotica sprinkled upon them. I also learned that in general whites (at least in New York) found West Indian Negroes to be more "intelligent, more reliable, more ambitious" than American "homegrown" Negroes. One of my more cynical friends was quick to point out, however, that there were any number of places where such ploys as the wearing of a turban or the faking of an accent would not make the slightest impact.

After six years of indirection at City (interspersed by frequent semester interruptions, during which I worked full time) I ended up with a smattering of comparative literature, journalism and a solemn pledge never to sit for an examination again as long as I lived. In April, 1960, I received a love letter from the Selective Service System, cordially inviting me to drop in at the draft board for a physical examination. By August I was a Private E-1 Army recruit at Fort Dix, New Jersey.

Hindsight tells me that I must have been temporarily insane, but at the time I welcomed being drafted. I looked forward to the simple orderliness that I supposed military life would bring. I even thought I would make one of the better soldiers. And so I submitted to all the indignities that basic training requires: taking orders from men who measure intelligence by height, eating rain-soaked powdered eggs at four-thirty in the morning by the light of a two-and-a-half-ton truck; scrubbing and rescrubbing toilet bowls that didn't need cleaning, only to have the first sergeant stride into the latrine and say, "This place looks like a goddamn cow licked it"; sharing a bivouac tent with someone smelling so foul that no dog would tolerate him in his kennel; standing at bedside while fully grown men conducted their daily probes for dust —on wall lockers, foot lockers, on towels, toothbrushes and razors, on Bibles, shoe tops, gas masks, on blankets, bed rails, laundry bags.

I tried very hard but never quite mastered the paraphernalia of warfare. In the classroom, I could explain all there was to explain about the M-1 rifle, the Browning automatic rifle, the Army pistol caliber .45, the machine gun, the carbine, the hand grenade and the flame thrower. But on the rifle range where it counted, I was a dud. My big trouble, as sergeants pointed out to me with loud impatience, was that I was flinching. Each time I took aim, I would anticipate the sound the shot made, jerk my arm and thereby eliminate any chance of hitting the target.

I suppose that an Army classification test must have shown that Private Moore, Gilbert D., had some extraordinary talent for sorting mail. After basic training and three more excruciatingly painful months of advanced infantry training, I was transferred from one side of Fort Dix to the other. I joined the ranks of the 22nd Base Post Office—then a small company of seventy-five, as pathetic an assemblage of troops as one was likely to find anywhere in the world. Our mission was to man and operate a half-dozen or so postal units scattered around Fort Dix, providing all the services of civilian post offices. None of the Dix soldiers seemed to know we existed, however, for stamp sales were pitifully low. We therefore spent most of our time fortifying these tiny post offices against the much hated enemy of the peacetime Army —dust.

Still, all the absurdities of my first twelve months in the Army were made more tolerable by the fact that Fort Dix was only an hour-and-a-half bus ride from New York City and, except for occasional lapses when my belt buckle was not properly shined for inspection, I usually went home on weekends.

But suddenly one day in October, 1961, the 22nd Base Post Office was summoned to serve a higher purpose. We were one of the many Army units designated "STRAC" (Strategic Army Command). Rough-and-ready fighting men that we were, we were at all times prepared to saddle up and "move out" on very short notice to whatever theater of operations we might be needed. And so it happened. The 22nd BPO was called to service in Germany, where, at the time, a newly erected wall was making the entire world nervous. We hastily packed our gear—a process which labored on for six weeks. Armed now with stamps, scales, postal manuals and carbines (which few of us could handle without self-destruction), the BPO set sail for Europe.

In Germany we set up shop in a town near the French border called Kaiserslautern. Though small in German population in comparison to Munich, Berlin and Hamburg, Kaiserslautern, or "K-Town" as we called it, had the largest American installation in all Germany and indeed was said then to have the largest concentration of Americans outside of the United States.

Abruptly the racial proportions of the 22nd BPO, which at Fort Dix had been of no particular consequence, came to be very important. A few significant things about our existence were now quite different. At Fort Dix we slept in the traditional Army barracks with its wide-open, unpartitioned floor space. Our new quarters, once occupied by Nazi officers, had separate rooms and, since there were not enough of them for each man to have his own, the necessity arose for our commanding officer to decide who would be roommates with whom. All the blacks, of whom the seventy-five-man company had nine, ended up rooming with each other in twos and threes. Left to our own choosing, some of us would have had whites in our midst, not in any crusade for "integration" but purely and simply because some of us had developed cross-racial friendships. Still others would have elected to room with precisely the Negroes the captain had designated. In any case, it was clear that by the CO's reckoning it would be better for all concerned for the Black Nine to be cordoned off by themselves.

The men of the 22nd "lived together" now in a way peculiarly enforced by new circumstance. Off duty at Fort Dix, we were all free to go our own social ways. In the case of us blacks, almost all of whom came from nearby New York and Philadelphia, this meant going home regularly to see families and girlfriends. In Germany there were no separate paths to take, no families to go home to on weekends. All of us, black and white, were Americans in a foreign country. If there was to be any social activity, it would all have to take place in downtown K-Town.

In my early, uniformed days in K-Town, I very rashly assumed that a bar was a bar and that I had only to scout around until I found one or two suitable to my taste and that would be that. Not so! The local townsfolk wanted nothing *less* than to fraternize with American soldiers—a pardonable prejudice, given the barbaric behavior of most GI's out on the town. We were thus socially confined to "GI joints," and, as I was to discover quite by accident, these were of two varieties—white and black.

One night I strolled into a bar, chosen at random, and took up a beer-drinking position in the center of the activity.

Eventually I got to talking to a German soldier who happened to be sitting there. Why he happened to be in this place, I never learned. Moments later, the bartender and owner, a stocky, middle-aged German with an agitated look about his eyes, came over to where we were sitting and whispered something in German to my new-found drinking companion. The German soldier nodded, and a look of great relief swept the bartender's face as he picked up our beer mugs and slid them down to the far end of the bar. Settled in our new seats, the young German smiled and explained the situation to me. It was not, he said, that ole Klaus the owner had anything against Negroes. It was simply that over the years his American clientele had come to be all white and they, in their social life, wanted it as much like home as possible, and while it was one thing to have to "soldier" with 'em all day, drinking with niggers was quite another. In short, I was in the wrong place. I glanced around the room and, sure enough, there wasn't another nigger in sight and we two were the focus of scowling attention. I got up off the stool and told my young German friend the situation wasn't any skin off my ass because the place was a dump when you got right down to it. The chicks in there all looked pretty scaggy and the beer tasted like cow piss so who needed it?

It was a first for me. I had become accustomed to racial indignity in all the myriad subtle forms it took in New York. But here now was racism—overt, unmistakable. Mild, of course, compared to getting chewed up by police dogs or being clubbed half to death for asserting one's right to sit down in a public place, but it strikes me that the violence wrought upon the *psyche* is hardly much different.

I did a little investigating among black soldiers who had been in Germany long before the 22nd got there and learned that the situation I had run into was commonplace in Kaiserslautern and indeed wherever there was an American military installation. What surprised them was that I had gotten out of the place without getting my head kicked in.

It was *not* that any of the black soldiers longed to taste some special luxury that they could find only in a white place; no such luxuries existed. Black GI joints, white GI joints—they were uniformly tawdry, and it didn't matter very much whether you hung out at the Dixie Bar, which was a white night spot, or at Johnny's Keller, which was black; you were going to find the same dreary surrounding in both places: drunken old sergeants weeping over their wasted lives, inflated liquor prices and German whores hustling GI's for drinks.

We began to hold meetings, we nine black soldiers of the 22nd Base Post Office, to decide what we could do about the Kaiserslautern race situation short of burning the town down. I was appointed to go have a friendly chat with the inspector general. The IG is usually a high-ranking officer who travels about from post to post listening to the complaints of the men and occasionally doing something about them. Theoretically, the complaining soldier does so in confidence and he need not go through the customary chain of command before getting a hearing.

We did not expect anything to come of this trip to the IG; nor did we think we were telling the United States Army something it did not already know. The peacetime Army is like a great calm lake. So long as no one gripes about anything it remains that way: the men go to work, eat their meals, get drunk at night and lieutenants make captain, captains make major. Everybody's happy. But as soon as someone makes an official complaint, particularly to the IG, papers get typed up in triplicate, ripples form on the waters and the tranquillity of the entire lake is disturbed. All we wanted was to shake up the lake a little bit.

I went to see our commanding officer and told him I wanted an appointment with the IG. He frowned as dark visions of a rippling lake danced in his head. But he had no choice. Within two days I was sitting, legs crossed, opposite the IG (a colonel) in his office. He was extremely cordial. Would I care for a cigarette? "Yes, thank you very much." How long had I been in Europe? About six months, except that it seemed to me that we were still in the United States because it appeared that the Army was going to such great lengths to keep us away from the local Germans. The Army provided drinking places, movies, cafeterias chock-full of hamburgers and apple pie, bus service in and out of town. All this plus a little "home-fried" racism. A careless soldier might be in Germany for a whole year without laying eyes on a single German. A soldier might get the idea that he was back home in Fort Benning, Georgia, someplace.

The colonel murmured something about a "balance of payments" problem. The Secretary of Defense, he said, wanted to discourage overseas troops from spending their dollars on the foreign market. As for the "racism," the colonel did not know what I was talking about. "The Army," he said with a straight face, "is interested only in the individual talents of individual men and does not concern itself with matters of race, color, creed and national origin."

Was the colonel aware that there was a full-fledged segregation system in operation in downtown Kaiserslautern? Was he further aware that there was great racial tension between white and black soldiers and that this tension regularly erupted into little wars? Did he know that there were sergeants given to running their platoons like plantations? Did the colonel ever notice in his trips to the PX that wives of white soldiers had all the jobs behind the sales counters and cash registers, and wives of the Negro soldiers had all the jobs behind the mops and dishrags? And having noticed it, did the colonel take exception to the practice?

No, the colonel was aware of very little of this. Again he had to point to the Army's strict policy regarding race, color, creed and national origin. He *did* understand that over the years white soldiers tended to go to certain bars and the Negroes tended to go to others, but he was inclined to think that Negroes preferred it that way. In any case, he would look into the matter. He would also investigate the other questions I had raised.

Whereupon my complaint was typed up in triplicate. A ripple formed on the lake; the lake promptly swallowed the ripple; tranquillity was restored. And that was that.

I cannot imagine being as happy as the day I was released from the Army. It was August 10, 1962. The two-year experience was not without its benefits. Army dentists had saved me the expense of a dental bill that might have run as high as two thousand dollars in civilian life. After twenty-four months of mopping and sweeping, I could now qualify for any janitorial position in America. I also learned that unending cynicism is one small part of being black in America. Lurking behind rifles, behind rosebuds, might very well be a racist.

While I was in the Army I convinced myself that I would never be contented unless I were writing novels—preferably great ones. But there were as yet no novels in me burning to be written. Besides, what was I to live on while these novels were being written? Confronted by similar circumstances, others have chosen one of three paths: (1.) They dropped the "great American novel" bullshit, went into public relations and made piles of money. (2.) They moved beard and baggage into a garret in Greenwich Village to play the starving-artist game. (3.) They became reporters, postponing the novel writing (indefinitely sometimes) until they gained enough "exposure."

I chose the latter course. I wanted to work for some organization that was big and powerful and so I made the rounds to all the "biggies": CBS-TV and Radio, NBC-TV and Radio, *Newsweek*, the *New York Times*, Time-Life. I had no friends in any of these places; I had no "connections" that would facilitate entry into one of these empires. I don't think I even knew what connections were.

My first office was on the twenty-sixth floor of the Time & Life Building. I shared it with about twenty-five other people. Principally our job was to eviscerate the *New York Times* with rulers and scissors and later to file away the enormous piles of newspaper clippings. After this and a number of other stints in Time Inc.'s Editorial Reference Library, I got a job working for the company's house organ. In 1966 I landed on the twenty-ninth floor as a reporter for *Life* magazine.

I spent a good deal of time at *Life* trying to thwart what appeared to me had become a journalistic rule of thumb: "black stories" should be given to black reporters.

There was a time, frighteningly recent, when there were *no* black reporters to send to this or that riot, to this or that press conference. And the news media, abruptly caught blackless when riots began to be commonplace summer events, were obliged to scurry about looking for black newsmen—unqualified, near-qualified or whatever. In the beginning the custom was to give these black hirelings "piecework," which is to say that when the riot was over, they were out of a job. The laughingstock of the black trade a few years ago was the "nigger newsman on a one-day contract."

Much of that has changed in recent times so that there is scarcely a radio or television station, scarcely a newspaper or magazine in the country, that cannot point a proud finger to a sprinkling of black faces on its staff.

But what kind of assignments shall they have? Shall a black reporter do black stories *to the exclusion of* everything else and, indeed, is the black reporter *capable* of doing a story that does not in some way involve a racial question? On these matters, black reporters are themselves not of one mind any more than they are of one mind on birth control, for instance. There are black reporters who have come to be "ghetto specialists," either because that role was slowly, surely thrust upon them by their editors or because they sought that role and won it. Some of them are good at it; some of them are awful at it. There are some black reporters who basically don't want to go within a hundred miles of a "black story," but do finally go because it seems to them, rightly or wrongly, that they have no choice. There are others who think it their special responsibility to themselves and to their people to report the news from the black community rather than leave it to be misunderstood or whitewashed by a nonblack reporter.

As for myself, I have always resisted the facile notion that as a black reporter I was *ipso facto* best qualified to do this or that story involving black people. (I have also been contemptuous of the idea that once taken away from the contemplation of my black novel, I would be quite useless as a reporter.) I have welcomed assignments that dealt with matters of race; I have welcomed others having no racial implications whatever, feeling no discomfort in either the acceptance or execution of the assignment.

In moments when racial preoccupations could be set aside, there was time to enjoy the spectacle of power and influence at work. Consider the difference between saying "This is John Doe calling" and "This is John Doe calling from *Life* magazine," and you have a small measure of the enormous power of such giants of the press as *Life*. Doors that would otherwise be bolted to bar your entrance fly open when you mention the magic name. People who would sooner spit on you fall humbly at your feet. For there is a continuous fever abroad: the already powerful are struggling to sustain their power; the powerless are struggling for one small sliver of recognition.

Working for *Life* was nothing if not luxurious. And if you were unaccustomed to luxury as I was, you became giddy in the whirlpool of cocktail parties, first-class air travel and expensive hotels. Eventually the initial champagne tide receded and I managed to do some work. I learned how to take oceans of written material and whittle it down to a paragraph. Some of those paragraphs, happily, were precision instruments; too often they were monstrous oversimplifications.

Life also afforded me glimpses of America that I wanted very much, but which I would otherwise probably not have gotten. I had been overseas without ever having been next door; I had been to Montego Bay, Madrid, Paris and Copenhagen, and never crossed the state line to Connecticut or Pennsylvania. Through *Life* I went to Indiana with Eugene McCarthy; to Medicine Hat, Canada, with Pierre Trudeau; to Martha's Vineyard to see William Styron; to Fairbanks, Alaska, to photograph a curious animal called the musk ox; to the customs checkpoint at Tijuana to photograph what must surely have been the highest pile of pot ever gathered in one place. And, what now seems a century ago, I had a cozy chat in Baltimore three years ago with a Republican gentleman named Spiro ("Just-call-me-Ted") Agnew. Maryland liberals in those olden days were earnestly praying that

Mr. Agnew would outstrip his Democratic opponent, George ("Your-home-is-your-castle") Mahoney. Agnew won.

I accepted a *Life* Black Panther assignment with great reluctance. I was afraid of getting my head blown off. I was afraid of not being able to communicate with them. I was afraid of communicating with them *all too well*. Had I known more about them at the time, I should probably not have accepted the assignment. I remembered vaguely that someone by the name of Eldridge Cleaver had published a book recently called *Soul on Ice* that some critics thought very highly of, but I had not read it. I remembered vaguely reading somewhere that someone by the name of Huey Newton was soon to go on trial for the murder of an Oakland policeman, but I didn't know what that was all about either.

The Panthers had not yet thrust themselves into national infamy, so the very fleeting impression I had of them was that they were this bizarre bunch of California niggers, talking bad and occasionally shooting someone.

I remember fearing that they would be a West Coast version of the Blackstone Rangers of Chicago, and the frustrations I had suffered there would be repeated in Oakland. I was quite wrong about that, as it turned out. The Black Panthers and the Blackstone Rangers, though they sprang from the same roots, could not have been more different.

But at that time, and this was the end of June, 1968, I remembered hoping that it was not the same naked square now about to go to Oakland as had gone to Chicago two years before to meet the Rangers. They're an organization, I thought then, and organizations have a reason for being; they have leaders and rules; they have a past and a future. But not the Blackstone Rangers; they were a loose coalition of armed hustlers, who, stripped of all else, lived to hustle—the world, the country, South Side Chicago, their women, each other and dumb motherfuckers that come from *Life* magazine to do stories on them.

I had forgotten about Harlem and those grand old gangs like the Royalistics, the Buccaneers and the Sabers. They were organizations too, but you don't approach them for a story in the same way that you might approach the American Medical Association, the American Philatelic Society. You just don't do it that way. It may simply be that they are unapproachable because everyone and everything outside of them has conspired to perpetuate their separateness. And if you are black and you have lived in some corner, any corner, of America, you know, you feel, you share some fraction of their despair. It doesn't matter very much what you own; though you may have risen to the dizziest of material heights, you feel it. The Blackstone Rangers, therefore, were not total strangers to me. Our despairs differed not in kind—only in degree. But they were contemptuous of our differences. Occasionally they would smile at me: *"You may think you into somethin', baby, but you ain't; you just as fucked up as you think we are."*

Anyway I left Chicago—I fled Chicago without a story. In another way, I had *one hell of a story;* but in the conventional terms of what makes a magazine piece I had nothing. I was trying to introduce order where there was none. I was trying to feel a complete solidarity with the Rangers when our separate paths had doomed us to a half-assed one. And since they were as gifted conning each other as outsiders, I got caught in a crossfire of conflicting hustles. Good-bye Chicago. Good-bye Mighty Blackstone.

In nervously going west to Oakland, I took some comfort in the fact that the photographer I would be working with was Howard Bingham. Howard was then, and remains joyously, "jes' plain folks." He grew up in Mississippi or "behind the Iron Curtain," as he was wont to say, and was now living in Los Angeles. He had done lots of work for *Life* before, but the Panther piece was his first major assignment. He was well known in what had come to be called "the Black Power periphery," having photographed the Black Muslims extensively from Elijah Muhammad to Muhammad Ali on down, and had photographed Stokely and Rap and Bobby Seale and Ron Karenga. There was scarcely a Black Power conference, small or large, that had not seen his familiar frame bobbing up and down with camera and strobe. He had no great pretensions to being an artist with his camera; he enjoyed taking pictures and enjoyed making money out of it. Nor did he look upon the Black Panther assignment as some staggering intellectual exercise. Not at all. As far as Howard was concerned, we were going over to Oakland to talk to some of the brothers and make some pictures and at the end of it all we would have a story. And that's all there was to it. I remember envying him for his unconcern. Here I was dragging my nerve endings cross-country and Bingham wasn't really sweating.

II

Black Is a Prior Felony

I mean we piss away a million dollars on Radio Free Europe, and don't know anything about the country within the country—don't know *anything* about these people.

—LENNY BRUCE

I hope a nigger gets you on a dark street and kills you, takes your fat wallets and your credit cards and cuts your throats. . . .

—ELDRIDGE CLEAVER

On OCTOBER 28, 1967, a policeman named John Frey was shot to death. Another man, Huey Percy Newton, was said to have been instrumental in his death. Did he kill John Frey with premeditation, with malice aforethought? Did he kill him under extreme provocation? Did he kill him in the heat of a great passion? Did he kill him in self-defense? Did he kill him *at all*?

Seven women and five men were brought together to decide. Seven women and five men: a lab technician, an engineer, a housewife, a secretary, a junior executive secretary, a bookkeeper, a bologna slicer, a drugstore clerk, a machinist, a bank lending officer, a bank trust officer and a landlady. They weighed the evidence, the testimony, the matter of Huey P. Newton's life, for four days. At 10:09 P.M. on September 8, 1968, the jury announced its verdict.

Superior Court of the State of California, in and for the County of Alameda, Department Number Eight, Action Number 41266, the People of the State of California, Plaintiff, versus Huey P. Newton, Defendant.

We the jury in the above entitled cause, find the above-

named defendant Huey P. Newton guilty of a felony, to wit,
voluntary manslaughter, a violation of Section 192 Subdivision
1 of the Penal Code of the State of California, a lesser and in-
cluded offense charged in the first count of the Indictment.

His Honor Superior Court Justice Monroe Friedman was
moved to say that the jury in its performance of eight weeks
of civic duty had done well: "Ladies and gentlemen, I want
to thank you very much for your services on behalf of all the
twenty judges of this court, and on behalf of the citizens of
the County of Alameda. I know that you have conscientiously
performed your duty as you saw it according to your lights.
I know you have been patient and that you have listened
carefully to all the proceedings in the court. It has been a
long trial. Every juror was present all the time, and it is
a splendid thing that we have the citizens of our country
who are willing to give up their time in order to serve in the
administration of justice."

On Friday, September 27, 1968, Huey P. Newton was
brought to court for sentencing. The defense moved that
there be a new trial.

Motion denied.

The defense moved that Huey Newton be released from
custody on bail pending the outcome of an appeal.

Motion denied.

Did Mr. Charles Garry, the attorney for the defense, have
any legal cause to show why the judgment of this Court
should not be pronounced against his client?

"No, Your Honor," Mr. Garry said.

Did Mr. Huey Newton have anything he wished to say
before sentence was passed against him? The defendant said
he did not.

"It is the judgment of this court and it is hereby ordered,
adjudged, and decreed that in punishment for said crime the

defendant be imprisoned in the State Prison of California for the term prescribed by law.

"It is further ordered, adjudged, and decreed that he be remanded to the custody of the Sheriff of Alameda County, to be by said Sheriff delivered to the Director of Corrections of the State of California at the California Medical Facility, Vacaville, California, to be by said Director imprisoned for the term prescribed by law in pursuance of this judgment.

"Please take the defendant upstairs," the judge said.

As the prisoner was being led from the courtroom, he raised a clenched tawny fist in salute to the spectators. In near unison, he and they proclaimed, "Power to the people!"

The press and the spectators waited outside the Alameda County Courthouse for one last glimpse of the prisoner. But the motion for a last glimpse of the prisoner was denied. In the interests of security, the prisoner was escorted from the building by a subterranean exit.

The order of the Court was carried out and Alameda County sheriff's deputies took the prisoner to Vacaville Medical Facility. Eventually Huey Newton was sent to the California Men's Colony at Los Padres, California.

The California Men's Colony at Los Padres is probably the most pleasant state prison in the country. It is secluded in the green of gentle rolling hills near the town of San Luis Obispo. The uniformed guards say "Good morning" and "How are you today," and they seem much more like watchers over a botanical garden than over a penal institution. Los Padres is proud of its emphasis upon rehabilitation of the prisoner rather than punishment. It has a drama group, a stamp club, a speech club, a puppeteers club, a singing troupe and a chapter of Alcoholics Anonymous. It has the facilities for playing volleyball, tennis, baseball, handball, basketball and boxing. It has an academic program for those who have the aptitude; it has vocational programs for those who have the skill. Perhaps the only worldly pleasures denied the inmates of the California Men's Colony at Los Padres is the freedom to leave the institution at will and the possibility of heterosexual intercourse.

Huey Newton became one of approximately 2,400 inmates in the east wing at Los Padres. The East Facility is what is described as a medium-security institution, which is to say that, among other things, the potential escapee has no surrounding wall to contend with in making good his flight. There is, however, a network of cyclone fences and eight watchtowers, four of which are manned twenty-four hours a day.

Escape from Los Padres would not have been a simple matter, particularly not for young Mr. Newton, that institution's most celebrated inmate. His cell was searched every day. He was skin-searched before and after he left the visiting room. He was skin-searched every time he walked across the prison yard. Otherwise Mr. Newton was accorded most of the privileges extended to his fellow prisoners. He, like his fellow prisoners, enjoyed the privacy of his own room. He might have as many as ten visitors, any of whom might spend up to five hours in his company, four times a week. They might visit with him in the large visitors' room allotted for that purpose or they might sit outside in an adjacent courtyard in the shade of birch trees.

Huey Newton was said to be cooperative with the staff of Los Padres except that he refused to work. He refused to make license plates or shoes. He refused to work in the laundry, the kitchen or hospital. He refused to work in the tobacco factory, the knitting mill or the industrial warehouse, unless he and his fellow prisoners were paid the state minimum wage instead of the penal rate.

By way of punishment, Mr. Newton was denied access to the prison library. Still his cell was not without reading matter: *The Economic and Philosophical Manuscripts* of Karl Marx (1884), *The Grapes of Wrath* by John Steinbeck, *The Warfare State* by Fred Smith, *Socialism in the Nuclear Age* by John Eaton and *The Race War* by Ronald Segal.

I was waiting to see Huey Newton at the reception desk at Los Padres one day in June, 1969. There was an elderly couple on line in front of me. They were waiting to see their son, who was going to be released on parole in two weeks. Huey poked his head through the window of the adjacent visitors' room. His hair was cropped close to the head. He wore the dowdy blue uniform of prisoners. The woman standing in front of me shuddered visibly as she seemed to recognize Newton. "Good God, is that him?" she asked her husband. "Is that the same one who started . . . ?" "That's him," her husband said. "Goodness, he doesn't look at all the way I thought . . . I mean he looks like such a nice young man. What a shame."

The "nice young man" was the baby of the Newton family. There was Leander (called Lee), then Myrtle, Leola, Walter, Jr., Doris, then Melvin, then Huey, Baby Huey. Baby Huey in the old album of pictures. Baby Huey, pampered Huey, three years old sitting on the horse, unafraid of the horse, unafraid of the cost of taking the picture. "It won't cost anything, Mommy. It won't cost anything for me to get on it." The man with the horse and the camera charged Mommy thirteen dollars. Baby Huey in cap and gown, a graduate of the Oakland Technical High School. Baby Huey in color, flagrantly retouched color, his cheeks, his countenance, rosier than a rose.

Baby Huey was two years old when his daddy left Monroe, Louisiana, in 1943 for Oakland, California, in the familiar immigrant hope that the place he was going up north was a far better place to live than the place he was leaving down south. Out west to Oakland!

Oakland—a century old, a self-conscious century in the shadow of San Francisco. Oakland—seventy-nine square miles of land and water and groves of oak trees. Oakland—waterfront haunt for Richard Henry Dana and Bret Harte and Robert Louis Stevenson.

Oakland—gateway to vacationland. West to San Francisco, east to Yosemite. South to Monterey and Big Sur. North to the hills and beaches of Marin.

Oakland—the second largest container cargo port in the world. Oakland—annual business in excess of three billion dollars.

Walter Newton, Senior, an ordained Baptist minister, went to work in the Oakland Naval Supply Depot. In 1948 he found what was to be more permanent work laying asphalt, tending to Oakland's manholes for the Oakland Streets Department. In 1945 Amelia Newton and seven children joined her husband.

The ensuing years were lean, but Baby Huey was shielded from most of the pain of pinching pennies, or living on the dirt floor of an Oakland basement. In grade school Baby Huey was what we used to call a scaredy-cat. A scaredy-cat was anybody who was afraid to fight, and fighting in school in Harlem (and apparently also in North Oakland) was as much a part of the curriculum as arithmetic. Baby Huey Newton in the course of attending the Santa Fe Grammar in North Oakland got his ass kicked at regular intervals.

Four years separated Huey from Melvin, his brother next in line. Four years and a welter of personality differences. They looked at the same world through very different eyes; they reacted to the same world with very different sensitivities. Huey stopped being a scaredy-cat after grade school. He learned how to fight—how to kick ass. He learned how to walk that black walk and talk that black talk. You walk so that it looks to a foreigner like something's wrong with your leg but ain't nothin' wrong with your leg—you walk that way 'cause you bad—you a *bad* motherfucker. Bad motherfuckers walked that way in Harlem, too, exactly the same way. Same way in Hough in Cleveland and South Side Chicago. They used to wear those long pointy red-brown shoes. All the bad cats—the bad dudes—the bad motherfuckers had taps on their shoes. Two or three cats would walk together in perfect cadence, their taps clacking away on the sidewalk. And of course if you walked "bad," you had to talk bad, too. You had to say to some defenseless square, "Hey, motherfucker—loan me a nickel," and if the motherfucker didn't loan you a nickel, you "stomped his ass."

Anyway, Huey was preoccupied in his early teens with getting an education on the block and wasn't much interested in any formal education he might get at the Oakland Technical High School. Not that that institution was any great stimulus for higher learning—but such as it had to offer, Huey pretty much rejected.

Melvin was different. "My brother," said Huey, "was a loner inside the school. He didn't associate with anyone. He didn't associate with the blacks, who were all illiterate. He's told me that when he first entered school he was going to prepare—he was preparing even then, in the first and second grade—to become a doctor, and that all of his energies were put into preparing himself for college. But he was very lonely. He worked after school just about full time since he was about eleven, and he never associated with the other students, and they, of course, ridiculed him and called him a square. . . ."

Huey didn't want to be like Melvin in those early high school days. No, he wanted to be like "Sonny Boy." Sonny Boy was Walter, Junior, one of his older brothers. Walter could walk and talk. Walter had all the right clothes and all the right places to hang out. Walter had all the chicks, too— the "fine" ones, the ugly ones—they all went for Walter.

While Huey was emulating Sonny Boy, studious Melvin was pressing ahead. He graduated from Oakland Technical High School, went on to get an Associate of Arts degree from Merritt College in Oakland, a B.A. degree from San Jose State, a Master's degree from the University of California at Berkeley and a B.A. and Master's in Social Welfare.

Melvin's scholarship, while it never quite neutralized "the Sonny Boy influence," was eventually to add a new dimension to Huey's life. Huey remembers that:

"All the way through high school, the instructors were telling me that I couldn't go to college. About the last year, I was telling them that I *was* going to college and they said, 'No, you can't go to college because you are not college material.' I wanted to show them that I could do anything that I wanted to.

"Right after high school, I started to read Plato's *Republic*. I read it through about five times until I could actually understand. My brother Melvin helped me—he was taking Philosophy 6A at the time. I used to follow him around his friends' houses where they would discuss various philosophies. I would listen and get in on the conversation and in the meantime I was struggling with Plato. . . .

"It was the Cave Allegory that impressed me most—it is symbolic of man discovering truth, gaining knowledge and wisdom. It takes you into a whole new world and you are able to distinguish between reality and things that are falsified.

"This was a trigger point in my life because after I finally succeeded in reading this book I sort of gobbled up everything I could get. And I found that, even with my limited ability to read from the start, I could grasp the essential point of the book. It was a very gratifying experience."

Huey in his junior year of high school, 1958, transferred from Oakland Tech to neighboring and somewhat more highly accredited Berkeley High School. The transfer was to last for only a semester. It was at Berkeley High School that Huey had his first official scrape with law enforcement. "I was walking over to a girlfriend's house on a Sunday. I was attacked by about seven other students and beat up pretty badly. And the next day I went to school with a carpenter's hammer, and at lunchtime the same seven guys came through the hall and they ridiculed me. Later we had an altercation downtown and I struck one of the boys with the hammer." Huey was taken into custody as a juvenile delinquent.

Returning to Oakland Tech, Huey graduated from that school the following year, in 1959. Later he went to Merritt College for two years, earning an Associate of Arts degree. From Merritt he went to San Francisco Law School, but dropped out after a semester. While going to school, Newton did a brief stint as a construction worker, worked for the Oakland Streets Department during summer vacations. He also put in five seasons at a fruit canning company, earning $2.45 an hour.

It wasn't so long ago, those years of 1962 and 1963 when Huey Newton was going to Merritt College in Oakland. It wasn't so long ago, and yet it was a century ago. A certain Malcolm X was alive, generating electricity before his time. A certain Martin Luther King was alive, boycotting, sitting in, presuming to be nonviolent in a nation of violence. John

F. Kennedy and American naval might were blockading Cuba. The vocabularies were different: integration and segregation, civil rights, discrimination had meaning in those ancient times. Black was not quite beautiful yet; it was (the word) still something of a curse.

It was in these times that Huey Newton discovered politics. And politics for him was more than a course in political science at school. To him it meant standing on the corner with an audience "runnin' it down" about Malcolm and what he said: "Whenever you're going after something that belongs to you, anyone who's depriving you of that right to have it is a criminal. Understand that. Whenever you are going after something that is yours, you are within your legal rights to lay claim to it, and anyone who puts forth any effort to deprive you of that which is yours, is breaking the law, is a criminal. . . . I believe in anything that is necessary to correct unjust conditions, political, economic, social, physical, anything that's necessary. I believe in it as long as it's intelligently directed and designed to get results. . . . It is criminal to teach a man not to defend himself when he is the constant victim of brutal attack. . . . We are anti-exploitation, antidegradation, antioppression. If the white man doesn't want us to be anti-him, then let him stop oppressing, degrading and exploiting us."

Politics for Huey was a living thing, and you lived it at school, down at Jo Ethel's Café, at home, at work, at the North Oakland Service Center. It meant joining the Afro-American Students Association at Merritt, but his disenchantment with them was to come very quickly. For one thing, the organization seemed to Huey to have been formed for the greater glory of Donald Warden, one of its founders. For another, it struck Huey that the members were, first and foremost, cultural nationalists. They were dedicated to the elevation of blackness, and the corollary of that principle was the downgrading of whiteness: Black is beautiful—white is ugly. You love black people, you hate white people. And these decisions on love and hate were made purely on the basis of skin color.

The cultural nationalists with their new-found blackness (the *nouveau noir*, as it were) gloried, wallowed in their negritude. Grow your hair high, wide and woolly and worship it. Shed your three-buttons suits and don dashikis. Learn Swahili. You're not Americans, you're Africans. Learn your black history, play your black music, worship your black god, read your black writers, love your black women. Buy black, think black, be black. . . .

But it seemed to Huey that if the supermarket on the corner belonged to a white and he charged an oppressive twenty-five cents a pound for flour, it didn't make any difference if that white man and his market were removed only to be replaced by a black man charging the same twenty-five cents a pound.

And you didn't stop living it because there were policemen around. Nor did you shrink from the confrontation when political debate gradually became a physical clash. He was still after all a "bad motherfucker," budding scholarship notwithstanding. In coming years, Huey was to have at least three "confrontations." By *his* terms they were political collisions carried to their natural physical extremes. But judges and prosecuting attorneys were, one day soon, to call them "criminal records."

Criminal records are written in indelible ink. There is a certain airtightness about the oral reading of them in courtrooms:

> In 1962 the defendant was convicted of a misdemeanor, to wit, battery on a police officer. In 1964 the defendant was con-

victed of a felony, to wit, assault with a deadly weapon, and in June 1967 the defendant was again convicted of a misdemeanor, to wit, interfering with an arresting officer. As far as is possible, ladies and gentlemen of the jury, the State wants you to ignore the circumstances of these convictions. The defendant is here, now charged with murder and while our system of justice demands that you presume him 100 per cent innocent of that crime his criminal record obviously reduces his innocence to forty percent. . . .

Along with politics at Merritt College Huey Newton found Bobby Seale. "I met Huey P. Newton," Bobby Seale wrote,

in the early Sixties during the time of the blockade that JFK enacted against Cuba, when there were numerous street rallies going on around Merritt Junior College in West Oakland. One particular day there was a lot of discussion about black people and the blockade against Cuba. People were out in front of the college, in the streets, grouped up in bunches of 200, 250, what have you—and there were these kind of gatherings and informal rallies at different times.

On this particular day that I met Huey, I don't remember exactly what day it was, but Huey was holding down a crowd of about 250 people who were standing around listening to him, and I was one of the participants. After he had held the conversation down to what in those days they called "shooting everybody down"—that means rapping off information and throwing facts—somebody would ask Huey a question or refer to something he said. They would try to shoot Huey down by citing some passage in a book. . . .

I guess I had the idea that I was supposed to ask questions, so I walked over to Huey and asked the brother, weren't all these civil rights laws the NAACP was trying to get for us, weren't they doing us some good? And he shot me down too, just like he shot a whole lot of other people down.

They began to hang out together, Huey Newton and this Bobby Seale who always seemed vaguely unhappy—Bobby Seale, who never seemed to smile unless it was absolutely necessary. They hung out together at the Afro-American Students Association and at Jo Ethel's Café, and the first Negro history course at Merritt.

They got in trouble together. On the record now it stands as assault on a policeman. On Bobby Seale's memory it sits somewhat differently. They were going to a record store in Berkeley one night—Huey, Bobby and another cat they used to call Weasel. They parked on Telegraph Avenue, the scene of a long procession of street rallies, campus demonstrations, hippie love-ins and assorted political, moral, philosophical, religious confrontations. They were near the legendary Forum Restaurant, an outdoor café, and Huey and Weasel asked Bobby to recite one of his poems, "Uncle Sammy Call Me Fulla Lucifer." By this time they were in front of the Forum and Weasel grabbed a chair and told Bobby to stand on it. From his soapbox Bobby declaimed:

"You school my naive heart to sing red-white-and-blue-stars-and-stripe songs and to pledge eternal allegiance to all things blue, true, blue-eyed blond, blond-haired, white chalk white skin with U.S.A. tattooed all over."

"Man, when I said that," Bobby later wrote of the incident, "this cop walks up and says, 'You're under arrest.'" (It was subsequently brought out in court that the policeman, off duty, was drunk, and it wasn't that Bobby the poet had violated any law but that the nigger was publicly, brazenly putting down America and laughing about it at the same time.)

Bobby got off the chair.

"What are you talking about, 'You're under arrest'? Under

arrest for what? What reason do you have for saying I'm under arrest?" And he says, "You're blocking the sidewalk." And I say, "What do you mean I'm blocking the sidewalk? I'm standing over here." I noticed Huey, standing to my left. Next thing I know, some people started grabbing on me. "You under arrest, you under arrest." I started snatching away from them, man. Next thing I know, Huey was battling up there, and three paddies had me down, tied down onto the ground. One of the paddies that had hold of me, Huey knocked him in the head a couple of times, and a couple of other brothers stomped on the paddies. I got loose. A big fight was going on. But boy, they say Huey whipped up some motherfuckers up there. They say Huey was throwing hands.

Anyway, a deal was made by which Bobby went free, an assault charge against him having been dropped, and Huey pleaded guilty to a misdemeanor—battery on the police officer. He was placed on probation for a year. The incident was trivial as convictions go, but it was to return to haunt him. Six years later he had to explain the matter again at his own murder trial: "I accepted the deal with the district attorney that if they freed Bobby Seale, gave me probation without a jail sentence, that I would not go back on Telegraph Avenue. I did this because of a lack of funds. Otherwise I would have to stand a chance of being tried by a racist jury here in Alameda County. So that was the deal and I accepted it and the record shows I pleaded guilty but I didn't feel I was guilty at any point."

There was another occasion when Huey didn't think he was guilty. A dean at Merritt College had him arrested on a charge of petty theft. He was accused of stealing a book. Huey came to the jury trial unrepresented: "Dean Olsen, why didn't you have me placed under arrest if you thought I had stolen the book?" Huey asked the plaintiff in his own defense. "Well, at that time, I just didn't know my rights as to whether or not I had the right to arrest you."

"Mr. Olsen," Huey continued, "you're a dean at the college; have a Ph.D. in education. Here I am a student in the college, learning my rights, and you've got a Ph.D., and you tell me you didn't know your *rights.*"

The jury acquitted Newton of petty theft, and while the incident might have died then and there in the courts, it circulated and lived on the campus. It made him something of a celebrity: "You don't mess with Huey—you don't mess with Huey no kinda way. . . ."

And yet there were still those who presumed to "mess with Huey": "The incident took place at a party. I believe it was a birthday party where they served a buffet dinner with steak, and people were playing cards and drinking and some standing and some sitting. I was involved in a conversation, as usual, and a number of people I was talking to I had been knowing for a number of years. Among them was Eddie Deems, who was with the Probation Department, also Henry Broom, who was also a probation officer. My brother Melvin was there. Most of the people there were academically inclined and were deep into a conversation on economics, and this one individual whom I didn't know at the time—I had the floor at the time—and this individual stepped up and asked me if I were an Afro-American. He was a black person and I told him that I didn't know what he meant exactly. But I responded by asking another question. 'If you're asking me whether I belong to Donald Warden's Afro-American Association, the answer is no, I am not an Afro-American. But if you are asking if I have African descent, yes, I am an Afro-American, just as you are.' And then he said, 'How do you know I am an Afro-American?'

And I said, 'Well, sir, I have 20-20 vision and I can see you have a black face just as mine, and your hair is kinky like mine and I am an Afro-American so you must therefore be exactly what I am.'

"And the people at the party thought this was pretty funny and so everyone laughed at him. . . . I turned around and started to cut my steak, and the individual grabbed me by the arm and pulled me around abruptly and said, 'Don't turn your back on me when I am talking to you.' And this upset me, because he laid his hands on me in a very rowdy fashion, and I told him, 'Don't ever put your hands on me again.' I pulled my arm away and started to cut my steak again. I didn't have any idea that the individual was going to fight.

"And then he turned me around again and said, 'You just don't know who you are talking to.' As he said this his hand went into his left hip pocket. He had a large scar on his face from his eye down to his mouth. It put terror into my heart, because in the ghetto, scars are signs of violence. I said, 'Don't draw a knife on me,' and I stabbed him. I stabbed him several times. He was still charging at me. My brother jumped up and pushed the guy and broke us up. . . . The guy collapsed in my brother's arms. . . . A lot of people didn't see what was happening and those who didn't see asked, 'Why did you stab him?' and my brother said, 'He stabbed him because he should have.'

"We backed out of the house together and I thought about pressing charges for assault but I didn't. And about two weeks later there was a warrant out for my arrest and I was arrested and I was convicted."

Thus in October, 1964, Huey Newton was convicted by a jury of a felony—assault with a deadly weapon. He was given three years' probation, with the first six months to be served in the county jail. To his own and surely to the enduring regret of his attorneys three years later, Huey insisted upon representing himself in the 1964 trial. It was probably that he had become cocky and, in premature self-assurance about his legal ability, took it upon himself to do what the most skillful, the most accomplished lawyers would shrink from doing—pleading his own case in court. Still, the Court may have been as remiss in the '64 proceedings as Newton. "You have been advised by the Court," the judge said then, "on at least one other occasion at the time your case was set for trial that you were entitled to [the right to be represented by an attorney] but I take it you wish to go on without the presence or the assistance of counsel; is that correct?"

"Well, if possible," Huey said, "I would like to have a legal adviser, but I would like to speak for myself."

"All right. You are asking me in effect, I take it," the judge went on, "to appoint the Public Defender as your legal adviser?" Huey said yes. "Your request is denied," the Court said.

The matter was to have extraordinary legal ramifications later.

Huey Newton had to spend six months in prison, where his inclinations to challenge what he could not abide grew stronger. In punishment for organizing a strike against food he thought unfit for human consumption, he was placed in solitary confinement for a month. His cell had no toilet, no running water.

He decided that the power the prison authorities had over him was the power to kill him, the power of the gun. He also decided that black people outside—in Oakland and in all of America's coast-to-coast ghettos—were similarly confined. If they made any serious attempt to radically change the quality of their lives, they would collide with blunt power—the power of the gun in the hands of police and National Guardsmen. The same fear that black people felt, Newton thought, had to be instilled in the keepers of their prisons.

The power of the gun!

And two years later Huey Newton and Bobby Seale moved to implement their thinking.

So here they were—two bad motherfuckers who were going to take on the whole city of Oakland. Nobody really believed that the cops turned into pigs when they came into West Oakland. Nobody really believed that cops were ripping down doors without search warrants and beating black heads without due process. Every so often some shrill voice would cry out "police brutality," but nobody but the brutalized would listen and the phrase had grown limp from overuse. Nobody really believed that cats were getting backed up against the wall on Saturday night to be stripped of their humanity and reduced to animals.

No, they didn't believe it. And who believed that cats were getting shot in the back for trying to steal a loaf of bread—'cause he didn't have the money to buy it, 'cause he didn't have a job, 'cause he didn't know how to do nothin', 'cause he didn't go to school, 'cause his mama didn't care, 'cause his papa wasn't there to care, 'cause they all good-for-nothin' niggers anyway and who really gives a shit? What wheat farmer in Kansas, what Senator from the sovereign State of Mississippi, what oilman from Dallas, what three-button Tom from New York? I mean, who really gives a shit?

So they were going to meet the cops—the pigs—head on. There wasn't going to be any more appeals, or petitions, or letters to the Oakland *Tribune,* or demonstrations at the

San Francisco Hall of Justice. No more pussyfooting around with the NAACP or the Urban League or the Afro-American Association. Fuck all that. All the cats do is talk anyway. All they do is talk—talk and set up commissions, and committees and subcommittees, and panels and seminars and study groups and task forces.

Power grows out of the barrel of a gun. We want power, so we are going to get some guns and when the pigs come to brutalize one of the brothers—whip out your power, your gun, and blow the motherfucker away.

And sometime in the spring of 1966 there came to be two Black Panthers—Huey Newton and Bobby Seale. There were "Black Panthers" before that, however. In northern California a group organized by one Mamadou Lumumba (Ken Freeman) were eclipsed by the Oakland organization. Both the Black Panther Party of Northern California and Huey Newton's Black Panthers in Oakland adopted the party name and symbol from the Black Panther Party of Lowndes County, Alabama.

Originally known as the Lowndes County Christian Movement for Human Rights, the Lowndes County Freedom Organization started in 1965 in an Alabama county where blacks were 80 percent of the population. The change in the name of the organization represented an important change in attitude. "The Negroes of Lowndes have learned," an early party pamphlet said, "that the whites who run the county have no respect for moral obligation, that they will respect only those who organize and challenge their power."

John Hulett, chairman of LCFO, explained in a speech why their group could no longer be a "civil rights" organization. "We fought for integration in this county. We fought that Negroes might have a right to get registered to vote. We protested at the school so that all the people could have

education—and for this we got nothing. We sat down together and discussed our problems. We thought about what
we were going to do with these 2,500 registered voters in
the county, whether or not we were going to join Lyndon
Johnson's party. Then we thought about the other people in
the State of Alabama who were working in this party. We
thought of the City Commissioner of Birmingham, Eugene
'Bull' Connor; George Wallace, who is now the Governor
of the State of Alabama; Al Lingo, who gave orders to those
who beat the people when they got ready to make the
march from Selma to Montgomery; the sheriff of Dallas
County, known as Jim Clark—these people control the Democratic Party in the State of Alabama.

"So the Negroes in Lowndes County decided that it's useless to stay in the Democratic Party or the Republican
Party in the State of Alabama. Through the years, these are
the people who kept Negroes from voting in the South and
in the State of Alabama. Why join the Democratic Party?"

The party to join was the Black Panther Party. Prominent
among its organizers were the workers in the Student Non-
violent Coordinating Committee and Stokely Carmichael,
who became SNCC chairman in May, 1966, after a year of
work in Lowndes County. Aside from refusing to work
within the existing political machinery, Carmichael said that
Alabama Black Panthers exercising the franchise would not
turn the other cheek if they were attacked by white racists:
"The Negroes won't take it this time. When they go down
to vote and they see the white man's got his guns, they're
going to go back home and get theirs. They're going to set
up armed teams to watch the ballot boxes. There's going to
be some shooting, some bloodshed. But they're going to
exercise their vote."

Few observers confronted in 1966 or now with the "ferocious" symbol of the Black Panther Party are prepared to believe that the symbol and/or the party name were conceived in innocence. But they were. Alabama law required that political parties have an animal symbol. The Democrats had the donkey; the Republicans had the elephant. The commercial artist who did the graphics for the LCFO was a New York friend of Carmichael's and in high school had been nicknamed "Black Panther."

Nevertheless, the symbolism of the Black Panther was appropriate, for as John Hulett pointed out: "This Black Panther is a vicious animal, as you know. Never bothers anything, but when you start pushing him, he moves backwards, backwards and backwards into his corner, and then he comes out to destroy everything that's before him."

But the Black Panthers who would come to be called a "threat to national security" were the Black Panthers of Oakland, California.

In the very beginning they had no guns; they had no money to buy them. So they went into business briefly to make money. Their commodity? The *Quotations from Chairman Mao Tse-tung*—the Red Book. They bought them at thirty cents a copy and resold them for a dollar on the campus of the University of California at Berkeley. "*Quotations from Chairman Mao Tse-tung*. Get your Red Book," Bobby Seale would say. "All you free-speechers up here who lost Mario Savio, read the Red Book and do it like the Red Guards did it."

Their first investment was in a High Standard shotgun. Eventually they bought .45-caliber pistols, 9-mm Lugers, .357 Magnums and M-1 rifles.

The Black Panther Party for Self-Defense. Huey P. Newton, Minister of Defense; Bobby Seale, Chairman. They were arrogant. And, indeed, was it not necessary to have an exaggerated sense of one's own importance to undertake the armed defense of thousands? The community needed defending, they said: "We have reached the point in history where we must claim that a black man, confronted by a bloodthirsty cop who is out to take his life out of a hatred for the black race, has a right to defend himself—even if this means picking up a gun and blowing that cop away." True enough! But who appointed Huey P. Newton and Bobby Seale defenders, as it were? The people? The Lord? Certainly not the Mayor of Oakland. They appointed themselves.

They were terrifying. Consider them walking across the urban stage for the first time, armed to the teeth: bandoliers across their chests, holstered .45's at their side, 12-gauge shotguns in their hands held at the port arms position. Consider them at their first press conference. No one in Oakland, black or white, had ever heard of the Black Panthers. Now comes Huey Newton, Baby Huey in black beret and baby brown face and black leather jacket and combat boots. Now comes Bobby Seale of Texas, sometime comedian, a mustache, a slight limp in his left leg, a studied ferocity about him.

They were terrifying, those two, as was Bobby Hutton, young sixteen-year-old Bobby Hutton, who would become the first of them to die. They were all terrifying because there is something particularly frightening about a black man with a gun. Anyone with a gun is to be feared, but there is tacit agreement among us all that black men with guns are infinitely more frightening. The unspoken understanding is that the black man, armed before us, is angry. He is smoldering with a rage that will very likely render him insane and thus more likely to shoot in blind, black, unreasonable hostility. And so we are afraid. And so the Black Panthers were terrifying.

But in the beginning there were no such blind acts of hostility. Their actions were all within the law, and they made every effort to see that they remained that way. There was no law in California at the time which prohibited the open bearing of arms. So a Black Panther or anyone else could walk the streets of Oakland, a 12-gauge shotgun strapped across his chest, with the same impunity a mother would have with an infant strapped on her back.

And so, completely within the law, Huey Newton, Bobby Seale, Bobby Hutton and their early recruits—these bad motherfuckers—had the temerity to begin patrolling the police. Huey Newton was to describe a typical patrol two years later in court at his own murder trial: "We would put three or four people into a car equipped with tape recorder, cameras and weapons and we would patrol the community. . . . If we saw anyone stopped, we would stay a reasonable distance from the person who is stopped by the police. We would have a lawbook with us to read the person his basic rights—his constitutional right to have an attorney present if he is going to answer any questions and the right to remain silent. We have also followed the police wagons to jails, bailing people out when we thought that the person was being done an injustice. . . ."

To many who caught those early glimpses of the Black Panthers, the likes of Bobby Seale were vaguely ludicrous:

IT'S ALL LEGAL
OAKLAND'S BLACK PANTHERS
WEAR GUNS, TALK REVOLUTION

said a headline in a spring 1967 story in the San Francisco *Chronicle*. "If a Hollywood director," the page-one story continued, were to choose them as stars of a movie melodrama of revolution, he would be accused of typecasting.

The leader: lithe, slender, saturnine and handsome. He looks out at the world with dark, slitted, suspicious eyes. He wears a uniform of black beret, black leather jacket. Across his chest slants a bandolier of shells. In his hands, at port arms, a blunt, ugly riot gun.

The chief lieutenant: also lithe and slender but taller. Face grim and tight, set off by a thick mustache. He wears the same uniform. Slung jauntily from his left shoulder, a holstered .45 caliber automatic pistol.

But these two are not actors and this is not Hollywood. This is Oakland, California. The melodrama is real, the guns are real. The two young men are real revolutionaries.

The leader is 25-year-old Huey Newton, a Negro who doesn't use that word but calls himself black. . . . [What man in his right mind would call himself black?]

There were others of course who caught early glimpses of the Panthers but for whom they were not the least bit terrifying or ludicrous. Among them was a Leroy Eldridge Cleaver, ex-convict, ex-Muslim, ex-bicycle thief, ex-rapist. A few months before seeing them for the first time, Cleaver had been released from Soledad Prison on parole, having served nine years of a sentence of one to fourteen years for rape. Cleaver had just then taken on a shield of "responsibility." He was now a senior editor on the masthead of *Ramparts* magazine. McGraw-Hill was soon to publish *Soul on Ice*, a collection of his writings in prison, and a phalanx of solid citizens of the San Francisco Bay Area were prepared to certify before the authorities that Leroy Eldridge Cleaver, then thirty-three, would be a good boy—from henceforth and even forevermore.

Now come Huey Newton and Bobby Seale:

I fell in love with the Black Panther Party immediately upon my first encounter with it; it was literally love at first sight. It happened one night at a meeting in a dingy little storefront on Scott Street in the Fillmore district, the heart of San Francisco's black ghetto. It was February 1967. The meeting was the latest in a series of weekly meetings held by a loose coalition functioning under the name of the Bay Area Grassroots Organizations Planning Committee. The purpose of the coalition was to coordinate three days of activities with the worthy ambition of involving the total black community in mass action commemorating the fourth anniversary of the assassination of Malcolm X. The highlight and culmination of the memorial was to be the appearance of Sister Betty Shabazz, Malcolm X's widow, who was to deliver the keynote speech at a mass meeting at the Bayview Community Center in Hunter's Point.

Among the topics on the agenda for this fortuitous meeting was the question of providing security for Sister Betty during the twenty-four hours she was to be our guest in the Bay Area. There was a paranoia around—which I did not share—that assassins by the dozens were lurking everywhere for the chance to shoot Sister Betty down. This fear, real or imagined, kept everybody uptight. . . .

Suddenly the room fell silent. The crackling undercurrent that for weeks had made it impossible to get one's point across when one had the floor was gone; there was only the sound of the lock clicking as the front door opened, and the soft shuffle of feet moving quietly toward the circle. Shadows danced on the walls. From the tension showing on the faces of the people before me, I thought the cops were invading the meeting, but there was a deep female gleam leaping out of one of the women's eyes that no cop who ever lived could elicit. I recognized that gleam out of the recesses of my soul, even though I had never seen it before in my life: the total admiration of a black woman for a black man. I spun round in my seat and saw the most beautiful sight I had ever seen: four black men wearing black berets, powder blue shirts, black leather jackets, black trousers, shiny black shoes—and each with a gun! In front was Huey P. Newton with a riot pump shotgun in his right hand, barrel pointed down to the floor. Beside him was Bobby Seale, the handle of a .45 caliber automatic showing from its holster on his right hip, just below the hem of his jacket. A few steps behind Seale was Bobby Hutton, the barrel of his shotgun at his feet. . . .

On April 25, 1967, five thousand copies of volume one, number one, of the *Black Panther,* the Black Community News Service, appeared in Oakland and environs. The newspaper, consisting of two mimeographed sheets stapled together, dealt almost entirely with the death of Denzil Dowell, twenty-two, who was shot and killed by a policeman in the neighboring ghetto of Richmond in the wee hours of April 1. A police investigation called the shooting "justifiable homicide" in that Dowell was shot fleeing the scene of a robbery.

But Mrs. Dowell thought otherwise: "I believe the police murdered my son," she said. The *Black Panther* reported what it called "the Dowell family point of view" and "questionable facts" in the police report. Newspaper and police reports said that three shots had been fired. The coroner's report and surrounding neighbors established that six to ten shots were fired. The police said that young Dowell was running and jumped over a fence to escape apprehension; the Dowell family said that Denzil had suffered a hip injury in a car accident several years before, rendering him unable to run very well and certainly incapable of jumping over a fence. The coroner reported, the *Black Panther* continued, that Dowell had bled to death, and yet no pool of blood was found by the body. Furthermore, it was said that the policeman knew Dowell by name and had stopped him several times before.

The *Black Panther* went on to report that the Dowell family and twelve hundred petition signatories demanded that there be a grand jury investigation. They requested that the officer who admitted to the shooting be removed from duty pending an investigation. "The sheriff refused our request."

All in all, the Dowell episode was a classic "Black Panther" case and had in it all the right ingredients for the Panthers to launch their cause. Was property so much more valuable than human life that the police should have the right to shoot and to kill in suspected-robbery cases? Implicit in their reporting of the incident was the warning that if black people didn't arm themselves, they stood an excellent chance of being gunned down like Denzil Dowell: "We believe we can end police brutality in our black community by organizing black self-defense groups that are dedicated to defending our black community from racist police oppression and brutality. The Second Amendment of the Constitution of the United States gives a right to bear arms. We therefore believe that all black people should arm themselves for self-defense."

"Arming for self-defense," while it was to remain the principal *raison d'être* of the Black Panthers, was, and is, only one item in their program. "What We Want, What We Believe"—the Black Panther manifesto—appeared in the second issue of the newspaper, May 15, 1967. Shedding its crude mimeograph beginnings, the paper had grown to full tabloid size. Few could quarrel with any of the points in the Ten Point Program. It called for black self-determination, full employment, decent housing, more relevant education, trial by a jury of peers and, finally, number ten said it all: "land, bread, housing, education, clothing, justice and peace."

Apart from the armed self-defense principle, the only other items that a reasonable man might take issue with were points six and eight: "We want all black men to be exempt from military service." "We want freedom for all black men held in federal, state, county and city prisons and jails." And yet their reasons for these demands did not seem so outrageous: "We believe that black people should not be forced to fight in the military service to defend a racist government that does not protect us. We will not fight and kill other people of color in the world who, like black people, are being victimized by the white racist government of America. . . ."

But probably very few ever got around to reading the Panther Ten Point Program, so hysterical was much of the early publicity attending the party. Part of the hysteria, the Panthers themselves courted. They were brazenly bearing arms in a city already terribly frightened of exploding into another Watts. But for every white middle-class heart that shrank in fear of the Black Panthers there was one young black soul of nineteen or twenty who, alienated from everything else, found comfort in joining the organization.

Their most celebrated exploit was to come on May 2, 1967. The Panthers had earned sufficient notoriety to prompt the California legislature to consider tighter gun-control laws. Heretofore, there had been no restrictions on the purchase of rifles or shotguns. Handguns could be sold to all but convicted felons, narcotics addicts, aliens and those under eighteen. On the day in question the Sacramento legislature was holding hearings on a bill, introduced by Republican Assemblyman Don Mulford, that would prohibit instruction in the use of firearms for the purpose of rioting and forbidding the carrying of loaded firearms on public streets and in public places by all except peace officers, guards and members of the armed forces.

The Panthers decided that they would go to Sacramento to protest the introduction of the bill. Huey, it was also decided, would not go. It might not be safe and they could not afford to lose him. He wanted to go, but was voted down. Thirty of them made the trip to Sacramento—six women and twenty-four men. Some of them, such as sixteen-year-old Bobby Hutton, were not quite men. They parked their caravan of automobiles. Twenty of them were armed—with .45's, with .357 Magnums, with all the weapons which by now had come to be conventional Black Panther arms. In scattered formation, their weapons pointed toward the sky, they moved nonchalantly toward the Capitol. People gaped at them in the street: *Who are the niggers? Where the hell are they going with those guns!* But they went ahead on their way, seemingly oblivious of the stir they were causing.

On the Capitol steps, Bobby Seale read a statement from the Minister of Defense of the Black Panther Party:

"The Black Panther Party for Self-Defense calls upon the American people in general and black people in particular to take careful note of the racist California legislature, which is now considering legislation aimed at keeping the black people disarmed and powerless at the very same time that racist police agencies throughout the country are intensifying the terror, brutality, murder and repression of black people. . . .

"Black people have begged, prayed, petitioned, demonstrated and everything else to get the racist power structure of America to right the wrongs which have historically been perpetrated against black people. All of these efforts have been answered by more repression, deceit and hypocrisy. . . .

"The Black Panther Party for Self-Defense believes that the time has come for black people to arm themselves against the terror before it is too late. The pending Mulford Act brings the hour of doom one step nearer. A people who have suffered so much for so long at the hands of a racist society must draw the line somewhere. . . ."

On the other side of the Capitol lawn the governor of the state was partaking of a picnic lunch with thirty youngsters from the Valley View Intermediate School.

The Black Panthers went inside. By now there was a retinue of reporters and photographers with them. There were guards and state police looking on who might have arrested them, but *goddamit all* there was nothing to arrest them for. It must have caused those guards and policemen terrible frustration: *Thirty niggers—not just one or two, mind you—thirty niggers strutting around the California legislature, scaring the shit out of everybody—and we can't arrest them. We can't touch them. What the fuck is this state, this country, coming to?*

But later on they *were* arrested. A swarm of state police and plain-clothesmen closed in as the Panthers were returning to their cars for the trip back to Oakland. No shots were fired, no one resisted arrest. They were variously charged with carrying loaded weapons in a motor vehicle—a violation of an obscure fish and game code law—and with conspiracy to commit a misdemeanor (i.e., disturbing the decorum of the legislature), with carrying concealed weapons and brandishing weapons in a threatening manner. Among those arrested were James and George Dowell, brothers of the late Denzil Dowell, Emory Douglas, a young man with a talent for drawing who was to become Minister of Culture, and of course Bobby Seale, who was to serve five months in jail following conviction. Also arrested (for violation of parole) was a *Ramparts* writer, Eldridge Cleaver—by now also a Black Panther—who went to Sacramento unarmed but for a camera to cover the "story."

Eldridge wrote of the incident:

> Although I was there as a reporter, with an assignment from my magazine, and with the advance permission of my parole agent, I was arrested by the Sacramento police; and then the parole authority slapped a "Hold" on me so that I could not get out on bail. To the surprise of both the cops and the parole authority, their investigations proved that my press credentials were in order, that I was indeed there on an assignment, and . . . that I had been armed with nothing more lethal than a camera and a ball point pen. Still the Sacramento cops would not drop the charges and the parole authority would not lift its "Hold" until the judge, citing the obvious "mistake" on the part of the cops, released me on my own recognizance. Then magnanimously, the parole authority lifted its "Hold."

If the point of the May, '67, "March on Sacramento" was to stifle the growth of a gun-control law budding in the legislature, then the Panthers' armed "invasion" of the legislature was a fiasco. It was largely *because of them* that the new law was introduced, and the May 2 foray served only to speed the bill's passage. Indeed, it resulted in an even tighter gun-control statute being passed than that earlier considered.

If the point was to publicize a still relatively unknown movement, the march was a resounding success. The story made the front pages of every major daily in the state, and television, true to its mission, did not fail to bring California live film coverage of the whole "bizarre episode." All in all, the news must have persuaded many a young black Oaklander that he ought to join the party: *These cats are serious!* The news must also have caused many a young Oakland policeman to shudder and say, *"These niggers have got to be stopped and stopped now before they get out of hand."*

And yet you could very easily overrationalize their motives. You could very easily say that Huey Newton decided to send the Black Panthers marching on Sacramento to get publicity or to kill a gun-control bill or for this reason or that reason or for some combination of reasons and you might be a little right. But you might also be a lot wrong because in clamoring for explanations you ignored all the slippery indefinables.

The thirty people, the thirty cats, who went to Sacramento were not the one nigger in a hundred that goes to Princeton, the one in ten with a lawn to mow and a Porsche to wash and wax on Saturday. These thirty weren't tennis-playing niggers or button-down niggers with big shiny hard-kicking cordovans when those are *the* shoes to wear or skinny little soft toes from Switzerland when those are the shoes to wear. These were not slick cocktail niggers shooting down slick white chicks at parties. These weren't smooth-talking niggers that could fool you on the telephone and make you think you were talking to Adlai Stevenson's son instead of Willie Lee Johnson's son. These weren't country club niggers with Diners' Club cards and African goatskin rugs and bullshit dashikis and oily elbows to hide the ashy skin.

No—these were the cats off the block. These were the bad motherfuckers, who came up hustling and pimping and taking numbers and kickin' ass just to stay alive just because they didn't know how to do anything else. These were the cats that hang out in the hallways that have more piss on one floor than all the urinals at Fort Bragg. These were the cats that hang out at pool halls where mean motherfuckers kick ass just to stay in shape. These were the niggers that get their heads slammed up against the wall at three o'clock in the morning by the police out looking for niggers to slam up against the wall. These were the cats that are sick of all that, sick of talking about it, sick of other niggers talking about it, sick of jive meetings and jive unenforced laws, and jive TV shows with jive niggers talking about what they don't know.

So when the California legislature decides it's time to take your guns away and give more guns to the police, you don't appeal to the NAACP for help. You get your M-1's and your .357 Magnums and your 12-gauge shotguns and you move. You *do* something. You take action. You cause a stir, a stink, anything. You *cause* things to happen.

No self-respecting Black Panther would ever concede the point, but their "March on Sacramento" was a terribly American thing to do. Americans have been marching on Sacramento for as long as they can remember. The same impatience with high-sounding debate, the same proclivity for spontaneity of action the Black Panthers demonstrated, are perhaps the qualities de Tocqueville saw as national characteristics more than a century ago:

> The citizen of the United States is taught from his earliest infancy to rely upon his own exertions, in order to resist the evils and the difficulties of life; he looks upon the social authority with an eye of mistrust and anxiety, and he only claims its assistance when he is quite unable to shift without it. . . . The same spirit pervades every act of social life. If a stoppage occurs in a thoroughfare, and the circulation of the public is hindered, the neighbors immediately constitute a deliberative body; and this extemporaneous assembly gives rise to an executive power, which remedies the inconvenience, before anybody has thought of recurring to an authority superior to that of the persons immediately concerned. . . . In the United

States associations are established to promote public order, commerce, industry, morality, and religion; for there is no end which the human will, seconded by the collective exertions of individuals, despairs of attaining.*

In search of a party symbol, Huey Newton, Bobby Seale and Eldridge Cleaver went to San Francisco to the apartment of Beverly Axelrod one evening in mid-May, 1967. A photographer was summoned and Eldridge went about the business of setting up the shot: a zebra-skin rug on the floor, a large rattan wicker chair with all its regal pretensions. On either side of the chair two African shields and seated in the chair the Minister of Defense of the Black Panther Party for Self-Defense, the Honorable Huey P. Newton. Huey was dressed in the familiar black beret and black leather jacket. In his left hand he held a spear, in his right hand a sawed-off shotgun. On his baby brown face he wore a scowl, a forced ferocity. Click, click, and a poster was born.

In the meantime the party went about its business: printing and selling a newspaper (twenty-five cents a copy), holding rallies and bail-fund parties, bailing "brothers" out of jail and of course patrolling the police. "We don't like the way you cops have been misusing the law and mistreating the people," the party said to the police. "You are civil servants, which means that the people—all the people—have delegated to you the task of securing the people in the daily exercise of their rights. . . . But because you have grossly defiled the very name—Peace Officer—by which you are known, you have become the enemy of the people; you have become a cancerous growth on the body politic. . . . We are here to civilize you. We are here to teach you how to

* Alexis de Tocqueville, *Democracy in America*, New York, Schocken Books, Inc., 1961.

love and serve the people. We are going to do the job whether you like it or not. . . ."

The Oakland police in turn began to track the Panthers: they knew the Panther cars, they knew where the Panthers lived. They went to Panther rallies, they watched, they stalked.

There was a bail-fund party held one night in Richmond in June, 1967. Huey Newton was there. The police were outside in a car—motor off, lights out. They waited outside almost all night until near dawn, when people who finally got tired of trying to outwait the police began to leave.

"We walked outside, got in our cars," as Huey remembers it, "and one guy made a U-turn in the middle of the block. As far as I know, that's perfectly legal in a residential area —I'm not sure about that, it may have been a violation, but anyway the police followed him. We watched and then we followed. They cut him off about a block away from the house. We stopped our cars—it must have been about fifteen or twenty people there. We stopped our cars, got out and just stood on the sidewalk. The guy had been drinking and didn't want to sign the ticket. I saw a fight coming so I walked over to the car and I told him to sign the ticket and that we could bring it up in the courts—but sign the ticket. They argued back and forth, and about five minutes later, seven or eight policemen showed up and stormed out of the car and this one very young policeman—he looked no more that twenty-two or twenty-three—starts to go around and step on everyone's feet. He was the only one doing this. . . . All of this time I'm trying to get the guy to sign the ticket. . . . The young policeman stepped on one guy's foot and the guy grabbed him and pushed him off and all the police charged in on this guy and I ran up to them and said, 'This is not necessary.' Then they started beating him with a club, and I said again, 'No one is armed, this is not necessary.' One of the cops turned around, charged me and backed me up onto the car and got me in a choke hold. The other people ran to me and said, 'Do you want us to help you?' and I said, 'No, I'll take an arrest, I'll take an arrest.' So no one did anything. . . .

"So I was arrested, the guy in the car was arrested and one other person. And then this big cop—he was about 6'8"—began to brutalize this other person. I didn't get beaten very badly because I didn't say anything. They would hurl profanities at me, but I didn't say anything. I kept telling the guys to shut up, but they wouldn't. But after this police-man finished beating the guy, he says, 'I have to go because I have to take my wife and kids to church at nine o'clock.'"

The three were convicted of a misdemeanor—interfering with an arresting officer. The two "guys" were sentenced to ten days' hard labor. Huey got sixty days.

But there was no letting up. In word and spirit, the Panthers continued to vent their fury against the police in Oakland and anywhere else in America they were to be found. Nor was there to be any letting up in their preaching the need for black people to arm themselves. The summer of 1967 saw violent racial upheaval in several American cities. Not the least of these was Newark, and the Panthers did not fail to point out the lessons to be learned from the "black liberation struggle" in that beleaguered New Jersey city. On the front page of the July 20 issue of the *Black Panther* there was a photograph, not very well reproduced, but clear enough so that readers could see a black man face down on the pavement of a city street, his hands hand-cuffed behind his back, with three white-helmeted police-men hovering over him.

The caption:

How can any black man in his right mind look at this picture in racist dog America and not understand what is happening? It is obvious that the brother on the ground is the underdog and that the arrogant gestapo dogs on top have the advantage. What is the essential difference between the man on the bottom and the pigs on top? If the brother had had his piece with him, it is obvious that the pigs would have had to deal with him in a different way. And the brother may have gotten something down—that is, if he knew how to shoot straight.

■   ■   ■

October 27, 1967. It was three years ago to the day that Huey Newton had been placed on probation and now it was over. It was a day for celebrating. Huey had a speaking engagement that afternoon at San Francisco State College. On the platform with him was Dr. Harry Edwards of San Jose State College, who was later to declare his solidarity with the Black Panther Party, who was also later to organize a black boycott against the United States Olympic teams. The subject of Huey's talk was "the future of the black liberation struggle." He received a seventy-five-dollar honorarium.

He had a date with his fiancée, LaVerne Williams, that night. Things might have happened very differently if she had been able to go with him. But she was not; she felt ill and told him to go and celebrate without her. Huey had been talking about having a good time the night his probation was up for so many months. Why should she be the one to spoil it for him? Huey borrowed her Volkswagen and went out.

He stopped at a bar, Bosun's Locker in Oakland, to have a drink and to cash his seventy-five-dollar check. From there he went to a church social, where he met a friend of his, Gene McKinney. And then there was a party to go to.

The party broke up around four in the morning, and Gene and Huey left and were heading for an all-night joint to get something to eat. They never got there. They were near the corner of Seventh and Willow streets in the ghetto that is West Oakland. Nearby was a construction site where a new post office was being built. Near also was Esther's Cocktail Lounge and Jenkins' Bar B-Que and Howard's Pool Hall.

A policeman in a patrol car signaled them to pull over. The policeman was John Frey. Frey got out of his car and came over to Huey and Gene McKinney in the Volkswagen. He knew the car of course. It was what had come to be called "a known Black Panther vehicle." And there could hardly have been a policeman in Oakland who did not have a list of "Black Panther vehicle" license plate numbers.

"Well, well, well," Frey said. "What do we have here? The great, great Huey P. Newton." He asked Huey for his driver's license and registration. Huey gave them to him. Frey returned the license, kept the registration card and went back to the patrol car. Moments later, another police car arrived. Frey had radioed for assistance. Patrolman Herbert Heanes had come to give a hand. Heanes got out of his car, paused momentarily to say something to Frey and then came up to Huey, who was still seated in LaVerne's Volkswagen.

"Mr. Williams, do you have any further identification?" Heanes asked Huey.

"I am Huey Newton."

Heanes nodded his head and said, "I know who you are."

Frey returned now from the first patrol car and ordered Huey out of the Volkswagen. Frey searched Huey as Heanes went around to the passenger side. McKinney got out of the car. Frey told Huey to walk back to the patrol car, he wanted to talk to him. Huey had a criminal lawbook in his hand. As they walked toward the patrol car, Huey pointed out that Frey had no reasonable cause to arrest him. He began to open his lawbook. "You can take that book and stick it in your ass, nigger," Frey said.

Precisely what happened in the ensuing moments is not clear. It may never be. What is known is that just before dawn on October 28, 1967, Officer Herbert Heanes of the Oakland Police Department sustained multiple bullet wounds; Huey Newton sustained one bullet wound to the abdomen; Gene McKinney vanished; and Officer John Frey was killed.

Two weeks later District Attorney J. Frank Coakley asked for a three-count indictment against Newton. The Alameda County Grand Jury pondered the matter for twenty-seven minutes. On November 13, 1967, Huey Newton was formally charged with the murder of John Frey, the felonious assault of Herbert Heanes and the kidnaping of a certain Dell Ross. (Dell Ross, it was alleged, was in his car near the scene of the shooting, when Newton, wounded, fleeing apprehension and in search of medical attention, forced Ross at gunpoint to drive him to a hospital.)

A cause was born: "Free Huey! Free Huey! Huey Must Be Set Free! If Huey Is Not Freed, the Sky Is the Limit." "Free Huey" buttons. "Free Huey" posters everywhere—on telephone poles, on palm trees, on the walls of broken-down tenement buildings. "Free Huey" bumper stickers, speeches, rallies, picnics, barbecues. "Free Huey!"

Directing most of this activity was Eldridge Cleaver, heretofore a model parolee. He had been warned before, in very blunt terms, that his parole was subject to immediate revocation by the California Adult Authority. And if he insisted upon making speeches of the offensive sort he made in April of that year in Kezar Stadium in San Francisco before 65,000 Vietnam war protesters, then very likely he would go back to jail. Thus between April and October, 1967, Eldridge cooled it; he stayed on ice: no flaming speeches against the war; no scorching indictments of the penal system; no pouring of vitriol upon His Excellency, the Governor of California. Obviously his association with the Black Panther Party for Self-Defense in this period had to be, at the very least, covert. When the Panthers trooped up to Sacramento to the legislature with their guns, Eldridge was there, but on the sidelines—taking pictures. And while he was already now editing their newspaper, as the Minister of Information, the *Black Panther* masthead, melodramatically, left him nameless and "underground."

But after the events of October 28 the lid was off. "I am finished," Eldridge was to write later in an open letter to Governor Ronald Reagan, "with the California Department of Correction, with the Adult Authority, with parole officers, with prisons, and all of their world of restraint, confinement, and punishment. I can't relate to them any more, because I am free. I am free man, Governor, and I no longer know how to submit and play the part of a debtor to society. . . ."

In February, 1968, *Soul on Ice* was published, one year after its author had been released from prison. The warm critical acclaim the book received, the ensuing television and radio appearances along with numerous newspaper and magazine interviews, very quickly provided Eldridge with a national forum. He used it.

The Black Panthers began to court support for the "Free Huey" movement from whites. Most significant in this drive was a coalition formed between the Panthers and the California Peace and Freedom Party, a young ambitious radical-left party born of a movement to end the war in Vietnam and determined to function "within an electoral process rigged to exclude it." Handicapped by lack of money, the Peace and Freedom Party nevertheless managed to nail down a spot on the ballot by inducing over 100,000 California citizens to join its fledgling ranks.

The union between the Panthers and PFP was by no means joyous. It was, as Eldridge described it, "narrow, limited, tentative and viewed with mutual suspicion." Each hoped to broaden its base through the other. Before now the PFP had done almost no registration work in the black communities. Before now the cries of "Free Huey" had come almost exclusively from black mouths. However frail the coalition, the union was consummated to the extent that the PFP endorsed the Black Panther Ten Point Program, took up the spreading "Free Huey" chant and nominated four Black Panthers to run for office under the PFP banner: Huey Newton for Alameda County's Seventh Congressional District, Bobby Seale for the Seventeenth Assembly District, Mrs. Eldridge Cleaver for the Eighteenth A.D. in San Francisco and, eventually, Eldridge himself as candidate for President.

The early clamor to free Huey produced another bond— the "merger" between the Black Panthers and the Student Nonviolent Coordinating Committee, but, like the coalition with the PFP, this last never quite jelled. Nevertheless, on February 17, 1968, a very convincing semblance of solidarity appeared. It was Huey's twenty-sixth birthday, and a crowd of more than seven thousand came to the Oakland Auditorium to see a speakers' platform shared by Eldridge Cleaver, Bobby Seale, Bob Avakian of the Peace and Freedom Party and three distinguished gentlemen from SNCC. The merger was formally announced, and Stokely Carmichael was drafted as the Prime Minister of the Black Panther Party, H. Rap Brown as Minister of Justice and James Foreman as Minister of Foreign Affairs.

And while the Panthers were busy mobilizing support for Huey, the police were busy mobilizing against the Panthers. It was said that a Black Panther could not scratch his ass without getting picked up by the police and charged with the willful and premeditated scratching of his ass. On January 15 at about three in the morning, members of the Special Tactical Squad of the San Francisco Police Department, unembarrassed by the lack of a search warrant, broke the door down and ransacked the Cleaver apartment looking for guns. At 3:30 A.M. on February 25, Bobby Seale was roused from his sleep to be charged by the Berkeley police with "conspiracy to commit murder"—a charge later dropped—and with the illegal possession of weapons.

On April 3 twelve Oakland police carrying 12-gauge shotguns (accompanied by two clergymen whose presence presumably sanctified the invasion) invaded St. Augustine's Episcopal church, apparently in search of Bobby Seale and Eldridge Cleaver. The church had come to be a regular Panther meeting place, but neither Seale nor Cleaver happened to be there at the time. Obviously disappointed, the police lowered their shotguns and left.

Eldridge has described the reaction of the Reverend Earl Neil, the young black pastor of the church, whose gentle temperament, then as now, seemed quite out of keeping with the ferocity of the Black Panthers:

> Father Neil, whose church it is, happened to be present to witness the entire event. Theretofore, criticism of the police had been just that, and although he was inclined to believe that there was some validity to all the complaints, it was all still pretty abstract to him because he had never witnessed

anything with his own eyes. Well, he had witnessed it now, and in his own church—with ugly shotguns thrown down on innocent, unarmed people who were holding a quiet peaceful assembly. Father Neil was outraged. He called a press conference next day at which he denounced the Oakland Police Department for behaving like Nazi storm troopers inside his church. However, Father Neil's press conference was upstaged by the fact that earlier in the day, his brother of the cloth, Martin Luther King, had got assassinated in Memphis, Tennessee.

The main Panther-police event of the season came two days later, on April 6. As usual, there were two very different versions of what happened that night. According to the Oakland police, a patrol car stopped to make a routine investigation of the occupants of three parked cars. It was thought that one of the cars with an out-of-state license plate might have been stolen. The police said that the eight Panthers in the cars started shooting without warning. The two patrolmen, slightly wounded, returned fire and radioed for help. When the reinforcements arrived seconds later, two of the cornered Panthers were promptly arrested and all but two of the others were apprehended shortly thereafter. Eldridge Cleaver and Bobby Hutton, the last of the eight, fled to a nearby house, but after a barrage of fire bombs, rifle and machine-gun fire they agreed to surrender. When they emerged from the building, there was a shout that Hutton still had a gun. He ran, the police said, and was shot and killed.

Two weeks later during the Alameda County Grand Jury proceedings, which ended with the Panthers being indicted for assault with intent to commit murder, the District Attorney presented the "confessions" of four of the accused Panthers. Collectively, the statements tended to fix the blame on

Eldridge Cleaver. It was *he* who had called the meeting that night (Bobby Seale was in Los Angeles at the time). It was Eldridge who distributed the weapons. It was Eldridge who said, "Let's go out and scout around and if the cops stop us we'll have a shoot-out with them." It was Eldridge who fired the first shot.

In his account of the April 6 shoot-out, Eldridge speculated that the Oakland police were deliberately trying to sabotage a widely advertised fund-raising picnic the Panthers were planning for the next day. They had, he wrote, experienced the same kind of harassment two months before with the February 17 "Free Huey" rally: police attempts to block issuance of a permit for the rally site and wholesale arrest of Panthers after the rally in an attempt to drain such money as might have been raised.

> So, in staging the barbecue picnic, we had this experience in mind, and we had cautioned all party members to be on their best behavior in order to avoid any incidents with the police that would provide a pretext for arrest. . . .
>
> It is a rule of our party that no well known member of the party is to be out on the Oakland streets at night unless accompanied by two or more other people, because we felt that if the Oakland cops ever caught one of us alone like that there was a chance that such a one might be killed and there would be only racist pig cops for witnesses: Verdict of the Coroner's Inquest, "Justifiable Homicide." Period. After the way they tried to murder our leader, Minister of Defense Huey P. Newton, we were not taking any chances. So on the night of April 6, the car I was driving was being followed by two carloads of Panthers and I was on my way to David Hilliard's house at 34th and Magnolia. In the car with me were David Hilliard, Wendell Wade, and John Scott, all members of the Black Panther Party.
>
> We were only a few blocks away from David's house when,

all of a sudden, I was overcome by an irresistible urge, a necessity, to urinate, and so I turned off the brightly lighted street we were on . . . pulled to the curb, stopped the car, got out and started relieving myself. The two Panther cars following us pulled up behind to wait. While I was in the middle in this call of nature, a car came around the corner from the direction that we ourselves had come, and I found myself in danger of being embarrassed, I thought, by a passing car. So I cut off the flow, then, and awkwardly hurried around to the other side of the car, to the sidewalk, to finish what had already been started and what was most difficult to stop—I recall that I did soil my trousers somewhat. But this car, instead of passing, stopped, and a spotlight from it was turned on and beamed my way. I could see it was the cops, two of them. They got out of the car and stood there, not leaving the car, each standing just outside. One of them shouted, "Hey, you, walk out into the middle of the street with your hands up, quick!"

Eldridge said he quickly zipped up his fly and started to come around the front of his car, when one policeman started shouting and the other started shooting. Later when he and "Li'l" Bobby Hutton were holed up in the house surrounded by policemen, Eldridge was struck in the chest by a tear-gas canister. Bobby helped him take all his clothes off trying to find the wound. Overcome by tear gas, their refuge now riddled with bullets, and Cleaver now shot in the leg, they decided to surrender. Eldridge threw Bobby's rifle outside.

Then Little Bobby helped me to my feet and we tumbled through the door. There were pigs in the windows above us in the house next door, with guns pointed at us. They told us not to move, to raise our hands. This we did, and an army of pigs ran up from the street. They started kicking and cursing us, but we were already beyond any pain, beyond feeling. The pigs told us to stand up. Little Bobby helped me to my feet. The pigs pointed to a squad car parked in the middle of the street and told us to run to it. I told them I couldn't run. Then they snatched Little Bobby away from me and shoved him forward, telling him to run to the car. It was a sickening sight. Little Bobby, coughing and choking on the night air that was burning his lungs as my own were burning from the tear gas, stumbled forward as best he could, and after he had traveled about ten yards the pigs cut loose on him with their guns.

Cleaver was subsequently taken to Vacaville State Prison as a parole violator. He had violated parole, the California Adult Authority said, by being in possession of a gun, by associating with people of bad reputation and by failure to cooperate with his parole agent. In addition, he was indicted on three counts of attempted murder of policemen and three counts of assault with a deadly weapon. Bail was set at $50,000.

To the outrage of many, to the joy of many others and surely to his own great surprise, Eldridge Cleaver was released from Vacaville two months later. His attorneys had petitioned for a writ of habeas corpus in Solano County, which incorporates Vacaville. To the utter astonishment of all concerned, Superior Court Judge Raymond J. Sherwin noted in a hearing:

"The record here is that though the petitioner was arrested and his parole cancelled more than two months ago, hearings before the Adult Authority have not even been scheduled. There is nothing to indicate why it was deemed necessary to cancel his parole before his trial on the pending of criminal charges of which he is presumed innocent. . . . It has to be stressed that the uncontradicted evidence presented to this Court indicated that the petitioner had been a model parolee. The peril to his parole status stemmed from no failure of personal rehabilitation, but from his undue eloquence in pursuing political goals, goals which were offensive to many of his contemporaries. Not only was there absence of cause for the cancellation of parole, it was the product of a type of pressure unbecoming, to say the least, to the law enforcement paraphernalia of this State."

In view of the $50,000 bail already set on Cleaver's other charges, Judge Sherwin was moved to fix bail (on Eldridge's parole status) at a mere $27.50. Shortly after three o'clock on the afternoon of June 13, 1968, Eldridge Cleaver was released from the State Medical Facility (so-called) at Vacaville.

It was about this time that *Life* magazine decided to do a story focused either on Eldridge Cleaver, on the Panthers in general or on Oakland, the "tinderbox about to explode."

I had been in San Francisco before but never to Oakland, its sister city across the bay. Appropriately enough, the San Francisco Bay Bridge linking the two is one of the longest bridges in the world. San Francisco, while it has its share of blight and decay, compensates for it by being so brashly cosmopolitan, so frantically happy. San Francisco and all that is in it are enthralled by the simple joy of motion. San Francisco swings.

A nagging sensation of death comes from walking through what purports to be a residential street of West Oakland. The sun shines brightly but not oppressively. There is just enough wind to keep palm trees aflutter. But the stillness is frightening. Policemen cruise in and out of the side streets in their glistening cars, their .30-caliber rifles slung over the dashboard as casually as St. Christopher medals. Too many of those grand old houses are boarded up—dead. As you pass by, the certainty sweeps over you that you are about to be shot through the head with high-powered accuracy.

■   ■   ■

There was a distinct click on the line the first time I tried to telephone Eldridge Cleaver; it was the familiar sound of a wire-tap being engaged. A peculiar feeling comes from knowing that you are speaking to at least two people when you choose to speak to only one.

Eldridge, as I expected, was not home, but Kathleen, his wife, invited me to stop by. The Cleavers lived then on Oak Street in San Francisco. As instructed, we rang the down-stairs doorbell three times. Kathleen peeped out of the window from three floors up, and I suppose that photographer Howard Bingham and I looked unforbidding enough so she let us in. Upstairs she apologized for all the cloak-and-dagger, but they had to be careful she said because the pigs were closing in. I nodded casually as though I knew per-fectly well how it felt when "the pigs were closing in."

Their living room was dominated by a grand wicker rattan chair and floor-to-ceiling shelves of books—Fanon, the *Auto-biography* of Malcolm X, *The Confessions of Nat Turner*, Dostoyevsky, Sartre, Mailer, Baldwin, *Black Rage, The Eco-nomic Transformation of Cuba*, among many others.

Kathleen sat on the wicker chair and handed me a folder full of newspaper clippings. She seemed so thoroughly in command of her movements, with elegant black boots hug-ging her legs to the knees and reddish-brown hair coiling to majestic heights above her head. And yet in another moment she looked so very frail, the belt around her waist drawn to its thinnest girth, her face looking so very soft. She was very young; twenty-three really is very young.

We didn't catch up with Eldridge until the next day. He had so many appearances to make that neither he nor anyone around him was ever quite sure where he would be from one moment to the next. Anyway, we got to the Berkeley campus just in time to watch him leaving the podium before a crowd of three hundred cheering students. He looked tall and mighty in the familiar black leather jacket and boots and the beginnings of a beard, but the thundering blackness of his clothing and dark glasses was softened by a beige turtleneck sweater and tiny multicolored beads around his neck.

I told him who we were, what we had come for. (Howard, meanwhile, had assumed his wide-angle crouch position and had begun shooting.) Eldridge smiled and nodded his tentative approval to our presence, but the hopeless feeling came over me that I was addressing an oak tree.

Abruptly he asked me: "Have you ever written about the black liberation struggle, man?"

And with as much authority as I could summon on such short notice I said, "Yes, of course I have." The moment froze, and we simply walked side by side to his car with nothing else to say to each other. He was too busy with his own private thoughts and I with mine.

We returned to the Berkeley campus the next day. The Berkeley City Council was holding public hearings to determine whether the Black Panthers, the Peace and Freedom Party, the hippies, the Yippies and assorted student groups against the war in Vietnam should be allowed to hold an outdoor rally on July 4. Bobby Seale was there. Three watchful Panthers were standing around him as he awaited his turn outside the campus building to appear before the Council. Seale looked as though he hadn't slept in a week. His hair was uncombed; his gaunt face was heavy with fatigue. Good photograph! I nudged Howard, who raised his camera about to shoot.

"You not taking no pictures in here—mother*fucker*," a voice behind us said. We spun around to confront another Panther. He couldn't have been more than eighteen, but his voice had all of the raspy authority of an Army master sergeant. Howard whipped out his press credentials. In his haste to show that he was "clean," his hand obscured half of the press pass. The visible portion read: "Los Angeles Police Department."

The Panther was astonished. "You a pig?" he asked. "Now I *know* you not takin' no pictures 'round here."

Bobby Seale came over, smiling. "It's all right, brother," he said to the young Panther.

"But these cats are pigs, Chairman Bobby. They—"

"No, it's okay," Bobby said.

"If you cats are gonna be taking pictures," Bobby warned us later, "better watch your step. These brothers are not playin'. "

■   ■   ■

The main office of the Black Panther Party was then a cramped store front on Grove Street in West Oakland, sandwiched between a tiny soul-food joint and an alley. A huge poster of Huey Newton stared at you as you walked in. Signs on the walls reminded the membership that alcohol or the drinking of it was not permitted on the premises. Nor would the presence of any form of narcotics be tolerated. Signs also reminded the membership that it was time to intensify the struggle and that power grew out of the barrel of the gun. Another sign demanded strict adherence to party rules:

1. No party member can have narcotics or weed in his possession while doing party work.
2. Any member found shooting narcotics will be expelled from this party.
3. No party member can be drunk while doing daily party work.

4. No party member will violate rules relating to office work and general meetings of the Black Panther Party, and meetings of the Black Panther Party anywhere.
5. No party member will point or fire a weapon unnecessarily at anyone other than the enemy.
6. No party member can join any other army or force other than the Black Liberation Army.
7. No party member can have a weapon in his possession while drunk or loaded on narcotics or weed.
8. No party member will commit any crimes against other Black people at all, and cannot steal or take from the people; not even a needle and a piece of thread.
9. When arrested, Black Panther Party members will give only name and address and will sign nothing. Legal first aid must be understood by all party members.
10. The Ten Point Program and platform of the Black Panther Party must be known and understood by each party member.

The telephone rang constantly. There was a sister seated at the cluttered desk to answer all the calls. Periodically she would come outside to inquire whether anyone had seen "Chairman Bobby" or "Captain David." Like her male fellows she wore black and powder blue and a rifle shell dangled from a chain around her neck. All telephone conversations ended with her saying "Power to the people!" or "Panther power!"

There was the loud screech of automobile tires coming from outside the office. An enormous yellow chariot pulled up to the curb. A man of about thirty-five sprang out of the freshly polished Cadillac. He wore the conventional Panther uniform, complete with beret and dark glasses. He had a limp in his right leg. He was introduced simply as "Captain Crutch." It amazed me that Captain Crutch looked so out of keeping with his fellow Panthers with his show of "middle-class decadence," brazenly parked curbside, and, what was more, his head was (as we used to say) "gassed." Where was his proud Afro haircut? I wondered.

We shook hands, whereupon he frowned impatiently and said, "We don't shake hands like that, brother. You better get yourself together." And then he demonstrated: a firm conventional handshake first, then a kind of upturned handshake, grasping thumbs, then another ordinary handshake, then a grasping of fingers, of shoulders, ordinary handshake again, then a snapping of fingers . . . it was an old African tribal ritual. I decided then that in the future I would use the first three steps, which struck me as adequate enough a fraternal greeting, and that I would skip the rest.

"See that fine yellow bitch over there?" Captain Crutch asked. "I got that when I was pimping. Now I use her in the struggle. She serves the people now."

The Black Panther political education classes for that area were held in St. Augustine's church, the Episcopal church in the black community of Oakland. Thirty brothers and sisters attended the class on this first day that I went. They were as young as sixteen. They were as old as forty-seven. They entered the church variously laughing, talking, reading. Each of them carried a tiny red volume—the Red Book, the *Quotations from Chairman Mao Tse-tung*. In an orderly precision they each took a folding chair from the corner rack, placing them in classroom-style rows of five and six. At the table in the front of the room sat the conductors of the class, David Hilliard, then National Headquarters Captain, and George Murray, Minister of Education. They were going to deal today with the *Catechism of the Revolutionist* by Mikhail Bakunin, a contemporary of Karl Marx, Minister Murray said.

And the brothers and sisters listened attentively to learn what their attitudes as revolutionists should be:

The revolutionist is a doomed man. He has no personal interests, no affairs, sentiments, attachments, property, not even a name of his own. Everything in him is absorbed by one exclusive interest, one thought, one passion—the revolution. . . . He despises public opinion. He despises and hates the present-day code of morals with all its motivations and manifestations. To him, whatever aids the triumph of the revolution is ethical; all that which hinders it is unethical and criminal. . . . The nature of a real revolutionist precludes every bit of sentimentality, romanticism, of infatuation and exaltation. It precludes even personal hatred and revenge. Revolutionary passion having become a normal phenomenon, it must be combined with cold calculation. At all times and places the revolutionist must not be that towards which he is impelled by personal impulses, but that which the general interests of the revolution dictate.

They were also going to get into what Chairman Mao had to say about "liberalism," Minister Murray said. Captain Hilliard reminded the brothers and sisters that in coming up to address the class they should not be ashamed or afraid to use their own words and the language they were used to.

And according to Chairman Mao, what is liberalism?

One young brother thought he had the answer. He was only eighteen and new to the party, but he seemed determined not to look eighteen and new. On his way up to the front of the class he tucked his shirt in and glanced at his proud "Free Huey" button to see if it was straight.

"There's lots of different kinds, different types o' liberalism," he began. "Like say I come into the party with another cat and we been friends, we been tight for a long time and we're still tight and I see this cat breaking the rules o' the party. Like say I see him smokin' pot or somethin' while he's workin' for the party. If I don't say somethin' to the brother about it, tryin' to stay tight with the cat and if I don't bring the thing up with somebody else in the party, it would be bad for the cat and bad for the party and bad for the people and jus' bad for everybody. And if I acted like that, Chairman Mao says that I would be 'gaging in a type of liberalism."

The young brother paused to gauge reaction to his performance before returning to his seat. The class approved and voiced their approval: "Right on, brother, right on!"

After that meeting in the church I began to wake up. After reading more, in the Panther paper, I began to wake up:

> Black people have already judged you, America . . . and have condemned you to death. And we also know that history has selected us, your slaves and chief victims, to be your executioner, the instrument of your destruction. . . .

Read on, read on.

> What a laugh! America the beautiful. Home of the brave. Friend of the underdog. You once had a beautiful dream—but even then, while you dreamed that dream, you were foul and corrupt and rotten in your heart, but you were a minor league brigand and then when you compared yourself to the tyrannies in the world, you looked innocent by contrast to their greater evil. The innocent blood they had shed was a vast and ancient ocean, and yours was a fresh new stream. But now your little stream has become vaster than the sky and your evil dwarfs everything that has gone before. Now you stand naked before the world, before yourself, a predatory, genocidal Dorian Gray, stripped of all egalitarian democratic makeup. . . .
>
> America, you will be cleansed by fire, by blood, by death. . . .

Now how do you make that palatable to the readers of *Life* magazine? How do you make that palatable to potato farmers in Idaho and little old Presbyterian ladies in Massachusetts and construction workers in Pittsburgh? And isn't there an enormous absurdity about your even trying?

I began to look for soft chinks in the granite. Sometimes I found them. "We do not claim the right to indiscriminate violence. We seek no bloodbath," Eldridge once said to me.

"The Panthers is a political organization; it's a third party. The Republican Party, the Democratic Party, we find, do not answer the desires of black people. We find it necessary to create a third party—or really we think of it as a second party because there's not very much difference between the Republicans and the Democrats." Huey Newton himself said that once in an interview, and wasn't that a pretty mild thing to say?

But for each soft chink I found there were ten cold nuggets of steel to offset them. There was absolutely no way that I could tell everything I was learning about the Black Panthers and somehow make it digestible to America. The realization was slow in coming, but it was coming.

■　　　　■　　　　■

I was hoping that the first time I met Huey Newton it would not be at a massive press conference with ten thousand reporters milling about with microphones and pencils and pads. I suppose I was wishing that at some point I could whisper into Huey's ear: *"You cats are just kidding, aren't you? All this Panther stuff about revolution is a big put-on, isn't it, Huey? You can tell me; I won't tell a soul."* But I was to have no such privacy.

Awaiting trial for murder, Huey Newton was kept behind bars in the Alameda County Jail on the tenth floor of the county courthouse in Oakland. Probably no prisoner in Oak-

land's penal history was held in tighter security. After rigor-
ously checking our press credentials, sheriff's deputies admitted us past a massive iron gate leading to a small
anteroom where Newton, his hands calmly folded before
him, was seated at a table. To my dismay, two local television stations had sent teams over and their crew was busy
readying their equipment for the curtain to go up. It had
always seemed to me that there was something about TV
lights that introduced a theatrical unreality to the grimmest
of realities.

Newton was dressed in baggy gray prison flannel. He was
badly in need of a shave and haircut, but few women, it
seemed to me, would deny that he was handsome. His still
childlike face assumed a broad smile as we entered the room.
The various reporters introduced themselves and shook his
hand. I decided I had to somehow distinguish myself from
the horde, and when it was my turn to greet him, I went into
the Black Panther handshake in all its seven-part grandeur.
Newton looked me in the eye and grinned. I looked him in
the eye and grinned. There was great warmth in that moment. It felt good; it felt right. For one wistful second I was
a Black Panther, full-fledged—unquestioning, unplagued by
ponderous doubts, unshackled from divided loyalty. Black
Panther, full-fledged.

But the moment passed. . . .

The TV men turned on their lights. The radio men
plugged in their microphones and the questioning began:

*Some of the news media have branded you and the Black
Panthers in general as antiwhite racists. Will you comment
on those charges, Mr. Newton?*

"The Black Panther Party is against racism; we're not
racists, but we stand to protect the black community, to rid
America of racism. We're subject to the tactics of racists by

the white establishment, but it's a very common thing for the people who are in control of the mass media to define the victim of racism as a racist. . . ."

How was he being treated in jail? someone else wanted to know.

The answers were coming as though from a computer. The questions had obviously all been asked dozens of times before, and Newton, just as obviously, was sick of answering them. But he went on. There had been so much pressure from the outside, he said, his incarceration had been so scrutinized that the authorities did not dare brutalize him as they most certainly would otherwise have done. He was being rigidly segregated from the other prisoners for fear that he would start a Black Panther movement right there in jail. But there was no physical brutality. He once got into a heated argument, he said, with one of the sheriff's deputies.

"I was asking one of the deputies something yesterday and he kept walking, then he abruptly turned around and he came back and said, 'Whenever you address me, you call me mister or you call me sir.' And I told him, 'Very fine,' that I would do that, but in return I would demand equal respect and that he would have to address *me* as sir or mister. He got very upset and stormed out. . . ."

How did he feel about other black nationalist groups such as Ron Karenga's U.S. organization in Los Angeles? I wanted to know.

"In the first place, the Black Panther Party is a political party. I don't believe that Ron Karenga claims to be a political organization. And secondly, Ron Karenga and some other nationalist groups seem to be somewhat hung-up on surviving Africanisms, or what we call cultural nationalism. Cultural nationalism deals with a return to the old culture of Africa and that we are somehow freed by identifying in this manner. As far as we are concerned, we believe that it is important for us to recognize our origins and to identify with the revolutionary black people of Africa and people of color throughout the world. But as far as returning per se to the ancient customs, we don't see any necessity in this. And also that the only culture worth holding on to is revolutionary culture for change for the better. We say the only way we're going to be free is by seizing political power, which comes through the barrel of a gun. We say that we will identify so that we will have this consolidation of people; so we will have strength and we will respect ourselves and have the dignity of our past, but there are many things connected to the culture that we don't feel it's necessary to return to."

Was he optimistic about the outcome of his trial? Did he think it would be a fair trial?

"Well, I think that black people will make sure that I receive a fair trial. I have no faith at all in the court system, because I've already suffered an injustice by being indicted by an all-white middle-class grand jury, and so from my prior experiences I would expect no change. I also expect black people to come to my aid and to put pressure and to see to it by any means necessary that all black men receive a fair trial—that's including those who are held in the various prisons and county jails at the present time. We're demanding release for them because we realize they've suffered the same kind of injustice that I'm suffering now."

Suppose he were acquitted—would he return to studying law, would he go into politics, or what?

"I have one desire, and that is to go on fighting for the liberation of black people throughout the world, and in particular here in America. I would like to relate to the Black Panther Party and our political stand that black people must arm themselves. I think that this has been misinter-

preted in a number of ways many times. We make the statement, quoting it from Chairman Mao, that political power
comes through the barrel of a gun. The Black Panther Party
has analyzed the statement and come up with a clear realization that any time a people are unarmed and that the administrators of that country maintain a regular police force and a
military, and the people of that country are unarmed, they
are either slaves or subject to slavery at any given moment
that the administrators desire to inflict the force of that military or police upon the people. So we say that as long as the
military or police force is armed, then black people should
arm themselves.

"Many people have spoken of violence or our advocating
violence. We're advocating that we defend ourselves from
aggression—that if America is armed, and if it's right for
America to commit violence throughout the world, then it's
right for black people to arm themselves. . . . This reminds
me of a statement that Ronald Reagan made shortly after
our appearance in Sacramento. He said something to the
effect that in these enlightened times people cannot and
should not influence other people by the use of physical force
and the gun. But at the same time we see throughout America that the police are being heavily armed. Not only are
they being heavily armed, but they are escalating the war
against black people in our black communities by ordering in
heavy military equipment. We think Reagan should take a
look at what he's doing and what the American Government
is doing before he criticizes black people for arming themselves in self-defense."

Huey paused to light up one of his Kools. He held the
cigarette in that stiff-armed fashion that nonhabitués hold
their occasional cigarettes. Now he was ready for us again.
Whenever he spoke, it was as though he were addressing a

rally of ten thousand. In answering he would look straight into the questioner's eyes, but somehow he seemed to be looking *through* him to a larger audience.

Could he see himself functioning as a politician in the present political structure? ("Forget it," I thought.)

"I think that the present political structure is bankrupt and this is what the game is all about. The present political structure has perpetuated and protected and inflicted racism, so we say that there has to be a drastic change. As far as my running for office, I would only serve one purpose there— as a spokesman to articulate the grievances of the black community. And as far as playing the game that some black politicians have traditionally played, the day has come for this kind of thing to stop. . . . In the past we thought if we put a representative in office we automatically got justice. But now it's being realized that to have a black man in office doesn't necessarily mean that you're going to get political justice."

What kind of system did he want to replace the present American system with?

"The Black Panther Party, you'll note, has demanded full employment, we've demanded decent housing, we've demanded good education and justice, and we feel that this system as it is now cannot give this to us. The American capitalistic system has never been able to employ all of its people, particularly because of the greed of the private owner and his so-called private enterprise. . . . But we've never been given a chance to participate in this system, and we say since we have never benefited from free enterprise and private ownership, this is not a goal for us. . . ."

And how did Mr. Newton view integration? Was it a positive or negative force in the total struggle?

"I don't think it's even a question of integration. I think it's a question of gaining human rights for people. As far as being anti-integration, I am not. I believe that people should be able to go wherever they choose and marry whomever they choose to marry. . . ."

One of the sheriff's deputies rapped on the thick glass partition and scowled at us through the bars. The party was over; it was time for us to leave. There were of course many questions that had gone unasked, unanswered. *When was the revolution coming? Who, Mr. Newton, is going to overthrow what? We understand what the black liberation struggle would mean in South Africa—the lines are clearly drawn. We understand what revolution meant in colonial Algeria. The Algerian colonists rose up and threw out the oppressive French colonialists; Algeria for the Algerians: Right on! But what does the black liberation struggle mean in these United States? Liberation from what, from whom? How? Who is the enemy—*precisely *who? Is it us 10 or 11 or 12 percent black against the rest? Are we talking about revolution or a series of bloody battles or civil war or what? Tell me, Mr. Newton; I don't know.*

I was the last to leave the room. I turned around in the doorway. Newton smiled and raised his fist in the Black Power salute. I returned the salute; it lacked Newton's spontaneity—my fingers were not as tightly clenched as his—but I returned the salute. The deputy who had signaled an end to the press conference was leaning against the adjacent wall. "I saw that," he said. "I saw that." I stared at him without answering. His right hand rested on his holstered pistol. His barrel of a stomach hung over the sides of his belt. His pink, splotchy face was one great jowl of flesh interrupted as though by afterthought by eyes, nose, mouth. His resemblance to a pig was staggering. There was massive hatred in those tiny eyes, and I think had we been alone, had that dingy room been a little darker . . .

■   ■   ■

Defemerry Park in West Oakland. The Black Panthers in their presumptuous might renamed it Bobby Hutton Memorial Park. A rally for Huey. Free Huey! The California sun was out in all its glory, but you could sit on the cool, clean grass under an oak tree if you found the sun oppressive. And if you grew hungry or the speakers got too boring, there was plenty to eat, to fill your stomach, to take your mind off politics, off the "struggle." Barbecued spare ribs, potato salad —pots and pots of it. Dollar a plate! And if you didn't go for ribs, there were half a dozen snack trucks spread out around the park selling hamburgers, hot dogs, chili dogs, french fries, root beer, Coke. There was plenty to read while you ate. The *Black Panther*, twenty-five cents a copy. The Berkeley *Barb*, the *Mid Peninsula Observer*.

They came in great numbers—the curious, the indolent, the gay, the radical, the raunchy, the paunchy—little ladies in pretty, pink floral frocks, their tiny tots strapped to their backs; perky, smart-set black chicks, their slender legs rushing on up to meet their tasty little bodies. The hippies, loving and hairy and funky, munching communally on their big loaves of black bread. Big, husky, breast-feedin' mamas trailed by their tykes, sucking happily on their lollipops. The police were there, scattered around the park's perimeter, on foot, in cars—armed and helmeted and happy to be keepers of the peace. They were in the sky, too, swooping and buzzing about in helicopters, awaiting a signal to declare open war upon their savage fellow citizens below. To be sure, the police were sprinkled here and there in the crowd as well, variously disguised as hippie, as Negro, as guileless spectators.

The crowd came to see and hear Melvin Newton, Huey's brother. They came to hear Jim Foreman of SNCC and lately of the Black Panthers. They came to hear Bobby Seale and Kathleen Cleaver, but mostly they came to hear Eldridge, resplendent in coat of leather, tunic of silk. "Something smells in Alameda County," he began, "and it smells like pork."

They loved that; they cheered.

"I would love to sit around on my ass drinking wine, smoking pot and making love to my wife, but I can't afford to be doing that while all these pigs are loose. . . . Here I am, a convict. A whole lot of respectable people have nominated me for President. I'm *not* going to get elected—you dig? I'm a Black Panther and a madman. I'm a symbol of dissent, of rejection. Every page of American history is written in human blood, and we can't endorse it. We cannot endorse it. Close it! Close the motherfucker and put it on the shelf. . . . It's too bad I'm not thirty-five. Then I could get elected President and realize that old American dream of going from rags to riches. I could go in poor and come out fat, funky and rich. But I am too young. But I say, fuck the White House, fuck the electoral system, fuck all the white power structure."

And the crowd reveled in his anger; they wallowed in his bitterness. *Right on, Eldridge, right on!*

He was in command of us all, and yet his arrogant, bigbooted stance up there at the microphone spoke of discomfort. You could see the occasional unease as he shifted his weight from left to right foot, and if you were close enough, you might see it betrayed in the corners of his mouth. I was sure that if I dared to snatch his dark glasses from his face, I would see all the discomfort registered in his eyes.

Perhaps in those restless moments he was beneath the platform with us, looking at himself, hearing himself. Perhaps the absurdity—the spinning, the circular, the monumental absurdity of it all—crowded in on him from time to time. Eldridge Cleaver, Black Panther, feloniously black, spokesman for a cause that America would have to do a triple somersault to embrace. Eldridge Cleaver, sometime rapist, occasional madman. Eldridge Cleaver, who had spent one-third of his life in prison, at once now celebrated and vilified. Eldridge Cleaver, another bastard of the West, serving up his bitterness in heaping portions, watching the objects of his rancor being more entertained than repentant. Eldridge Cleaver, suddenly besieged by a nation's press, hungry for pictures, for anecdotes, for droppings from his life. Eldridge Cleaver, the husband, so adored by his wife Kathleen that she would follow him wherever his plight might dictate. Eldridge Cleaver, the high-steppin', big-talkin' nigger, so wantonly hated by the Oakland Police Department that at any moment anyone in their seething ranks was liable to step forward, bayonet at the ready, to cut the very liver out of him. Eldridge Cleaver, the cocksman, casting an occasional lustful eye upon the behind-switchin', big-legged sisters, grinning with self-satisfaction when his other lady fans showed themselves so obviously eager to impale their quivering white bodies upon what they perceived to be the revolutionary phallus, sturdy, glistening and black.

But these moments of discomfort were fleeting, particularly when he was addressing a roaringly partisan crowd in Bobby Hutton Memorial Park. "We say that a government, a society, owes to all its people," he went on that day, "to provide them with the highest standard of living its technology can produce. . . ."

He was the polemicist, and many paid well to hear his polemics. *Tell us where to go, Eldridge. Tell us to fuck off. Ram your spear through our masochistic hearts, Eldridge.* And he would oblige. Consider Eldridge on the podium before the grandeur of the San Francisco Barristers Club. The elite legal establishment there is prepared to be excoriated for their sins. Eldridge accommodated them. He said that he loved those few of them who were on his side. As for the rest: "I say, fuck you, all of you. I hope a nigger gets you on a dark street and kills you, takes your fat wallets and your credit cards and cuts your throats. . . ."

In the course of trailing Eldridge Cleaver about for a couple weeks, in the course of going to Black Panther rallies and "political education" classes, the realization seeped into me that essentially neither Huey, Bobby Seale nor Eldridge Cleaver gave a rat's ass whether *Life* magazine did a story on the movement or not.

"Prior arrangements" had been made with the Black Panthers, but, as I suspected, they didn't mean anything—nothing whatever. No one, least of all Eldridge, felt any particular obligation to be at some agreed place at some agreed time. The Black Panthers were not, after all, some bureaucratic machine functioning on master plans and rigid timetables. Covering their activities was therefore largely a matter of "hanging out"—at Eldridge's apartment, at courthouses, at their disheveled headquarters on Grove Street in Oakland, and if you hung around long enough, eventually someone would say to you at the last minute: "Hey, brother, somethin' goin' on tonight at Chairman Bobby's house. You oughta make it."

Hanging around could be a simple matter sometimes. I tried very hard not to stick out very obviously as some "outsider." I always dressed as casually as I could, shunning tweeds and ties for khaki and turtlenecks—not that I bought any special clothing; I simply wore the things least likely to brand me as a yo-yo. To this extent, being black was an advantage for rarely did anyone feel inclined to say, "Well, who the fuck are *you*, and whatcha hangin' around all the time for?"

Still, there were other times of great discomfort, when I could not unobtrusively look and listen. More often than not, these were the times when I was with Howard Bingham, my photographer. There is just *no* way that you can be unobtrusive in the company of a photographer who has a light meter and two or three cameras around his neck, who is bobbing and weaving, now here, now there, grabbing head shots, grabbing angle shots. Not that he had any choice—we came there to get photographs, and how else could worthwhile ones be gotten but by moving in and out among Black Panthers, shooting?

Unless one is dealing with clients or models in a studio, there remains something clandestine about the act of tripping the shutter to take a photograph. The photographers move catlike, noiselessly, stealthily. Fleeting facial expressions are captured, moments are stolen. In any case, Howard was not concerned with these abstractions and simply went his merry way making pictures. What was more, he was not shackled by the fear of blowing his cool. He wore for this assignment what he might have worn if he were shooting Nixon putting on a California golf course—white, spotlessly white tennis sneakers and sometimes bright blue polo shirts à-la-Perry Como.

There were other moments of mental unease. Frequently

it seemed that at any moment a Black Panther would say, "Now wait a minute—wait just a motherfuckin' minute. What are you cats doin' here anyway? We out here trying to get rid of this system and you cats come here from *Life* magazine with your milk and honey and bullshit about you wanna do a fair story but there ain't gonna be no fair story 'cause you cats are just plain bootlickers. You either greedy or stupid 'cause you don't care you're being used or you don't know it. Like Brother Eldridge say, 'You either part of the solution or you part of the problem,' and we know goddamn well you can't work for *Life* magazine and be part of the solution at the same time. So you got to be part of the problem. . . ."

But no one ever got around to saying that, at least not explicitly. Bobby Seale once said to me that there were at least two kinds of bootlickers. The first variety moves very slowly and obviously in its bootlicking acts; the other moves with great stealth and subtlety. "Gil, I don't know whether you're a bootlicker or not," he said smiling, "but I know one thing: if you are, you're moving fast while you're doing it. You see some of these black bootlicking politicians out here so clumsy while they licking boots that they end up with shoe polish all over their mouths. But these other cats are too slick for that. They know enough that when they come to face their people, they have to at least not get any polish on around their mouths in the first place or else make sure and wipe it off before they come out in public."

Eldridge Cleaver, on the other hand, had a strong suspicion that I might be a cop. "Man, you *sure* you not a pig?" he used to say to me. "If you a pig, we gonna know sooner or later 'cause pigs can't hide from us but so long." The Black Panthers had already then been variously infiltrated by the FBI, *agents provocateurs* and by what Eldridge called "assorted swine." The fact that an outsider might be black did not make him any the less suspect. "Pigs come in all colors," Eldridge was wont to observe.

Suspected pig or not, I hung around. And shortly after, when Eldridge and a contingent of Oakland Panthers had business in New York, I followed them. I didn't find out they were going to New York or the reason for the trip until they were already there. They were going to the United Nations to apply for special status as a "nongovernmental organization." They were also seeking a UN-supervised plebiscite. "The position of the Black Panther Party," Eldridge once said,

is that in the past there have been too many people, too many splinter organizations coming along—"We speak for all black people, we want to be integrated"; "We speak for all black people and we want to be separated." We say that there's no organization, no man in history has ever had a mandate from black people on that particular issue, on separation or integration. And so we feel that the only way that it can be decided is through a democratic process, not through some of these rigged polls. The question has to be decided by a United Nations–supervised plebiscite. Machinery should be set up throughout this country that will allow black people to go into a voting booth and cast a ballot, stating whether or not they want to be integrated or whether or not they want to be separated, and have this land partitioned, so that they can build a nation of their own, or do they want to be part of the American stew here in the Babylonian melting pot? . . .

As a matter of fact, I would favor two plebiscites. I would like to have a plebiscite that will allow white people to go on record and let us know once and for all: do you want to be in a nation where black people are part of the citizenry, or do you want to be separated into your own white country? I think we need two plebiscites in this country, so that we will know whether or not to get behind George Wallace and Elijah Muhammad, to get behind the many others who speak of many other alternatives. We need to know that; it has to become part of the record. Once we have that information, we can move on to solve the problem, because our direction will be clear, our tactics will flow from that decision. The Black Panther Party takes that position.

Consider now the notion—farfetched but tantalizing—that constituted authority as high as the presidency backs up the Cleaver plebiscite idea. A Nixon, a Johnson goes before network television cameras: "My fellow Americans," he says, "come Tuesday, we're gonna have ourselves a plebiscite —no, *two* plebiscites: one for black folks and the other one for all the rest of us—meaning white folks." (*Let me make one thing perfectly clear, my fellow Americans. You will not be voting on some abstract proposition. Whatever the majority of people decide will be implemented—not gradually, not with all deliberate speed, but forthwith.*)

It seems to me the voter turnout would be massive, without parallel in American history. Burly white construction workers from Cleveland, wizened little ladies from Boston, chubby-cheeked black nannies on Long Island, baldheaded pawnbrokers, sweaty black preachers, stiff-spined Wall Street brokers, Oakland policemen, Harvard graduate students, West Virginia coal miners, fierce young men in dashikis, mild-mannered young men in dashikis, Arkansas sheriffs—your Strom Thurmonds, your Julian Bonds—George Wallace, Eugene McCarthy, Richard Daley, Ron Karenga, Norman Mailer, Robert Welch, Elijah Muhammad, Jonathan Winters, David Rockefeller, Whitney Young, Dick Gregory, Liberace—one man, one vote.

Both plebiscites would have to be held at the same time because the outcome of one might tend to influence the outcome of the other. It seems to me that if both plebiscites were held tomorrow, the blacks would vote 60 to 40 against separation and the whites would vote 60 to 40 in favor of separation.

Consider now America joyously detached from its black tumor. Every last nigger, gone, outa sight. The meek ones, the sassy ones, the slick ones, the dumb ones, the NAACP, the Student Nonviolent Coordinating Committee, the Black Panthers, the Black Firemen's Association, the Black Lettuce Growers Association, all gone. What a relief.

■   ■   ■

That July, 1968, New York City gave the Black Panthers the same indifferent shrug it gives all newcomers to its shores. Brooklyn's Bedford Stuyvesant already had its Black Panthers, but no one outside of a small inner circle had yet heard of them. Eldridge Cleaver and his party of about fifteen had come on what they judged to be very serious business, but the big city was just not impressed. Howard and I had prevailed upon them that sunny afternoon in July to stand still for a moment for a group picture on the sidewalk in front of the Secretariat. Eldridge, tall and familiarly ominous in his dark glasses, leather jacket and black attaché case, stood in the center; the others fanned out to his right and left. Howard started clicking away. For a moment it all seemed ludicrous to me. Here was as fierce a collection of young men as America could produce posing for pictures in front of the United Nations with as much of the earnest out-of-town squareness in their faces as those spry little ladies just in from Omaha, Nebraska, sitting for Kodak Instamatic portraits in Rockefeller Plaza. ("You take one of me, Pa, then I'll take one of you.")

Taxi drivers and an occasional pedestrian paused to gawk at this peculiar leather-jacket assemblage, but largely New York was indifferent to its revolutionary guests.

A press conference was held in a UN building across the street from the Secretariat. The local media showed modest interest, probably responding not so much to the little-known Black Panthers as to Eldridge Cleaver, whose book, *Soul on Ice*, was bringing him national attention.

Facing the gathering of about twenty television, radio and newspaper reporters, Eldridge stood in the center of a scowling row of Panthers. On either side of him at the long table stood two bodyguards, their arms folded with military rigidity across their leathery chests, their black berets cocked rakishly to one side.

Eldridge said in an opening statement: "We call on member nations of the United Nations to authorize the stationing of observer teams throughout the cities of North America where black people are cooped up in wretched ghettos. . . . This action is necessary because the racist power structure of this imperialist country is preparing to unleash a war of genocide against the black colonial subjects. We have assurances from the Cuban and Tanzanian missions that they will support us in the introduction of this resolution in the UN General Assembly. . . ."

Eldridge moved on to another pressing subject. "At this moment our leader, Brother Huey P. Newton, is being tried by old baldheaded racists who are predetermined to send him to the gas chamber. But they will carry out the sentence over our dead bodies. There seems to be little hope of avoiding open armed war in the streets of California and of preventing it from sweeping across the nation.

"If there has to be war, then let there be war."

"Good God, who *are* these cats?" a black reporter friend

of mine asked me after the press conference. His face reflected the bewilderment of the press corps, black and white. I smiled cryptically, as though privy to special knowledge. "They're revolutionaries, brother," I said, "and you better get yourself together. If you not part of the solution, you're part of the problem."

■   ■   ■

The visitors from California were huddled together on the floor of a Manhattan apartment when I walked in. Huey's brother Walter was there. Bobby Seale, looking his customarily sullen self, was fairly buried in the thick softness of an upholstered chair. In their midst smiling warmly sat a bespectacled black priest, his small frame resting against an upright piano. He was the Reverend Earl Neil, and as always he offered a jarring contrast to his companions.

I shook Eldridge's hand. "You brothers all know Gil Moore, don't you?" he asked them with planned mischief. "He says he's a writer, but I think the motherfucker's a pig."

"Maybe they're the same thing," I said, laughing—not without *some* tension.

"What do you think, Bobby?" Eldridge continued.

Bobby shook his head.

"What do you think, David? Is Gil Moore a pig?"

David Hilliard, then the Black Panther National Headquarters Captain, didn't think so either.

Eldridge liked to do that. He always had to let you know, particularly when you thought you were inching your way into his confidence, that he didn't trust you—that he didn't trust anybody.

It became clear that evening that the party was going to have a housing problem. Eldridge said that they would rough through that night on the floor, and I offered to get them into a hotel—at *Life's* expense.

The next day we all showed up at the Sheraton-Atlantic Hotel—scarcely New York's finest, but no dump either. To avoid any undue panic at the desk I wore a dark business suit and tie. Howard had on his cameras, a pair of freshly starched chinos and another one of his Perry Como golf shirts. The Reverend Neil came in full clerical garb. Eldridge and the Panthers, of course, wore what they always wore: black leather jackets, berets, dark glasses and "Free Huey" buttons. The hotel lobby was bristling with the summer trade: bellhops were scurrying about, lugging suitcases to the elevators; big-shouldered conventioneers stood all around in clusters, hefty cigars clenched in their teeth, carefully lettered name-tags proudly pinned to their lapels; tall Midwestern daddies were waiting patiently for service, in one hand clutching a Kodak Instamatic, in the other a wife and 2.4 children. *New York is a summer festival!*

There was a noticeable decline in activity when we came into full view. The bellhops stopped lugging for a moment; the conventioneers laid off of their big cigars; and the Midwestern daddies poked their wives in the ribs to call the little women's attention to what they had just seen.

In alternating seconds they were afraid and outraged and bewildered. Afraid that, whoever these stiff-lipped folks were, they looked like they were going to *turn the place out*, they looked like at any moment they might pounce upon them, sinking their fangs into all the defenseless white necks. Outraged that the waspish splendor of that lobby should now be befouled by a band of niggers. Then finally they were bewildered because while we were obviously all together, it did not seem that we ought to be. There was Howard, as usual, cheerfully at work, looking himself very much like a tourist but for the professional demeanor of his Nikons. There was the Reverend Neil, his friendly face radiant with the warmth of Christian fellowship. There was Eldridge Cleaver and his party—to a man, surly and grim in leather and the darkest of dark glasses. And finally the onlookers had to contemplate me—fairly glistening with respectability—so respectable, indeed, as to be almost white. Yet black. What a puzzlement!

"I made a telephone reservation yesterday for two adjoining suites," I told our man at the desk.

"What is your name, sir?" he asked without looking at me.

"Moore—Gilbert Moore—of *Life* magazine."

"Will you wait just a moment, sir, while I check on that?" he said, looking up past me at Eldridge and company. He went away to take the matter up with someone else. In five minutes he was back again.

"Yes, sir," he said, "I see we do have that reservation. Are those gentlemen all in your party?"

"Well—yes and no. Actually, the gentleman standing over there with his arms folded and six of the gentlemen with him will be occupying the rooms."

"I see. Shall I put the rooms in his name?"

"Yes, but please send the bill to me at *Life* magazine. His name is Cleaver—Eldridge Cleaver." Our man at the desk winced and looked quickly at Eldridge again.

"Could I have that name again?"

"Cleaver. 'C' as in 'catastrophe'—L–E–A–V–E–R. *Eldridge* Cleaver." I didn't really think the name would mean anything to him, but apparently it did.

"Is he the one who—"

"He's the one," I cut in. He began to rummage around in some papers before him, then excused himself and went into the back room for another conference.

"Is there a problem?" I asked him when he came back.

"No, no problem." With resignation in his eyes, he handed me the keys.

"You'll be in rooms 401 and '2," he said.

I couldn't resist it: "Are there no bellhops to see us upstairs?" I said. "Mr. Cleaver will need help carrying his rifles."

Eldridge Cleaver and six Black Panthers were duly registered in rooms 401 and 402 of the Sheraton-Atlantic Hotel for the night. I didn't find out about it until two weeks later, but they had one hell of a party that night. The room-service bill came to four hundred and forty-six dollars and twenty cents, which is not bad for a night's play.

One day in San Francisco Eldridge called my attention to this strange bill he said he had received from the Sheraton-Atlantic Hotel. I told him to ignore the bill and that I would take care of it, and that the four-hundred-dollar amount was probably a mistake. I checked with the hotel accountants, and it turned out of course there was no mistake.

On the other hand, I was relieved that the Black Panthers should have had a party because I was beginning to think that there was nothing the least bit human about them, that they were fixed on this abstract course called revolution and that there was to be no dillydallying en route for such mundane things as laughing or spanking children or going to the movies or making love or having expensive parties in expensive hotel rooms.

A month later on a return trip to Oakland, I had an idea I would go to Eldridge and warn him that having blasts of the kind they had at the hotel was a practice that could very easily be used against them. He had always said he didn't trust me. Suppose he were right in that mistrust; suppose my sole mission in being around them was to discredit the movement in some way? How easy he was making it for me.

So in telling Eldridge all of this, in showing him the folly in what they had done in New York, maybe—just maybe—he would trust me a little more.

Or would he?

He looked at me askance. He didn't have his glasses on, so you could see the cynicism in his eyes.

Was I worried about the Black Panthers' welfare or was I *really* worried about accounting to the *Man* for a huge one-night hotel bill? Eldridge wanted to know.

"No, no," I protested. There would be no problem at all about the bill.

"Well, all right then," Eldridge said smiling. "You're not worried about it, *Life* magazine ain't worried about it and we for *damn sure* ain't worried about it. So everything's cool. . . ."

After their four-day sojourn in New York, Eldridge and the Panthers who came with him flew back to Oakland; Howard Bingham flew back to Los Angeles, and I went up to the Time & Life Building to explain to my editor why the hell it was taking so long to do a simple little story on the Black Panthers.

It was very hard to justify my going back to Oakland. We had already taken truckloads of pictures—Eldridge at home, Eldridge on the podium, Kathleen at home, Kathleen on the podium, Panther rallies, Panther marches, Panther lawyers, Panther handshakes. I ventured the opinion that Huey Newton's trial was going to have very wide political implications and that we should cover it. I wasn't really sure that that was so, but I said it anyway. For reasons which I did not then understand, I felt that *I had to be at that trial.*

A few days after that Howard called me from L.A. to say

that three Panthers had been killed in a gun battle with the police and that all hell was about to break loose. Without asking anyone whether or not it was a good idea, I got on a plane and went back to California for a period of time that would come to seem like a hundred years.

III

Hang Huey! Free Huey!

Being unable to make what is just strong, we have made what is strong just.

—PASCAL

IT WAS ALMOST AS THOUGH Huey P. Newton were already dead. In those weeks and months after October 28, 1967, a single human being was being transformed—in that indefinable way that such transformations take place—into a shrine. A shrine at which some would worship, a shrine for others to spit upon. We usually require of those among us who would be symbols that they first cease to breathe and be buried before claiming the exalted status. But even as Huey Newton continued to be mortal, the throne was his. His mortality persisted—even as slogans were born, even as speakers mounted podiums, even as posters were hung, even as forces united to eradicate his legacy.

On that fateful Saturday morning, he had been shot once through the abdomen. The bullet penetrated an area near the navel, perforated some bowel tissue and came out through his back. For medical attention, he fled (or was taken—we still don't know which) to Kaiser Hospital in Oakland. He arrived at the hospital at about ten minutes to six in the morning. The nurse on duty at the emergency reception desk saw fit to telephone the police before she summoned the doctor. The doctor came to the emergency to find the police already there and in the process of handcuffing the "patient" to a hospital gurney.

All in all, it was about twenty-five minutes from the time that Huey arrived at Kaiser until he received any medical attention. In this period a much publicized photograph was taken of the celebrated patient by a photographer of the San Francisco *Examiner*. It showed a rather startled policeman in the foreground, a nurse in the background and Huey Newton, the patient, manacled to a stretcher. This photograph appeared in several of the San Francisco Bay Area newspapers and was subsequently published and republished to obvious advantage in the Black Panther newspaper. The picture's wide circulation led to a moving apology to Huey by Dr. Mary Jane Aguilar, a forty-three-year-old Oakland-born physician. In a letter to the Panther newspaper she wrote:

> I can remember nothing in my medical training which suggested that, in the care of an acute abdominal injury, severe pain and hemorrhage are best treated by manacling the patient to the examining table in such a way that the back is arched and belly tensed. Yet this is precisely the picture of current emergency room procedure which appeared on the front page of a local newspaper last weekend. Looming large in the foreground of the same picture, so large as to suggest a caricature, was a police officer. Could it have been he who distracted the doctor in charge of the case to position the patient in this curious way?
>
> Unusual as it was, this picture probably did not disrupt very much the pleasant weekend enjoyed by my neighbors nor disturb more than momentarily the consciences of my medical colleagues. To me, upon whose mind's eye it is permanently engraved, this photograph is a portentous document of modern

history; it represents an end and a beginning. Further, for me, there has been enough of listening, of reading, of pondering. The time has now come to speak, to act, to fight back. . . .

The beginning again for me dates from the last time I saw the patient [Huey Newton], several weeks ago, in a discussion with a group of people, many of whom came by, listened awhile and left. One such young man called later in the evening to say that he was in jail. He had been detained by the police for what they suspected might be a minor infraction of the Motor Vehicle Code, mistakenly, as it turned out, for they quickly determined that no law had been broken. Not content, the police undertook a lengthy investigation which ultimately revealed that the young man had not satisfactorily replied to a charge of driving with an invalid license *one year ago*. For this reason he was now jailed, with bail set at $550. It took three hours to fill out the requisite forms, pay the requisite fees, and see the requisite people, in order to extricate this black boy from his cell.

Two days later I was driving with a friend on the highway when she was apprehended because of four concurrent infractions of the Motor Vehicle Code: including driving with an invalid license, without an auto registration and without a valid permit for the trailer we were pulling. Nothing happened. In spite of the fact we were detained momentarily some miles farther on for still another infraction—this time a moving violation—we still arrived home in time for dinner, two white ladies to their comfortable white neighborhood. My friend told me later that her *total* bail for all of this lawlessness came to $15. So please do not waste my time, my white brothers and sisters, in telling me that justice is dispensed equally under the law to all Americans. I will not believe you.

I apologize, Mr. Newton, for any aggravation of suffering inflicted upon you during the course of treatment of your injuries. I apologize for the subhuman conditions and horrors of the ghetto in which we force you to exist. I apologize for living too quietly within an immoral political and social system, a system which makes it inevitable that men like you are gunned down in the streets of our town.

MARY JANE AGUILAR, M.D.

Huey Newton was transferred to another hospital; subsequently he was moved to San Quentin for "safekeeping," and then to the Alameda County Jail in Oakland, where he would remain until September, 1968.

In the meantime, the legal wrangling began. Before it was over, Newton's attorney, Charles Garry, would succeed in delaying the trial at least eleven times.

Among other moves, Garry sought to have the murder charge against Newton dropped on the grounds that the grand jury had indicted him without sufficient evidence. Garry claimed that the prosecution had presented only minimal circumstantial evidence which, while it placed Newton at the scene of the shooting, failed to produce the murder weapon, failed to explain the absence of said weapon, failed to show that Newton fired or even possessed a weapon in the October 28 shooting. Based on the evidence, Garry continued, "It is just as reasonable to assume Heanes [the other police officer] shot and killed Frey as to assume Newton did it." But all motions for dismissal failed.

Huey Newton's attorneys also challenged the validity of the three-count indictment which came after the grand jury had "deliberated" a scant twenty-seven minutes—a period which the defense pointed out included the movement of the fourteen-man jury from room to room, a roll call and several exits of the District Attorney and staff.

Then came the broadside attack on the Alameda County grand jury system:

"The indictment under which defendant was tried was returned by a grand jury which was selected in a manner

which violated defendant's right under the Fourteenth
Amendment. The Alameda County procedure for selecting
a grand jury systematically excludes representation of young
persons, lower-income groups, and members of the black
community. Defendant's conviction under such an indictment must be reversed under settled and well-established
principles of constitutional law. . . ."

The defense motions to quash the grand jury indictments
against Newton were denied in succession by the Alameda
County Superior Court, the State District Court of Appeals
and the California State Supreme Court.

In June, 1968, the defense, having failed in its challenge
to the Alameda County grand jury system, brought legal
muscle to bear upon the petit jury system of selection on
substantially the same grounds. A motion was introduced to
quash the entire master panel of jurors from which twelve
men and women would subsequently be selected for services
in the Newton trial. The motion pointed out:

> The traditional process of all other ethnic immigrant groups
> to America, involving occupational mobility and the ethnic's
> increasing contact with dominant institutions, especially edu-
> cation, does not fit the cultural experience of most Afro-Ameri-
> cans. . . . The black man did not enter this country with a
> group identity as a Negro. This group category could only be
> forced by the slave-making operation which vitiated the mean-
> ing and relevance of the traditional African identities. The cul-
> tural process could therefore not be one of movement from
> ethnic group to assimilation, since Negroes were not an ethnic
> group. . . . It is because black Americans have undergone
> unique experiences in America, experiences that no other na-
> tional or racial minority or lower-class group have shared, that
> a distinctive ethnic culture has evolved. . . . The single most
> dominant factor from today's urban black experience that sets
> him apart from his white counterpart is contact with the police,

described in the Kerner Report as the chief complaint of all black communities, and resonant with overtones of police brutality. The chief component of black experience, the white American, whether racist or not, does not and cannot share. It is a vital issue in the present proceeding and points up the impossibility of a jury of substantially white persons being able to perceive and objectively render fair judgement in the present case within the meaning of due process of law and equal protection of the laws. . . .

In the black community, in different ways than in the white, economic pressures strain the family and matriarchal trends are visible. Particular styles of music, language, style of dress and movement are consciously cultivated. A sense of fatalism, even apathy or quasi-paranoid outlooks pervade the streets. Against some of this, and yet incorporating some of the black heritage and style, the modern national liberation black groups struggle for manhood and a new identity as blacks. *As a member of this subculture and this militant liberation group, the defendant herein is virtually a stranger to most of the white American voters who will make up the jury under prevailing practice. They are not his peers.* . . . [Emphasis added.]

The motion to disrupt the entire Alameda County jury system was denied.

And so the last of the legal machinery had been exhausted. The trial date in the case of *The People of the State of California, Plaintiff,* vs. *Huey P. Newton, Defendant,* was fixed for July 15, 1968. Presiding judge: the Honorable Monroe Friedman, a man with the demeanor, the gentle forbearance, the myopia of an aging beagle.

■   ■   ■

They began to arrive at the courthouse as early as eight o'clock. They walked; they popped out of private cars, out of city buses, off bicycles: Black Panthers, high school science teachers, the Western Mobilization Against War, Brown Berets, housewives, the Peace and Freedom Party, the Iranian Students Association, Asian-American Political Alliance, students from Berkeley, dropouts from San Francisco State, black folks, white folks, Mexicans, Japanese. They brought their young, posters, banners, bullhorns, buttons.

By ten o'clock they were three thousand. Their numbers stretched three times, four times, around the impregnable fortress the Alameda County Courthouse was that day. Their number spilled over into the streets—on Twelfth Street, on Thirteenth, on Fallon and Oak. And onto the grass by Lake Merritt, by the forlorn bust of Lincoln put there "in memory of the heroes of the Spanish Civil War who gave their lives that liberty shall not perish."

They marched in cadence to their chants:

> Roast the pigs
> Free Huey!
> Off the pigs
> Free Huey!
> Black is beautiful
> Free Huey!

Rocking, clapping, singing:

> Power to the people
> Free Huey!

And around them sauntered those who knew little of Huey, those who heard that there would be a spectacle on this day. Enchanted by spectacles, they came.

Some deplored the spectacle, for it blocked them from the commission of their courthouse business: the paying of fines, getting licenses—to drive, to marry.

Here and there were pockets of hatred for Huey. Husky, hard-working Oaklanders, they looked to be. The chanting, the marching, the singing disgusted them, angered them. But this was not their day; nor was it their arena and they had to keep their tempers muzzled. Now and then it would come bursting out of their chests: "Jesus Christ, what is this country comin' to? Free Huey—my ass! They oughta burn the son of a bitch!"

But the crowd, circling and recircling the courthouse, were oblivious of these isolated minorities. Attention turned momentarily to the two flags flapping in the wind: California's own—the bear and the red star—and the Stars and Stripes. Someone shouted: "Cut the rope! Take the fuckin' flag down!" And as the soundness of the idea spread, a volunteer stepped forward to do the cutting. They cheered as the American flag came tumbling down into his arms. But the Oakland police moved in to make the arrest for a crime they swiftly appraised to be petty theft. Robert Avakian, the petty thief, twenty-five-year-old son of Judge Spurgeon Avakian of the Alameda County Superior Court, was led away to jail.

The peace officers were dressed for war. For a moment—for just a flash of a moment—they looked like little boys on Christmas morning who had opened all their presents to find shiny, baby-blue space helmets, rubber billy clubs, toy badges saying "Oakland Sheriff's Department," Daisy rifles and two guns each. But when you heard them thirsting to keep the peace, you knew otherwise.

Squads of four, five and more guarded every ground-level entrance to the courthouse. And lest some sly devil try to sneak into the building via one of the underground passageways, armed sheriff's deputies stood guard at those vantage points as well. In order to get past them you had to demonstrate that you had come to court on "legitimate" business.

Indoors the security, the insecurity, thickened. More police, more sheriff's deputies. Whispering secret things into their walkie-talkies, they guarded the corridors, the stairways, the elevators. Only one of the four elevators goes to the seventh floor, where the Newton trial would be held. That elevator had a special armed guard. The obsequious black elevator man had firm instructions to stop nowhere else but the seventh floor.

The ladies and gentlemen of the press gathered in a raucous cluster outside the sheriff's office on the second floor to hear the ground rules for covering the trial. The word came from a brooding plain-clothesman, who stood in the doorway of the office to address the restless horde. The courtroom in question had sixty-two spectator seats. Twenty-one of those seats would daily be reserved for the press. "All reporters must obtain a different pass *each day* of the trial. Passes will be issued on a first-come, first-served basis."

Reporters had come from as far away as London. The Boston *Globe* was there, the *New York Times*, the Los Angeles *Times*. The Bay Area three major dailies were there: the San Francisco *Chronicle*, the San Francisco *Examiner*, the Oakland *Tribune*. Network television men were there; local TV men. Network radio, local radio. The wire services were represented. The radical press, the "underground," were there in abundance: the Berkeley *Barb*, the *National Guardian*, the San Francisco *Guardian*, the *Mid Peninsula Observer*, *People's World* and on and on. Now come the *Sun Reporter*, the *Berkeley Gazette*. Now come the national weeklies: *Time, Newsweek, Life*. On that first day about twenty-five reporters were there to claim twenty-one seats. We pushed and shoved and shouted and some of us got in.

The attorneys for the defense came late. They were busy

in last-minute attempts to halt the trial. The State Supreme Court had been asked to expunge Newton's 1964 conviction (assault with a deadly weapon) from the records. The motion claimed that the defendant had not been properly represented in that trial. The prosecution would now use that conviction to influence the jury. The U.S. District Court in San Francisco had also been asked for a stay. But all these motions were denied.

■   ■   ■

Court was convened at 11:13 A.M. A panel of jurors took their places in the jury box. Cheerless sheriff's deputies ushered reporters, and such few Oakland citizens as had managed to worm their way in, to their seats. For all the teeming thousands outside, there were still empty seats, so vigorous had the guards been in barring the public entry. And then the bailiff escorted Huey Newton into the court-room from a side door. He had come down a staircase con-necting the tenth-floor jail to the seventh-floor court. He looked markedly different from the weary, unkempt prisoner I had seen two weeks before. A brand-new haircut had re-placed his uncombed Afro. And instead of the drab prison garb, he now wore a handsome gray sharkskin suit and black turtleneck sweater. All of these (as I learned later) had been carefully selected by his brother Walter. En route to his chair at the counsel table, Newton smiled, raised a clenched fist in the inevitable salute.

The court clerk read the roll of jurors, whereupon they were promptly dismissed until nine-forty-five tomorrow morning. There were "certain matters of law" the defense had to take up with the Court. Judge Friedman admonished the jury in the same words that he would use hundreds of times in the weeks to come: "I admonish each of you not to discuss anything pertaining to this case among yourselves, with anyone else or with the press or any of the communications media. I also admonish you not to listen to any television or radio programs concerning the case. I also admonish you not to read in the press or any publication anything pertaining to this case. I also remind you that you are not to fraternize or converse with any of the attorneys or the parties or any witnesses connected with this case. These rules that I have given you and admonitions apply during such time as you are a member of this panel: The jury is now excused. . . ."

The court would now hear defense argument on two motions: (1) "that persons who have complete and total objection to the death penalty . . . should not be excluded for cause from this jury"; and (2) the earlier motion to quash the entire jury panel on the grounds that racial minorities and lower-income citizens were underrepresented on the panel. In support of these motions the defense presented as distinguished an academic body as an Oakland court had ever heard. Among the witnesses, in what amounted to a two-day discourse in sociology, were: Jan Dizard, assistant professor of sociology at the University of California, Berkeley; Dr. Floyd Hunter, sociologist, author of *Top Leadership, U.S.A.*, a study of power relationships in urban planning, and founder-director of the Social Science Research and Development Corporation, Oakland; Dr. Hans Zeisel, professor of law and sociology at the University of Chicago Law School and co-author of *The American Jury*, a widely respected study of the jury system; Dr. Nevitt Sanford, professor of psychology in education and director of the Institute for the Study of Human Problems at Stanford University; Sheldon Messinger, vice chairman of the

Center for the Study of Law and Society at the University of California, Berkeley; Dr. Robert Blauner, associate professor of sociology at Berkeley; and Dr. Bernard L. Diamond, psychiatrist, professor of criminology and law and a familiar face in the Alameda and San Francisco County Court systems.

As the American flag was falling, seven stories below, as the Panthers threatened, "The sky's the limit if Huey's not freed," the first witness took the stand. He was Jury Commissioner for the Alameda County Superior Court, a Mr. Edward T. Schnaar. It became clear that it was Mr. Schnaar's role to set up the tenpins so that the high-powered academicians could knock them all down.

The names of potential jurors, Mr. Schnaar said, "were procured from the register of voters of Alameda County taking the persons from each precinct of Alameda County arriving at a specified projected number to produce sufficient jurors for the court." Seven thousand potential jurors for the six-month court session had been chosen "at random" from the list of registered voters, by use of a key number system.

Gradually the seven thousand had been whittled down to eighteen hundred, then to nine hundred. Schnaar pointed out that some names were dropped from the original panel when it turned out that the potential juror had moved out of the county. The list was further shortened by those jurors claiming occupational exemption, i.e., members of the armed forces, government workers, lawyers, policemen, clergymen, etc., and by "hardship" cases. Defense Attorney Garry pressed Schnaar, time and time again, for percentages of exemptions in the various categories, but the witness had no such data immediately available.

The questioning was turned over to Assistant District Attorney Lowell Jensen, a man marked by great calm—a calm that throughout the seven-week proceedings would betray not a ripple. In cross-examining Schnaar, Jensen carefully tucked all of the Jury Commissioner's activities under the protective mantle of the Court. "Mr. Schnaar," he asked, "where is it that you get your orders or your directives . . . in producing jurors for the Superior Court of Alameda County?"

"The judges of the Court," said Mr. Schnaar.

". . . You use the voter registration lists and a key number system to produce a series of names, is that right? . . . Now who told you to do that?" asked Jensen at another point.

And Schnaar replied, "That is just the policy that has been followed in this Court for a number of years prior to the time I became Jury Commissioner."

Jensen's clincher questions came later. Were there any directives emanating either from the Court, from Mr. Schnaar himself as Jury Commissioner, or from anyone on his staff "that are directed toward systematically excluding any person on the basis of his race, creed, color or economic status?"

No—of course not!

■   ■   ■

First witness asked to peck away at the Alameda County system of jury selection was Professor Dizard of Berkeley. Dizard testified that his studies of white/black voting patterns revealed that the county (about 10 percent black) had a voter registration rate of 82 percent; whereas the registration rate in the West Oakland ghetto (71.3 percent black) was only 52.5 percent. Adept in the rigors of simple arithmetic, Judge Friedman interjected that the discrepancy was close to 30 percent. The defense quickly asked Professor Dizard to account for the wide difference in the voting patterns. Predictably, the prosecution objected to the question on the ground that it called for the opinion and conclusion of the witness. Stirred, however briefly, from his sociological slumber, Judge Friedman wanted to hear Dizard's explanation anyway. He allowed him to answer the question. Dizard ventured the opinion that "Low-income people in general, and, more specifically, the Negro population, is more apathetic vis-à-vis the political process. It is a case of having less to gain from the political process. The political leadership that they are confronted with is much more distant and frequently unamenable to their plight and their dilemma. In short, the political system in my opinion has been historically and remains contemporarily, although perhaps in reduced amount, a relatively closed and foreign apparatus vis-à-vis the Negro population."

"You mean in Alameda County that is why they don't register?" asked Judge Friedman, preparing to resume his slumber.

"Yes, I would suggest that that is at least one reason," Professor Dizard replied.

"There is nothing," the judge wanted to know, "that stops them [meaning us] from registering. . . . There is no physical or legal barriers to stop them from registering. . . . It isn't your contention that anybody in Alameda County can't register as a voter if they want to?"

No, that wasn't the professor's contention at all. But the judge was resting peacefully now, comfortable in the knowledge that no one in the county was getting kicked in the head for daring to vote. He would have been genuinely disturbed had he learned otherwise, but thank God, this was dear ole Alameda where such things did not happen.

Dr. Hunter buttressed Dizard's testimony by furnishing more recent statistics (garnered after the 1960 Census). His studies, undertaken in 1966 for the U.S. Department of Commerce, indicated that in 1960 Oakland's white population was 73.9 percent, its black population 22.6 percent. In 1966 the white population had fallen off to 66.4 percent of the whole; the black population had jumped to 30.4 percent. Dr. Hunter said that his study pointed up the same black apathy to the political process that Professor Dizard had spoken of.

In one of his rare attempts at humor, Judge Friedman later asked Sheldon Messinger if he thought it was a better idea to draw up jury panels using the telephone book. Messinger took the question seriously: "I think that a partial solution to the problem might be to seek means of supplementing the voters roll and the telephone book might provide one source which would help supplement. . . . I would suspect there are many otherwise qualified voters who are in the telephone book who are not on the voters roll. On the other hand, this wouldn't be perfect either. I suggest that we might not be able to achieve a perfect system, but the burden of my testimony was . . . that the use of the voters registration lists was so imperfect and so apparently imperfect once one understood the problem, that I feel the Court should seek some means of supplementing it."

Sociologist Dr. Blauner, who in 1965 had acted as a consultant to California's McCone Commission which investigated the Watts riot, lectured the Court on the pervasiveness of white racism in American society. It was impossible, he said, to live in America, be white and be completely free of racism.

Was that true of *all* white people? Judge Friedman

wanted to know. Yes, it was, Dr. Blauner said, stroking his beard.

"Do you consider yourself a white racist?" Judge Friedman pressed.

The point was made—*even* sociologists could be racists. Young Dr. Blauner squirmed a bit but manfully confessed his sins: "I consider myself someone who may be less racist than some other people because I am aware of the racism which is part of me, because I have grown up in the society and under this whole heritage of Western culture. . . . Yes, I certainly am a racist."

The defense's key question, the one which more than any other Blauner was put on the stand to answer, was disallowed. Early in the testimony Garry asked Blauner: "I want you to assume that a black man is on trial in Alameda County. The black man is charged with killing a police officer and wounding another. This black man is a head of a militant black liberation movement. . . . Can that person get a fair trial by a society that is admitted by certain reports and studies to be inherently white racist?"

The prosecution objected to the question. It called for an opinion and conclusion from the witness. What's more, the question was ambiguous.

Objection sustained.

Last to be heard on the defense motion to quash the entire jury panel was Psychiatrist Bernard Diamond. The questioning brought out what Dr. Diamond had already written in a memorandum to the Court:

A large number of white persons in California today have attitudes of racism and prejudice towards black people and other minority groups. Many such persons possess and express such prejudicial attitudes without conscious awareness of doing so. They have become so accustomed to prejudice and bias in themselves and in the people they associate with that they are able to deceive themselves into believing that they are fair-minded and free of racist attitudes.

Attitudes of racism, prejudice and bias affect perception, behavior, and decision-making, and impair the capacity for fair, objective judgement. This is true whether the racist attitudes are conscious or unconscious, acknowledged or unacknowledged, and make it unlikely that such persons will make impartial judgements concerning members of minority groups.

Identification of such prejudicial and racist attitudes in prospective jurors . . . would require psychological techniques much too extensive for courtroom application. Certainly the ordinary *voir dire* questioning is not an adequate or sufficient way of eliciting such attitudes in a public courtroom. . . .

In support of the motion that prospective jurors having a "complete and total objection to the death penalty" should not be excluded from the jury, the Court heard the learned testimony of Dr. Hans Zeisel and Dr. Nevitt Sanford. Zeisel, whose jury studies in Chicago and New York had been cited in a recent Supreme Court decision, said that his findings showed that "Being for or against capital punishment is part of a larger personality syndrome, distinguishable by race, by sex, and by other characteristics and having predictable opinions on certain matters of social debate such as race issues or the John Birch Society." Those in favor of capital punishment, Zeisel continued, "are more likely to side with prosecution on the issue of the defendant's guilt. . . ."

Dr. Sanford expounded on that distinct cluster of attitudes which sociologists and psychologists have come to call the "authoritarian personality": "an oversubmissiveness to authority and uncritical acceptance of authority . . . a rigid adherence to conventional values to the degree that the individual involved is easily outraged by violations of conventional standards; a special kind of aggressiveness . . . directed particularly to people who are believed to be violating conventional standards."

And so the social scholars folded and packed away their charts and diagrams and returned to the serenity of their respective academic enclaves. The defense made an impassioned plea in support of his motions; the prosecution rose to make its controlled rebuttal. The decisions now rested with the seventy-two-year-old Judge Friedman.

Not that there was ever any particular doubt about how the judge would decide. At times he seemed to be thoroughly absorbed by what the learned professors were saying about juries and racial attitudes, but fundamentally he was unmoved. "We are not concerned," he pointed out several times, "with what happens in different parts of the world or different parts of the United States. We have the problem here in Alameda County. Now let's hold ourselves to it. . . ."

His own experience had taught the judge that blacks stood an excellent chance of getting a fair trial in his county. "Just a few weeks ago," he told Dr. Zeisel, "I had a Negro defendant charged with stealing a car. The jury consisted of eleven white persons and one black person. They went out, studied it for about three hours, and came back with a not guilty verdict."

So what on earth could Huey Newton be so worried about?

The motion to quash the master panel of jurors was denied.

The other motion regarding juror attitudes toward capital punishment would be granted in part, Judge Friedman said: The Court would abide by the recent (June, '68) Supreme Court ruling in the *Witherspoon* case. Only if a potential juror stated explicitly that under no circumstances would he vote for the death penalty, could that juror be eliminated.

In their customary fervor, the Black Panthers and their supporters pledged that they would encircle the Alameda County Courthouse every day that their Minister of Defense was on trial, but on Tuesday, July 16, the second day of the trial, their numbers dropped sharply from thousands to hundreds. Undaunted, Kathleen Cleaver, bullhorn in hand, voice raspy from cries of "Free Huey," led the troops in the procession around the building.

However, the courthouse remained the nearly impenetrable fortress it had been the day before. As on that day, armed sheriff's deputies manned their posts at all entrances, stairways, elevators and underground passageways, imposing all the same restrictions.

On a show of my tattered press credentials I got past the cluster of guards up to the second floor, to find a swarm of angry bees waiting for press passes to get into the courtroom. The "first-come, first-served" dictum had been summarily trampled as a deputy at the door began to distribute the precious "tickets" largely according to which voice could assert the priority of its publication the loudest. Representing *Life*, as I was, with the enormity of the magazine's clout ever preceding me, I was unaccustomed to jostling with the press "masses" in order to gain admission to *anything anywhere.*

Later that week, an order—repugnant to all but a handful —was handed down by Judge Friedman. In the daily distribution of passes for the seats reserved for the press, the local media would be favored. Top priority would be given to representatives of local daily newspapers, television and radio and the two wire services, Associated Press and United Press International. Now twenty-five seats would go to reporters in this category. All the rest of us would have to fight each other for three additional seats, and such other passes as were not claimed by 9:30 A.M.

Not that Judge Friedman's order might not have been circumvented. I was sure, for example, that if I telephoned some high-powered *Life* editor in New York, he could bring some big-magazine muscle to bear upon the Court to assure me a daily seat in the courtroom. But as tempting as that tactic was, I quickly dismissed it. I had already been covering the Black Panthers for some two weeks and already had more than enough material for a "story." To call New York would be to incur the high risk of having someone say, "Come on home and write the story—no need to cover the whole damn trial."

And so with an interest in the trial that was rapidly becoming an obsession, I stayed on to suffer all the discomforts required of anyone who insisted upon getting into the courtroom every day. On some days I would get up as early as two in the morning to stand on line with the similarly hapless radical press. One of the earlier absurdities of the trial of Huey P. Newton was that *Life* magazine and the Berkeley *Barb* were somehow made bedfellows.

The procession of sociologists having ended on Wednesday, July 17, the motion to quash the jury panel having been denied, the arduous process of selecting twelve jurors and four alternates began Thursday morning. To the first batch of jurors and to all succeeding panels of jurors, Judge Friedman outlined the specifications of the case:

"The defendant Huey P. Newton has been charged by the Grand Jury of the Court of Alameda in an indictment with three counts. The first count is a felony, to wit, murder, a violation of Section 187 of the Penal Code of the State of California, he murdered John Frey; the second count is a felony, violation of Section 245-B of the Penal Code of the State of California, in that on or about the 28th of October, 1967, in the County of Alameda, State of California, he assaulted with a deadly weapon, Herbert Heanes of the Oakland Police Department, knowing or having reasonable cause to know that said officer was a peace officer engaged in the performance of his duty; the third count he is charged with, the commission of a felony, to wit, kidnapping, a violation of Section 207 of the Penal Code of the State of California in that on or about the 28th day October, 1967, in the County of Alameda, State of California, he did forcibly steal and take Dell Ross and carry him into another part of the county. . . ."

In whittling down the large jury panel of several hundred to twelve, the defense, far more than the prosecution, had to exercise caution. To a degree difficult for anyone then living outside the San Francisco Bay Area to appreciate, the Black Panthers and the Huey Newton trial had evoked fierce community passions. Few could claim an honest indifference to their cause. You were either fervent in your support of them or raucous in denouncing them. There was little room for marginal positions. Some mounted platforms to trumpet their views; some dared only to whisper their thinking in the privacy of living rooms. "Huey is guilty. Gas him!" "Huey is innocent. Free him!"

But few of those partial to the Panthers were likely to pass through the Alameda Courthouse as prospective jurors. No—overwhelmingly, potential jurors would be white and middle-class and detached from the indignities that is life in the black enclave of West Oakland and a thousand enclaves across the country just like it. Almost uniformly these potential jurors would be people who would surely say that they had worked hard like their parents before them, that they had struggled and pinched pennies and saved to the point where they could buy homes and lawn sprinklers and station wagons and Magnavox color TV.

The parade of potential jurors began around nine-fifty-five that Wednesday morning and labored on for two weeks until August 2. Few jury panels have ever undergone so thorough a scrutiny. The scene took on a theatrical quality: the cynical producer and director searching for talent for a major Broadway production sit in the seventh row of an otherwise empty theater as a procession of starlets, actors and hopeful young singers prance on stage to display their artistic wares—only to be rejected by the hundreds by the jaded connoisseurs in the seventh row. Except that in our Alameda County Courthouse production almost none of the "talent" wanted to be in the show.

There were of course many among the Huey Newton jury panel for whom assignment to the case would have been "inconvenient" for all the usual reasons that jury duty can be inconvenient: "If I serve on this case, I'll lose a lot of pay on my job and I just can't afford it"; "I have two babies at home and no one to take care of them"; "My sister is getting married next week and I just wouldn't want to miss it"; etc.

Then there were a great many people who might otherwise have loved to have been assigned to an "interesting case," but who found the Huey Newton case much *too* interesting. Very simply, there were a great many who were *afraid* to be in any way involved with it. Few Bay Area TV watchers, few regular or even casual readers of the Oakland *Tribune*, the San Francisco *Chronicle*, could come away with the notion that the Huey Newton affair was anything but an open-and-shut case. Huey Newton, head of a bunch of gun-totin' niggers calling themselves the Black Panthers, had finally gone out and shot himself a cop. Now it was time for the law to take its course, but no one particularly wanted to be on "that jury that sent Huey Newton to the gas chamber." The Black Panthers had, after all, threatened in their scary, superb ambiguity, "The Sky Is the Limit."

Open to those who wanted to cop out on their "civic duties" were at least two ploys. The potential juror had only to "confess" that he had prejudged the case. One prospective alternate juror promptly blurted out, "I don't think I can be a fair juror in this case because I have an opinion." Judge Friedman wanted to know whether it was a "fixed" opinion that couldn't be set aside.

"No, I don't think I could, Your Honor. I would side with the police," the juror replied.

The defense rose to challenge the juror for cause; Judge Friedman allowed the challenge and dismissed the juror, who fled home to his wife and kids.

The other way of getting off the hook was by dint of the "death penalty" ploy. Some jurors, of course, honestly felt that they could not condemn Huey Newton or anyone else to death, and the *voir dire* questioning of such people clearly showed their sincerity. On the other hand, scores of others simply used the issue as an escape hatch. The panel of jurors had been told at the outset that the "big twelve" who would eventually sit in judgment of Huey might have to try the case in two phases. Regarding the charge of murder, four verdicts were open to the jury. They could find him innocent; they could find him guilty of first degree murder, of second degree murder or of manslaughter. If a verdict of first degree murder were returned, the jury would then have to go into phase two of the trial, which would decide whether Newton should be put to death or sentenced to life imprisonment.

Because Judge Friedman would abide by the findings of the *Witherspoon* case, the potential juror could escape serving by saying that under no circumstances would he vote for the death penalty.

Not that Alameda County jurors were necessarily versed in all these legal tangles before they came to court. No, many of those who did not want to serve on the Newton case picked up the techniques in court, watching as their fellow jurors were questioned by prosecution and defense.

Prosecutor Lowell Jensen, reasonably assured that most of the prospective jurors he would question were predisposed to finding the defendant guilty, could afford to conduct a fairly leisurely examination. In a typical *voir dire* examination he would establish the juror's occupation, place of employment, the makeup of his immediate family. Then on to stage two: Had the juror heard about the case before he came to court? Did the juror understand that what he had heard or read of the Newton case outside the courtroom was not evidence and could not be used in reaching a verdict? And in phase three: the prosecution would elicit the juror's reaction to capital punishment, challenging "for cause" all those who affirmed that they would *never* condemn a man to death. All in all, Assistant District Attorney Lowell Jensen was in the happy position of being a man with a passion for apples seated in the middle of an apple orchard.

Every so often, however, amidst bushel upon bushel of apples, an orange would turn up. Prospective juror Gordon Beam, a young white resident of Berkeley, told the Court that he was a sometime taxi driver and potter—a maker of "ceremonial tea bowls." Like everyone else, he had read about the Newton case long before being summoned to serve as a juror, but lo and behold, his principal source of information had been not the mass media—not the San Francisco *Examiner* or the Oakland *Tribune*—but the radical Berkeley *Barb*. At one point Mr. Beam referred to what he called "Mr. Newton's unfortunate thing." Jensen pressed for more information as the faint odor of citrus filtered through the courtroom.

"You have an opinion about the case?" Jensen asked.

Beam wriggled and squirmed. His answer was disjointed. He never really said all the things that were on his mind, but there was no mistaking it. Gordon Beam was an orange:

"Well, I understand, you know, the impartiality that is required of a juror, but I also have an opinion. I mean, in the sense that—I think he is innocent which—but it is little ambiguous. It is sort of broad. I really don't have any facts. . . ."

Turns out that young Gordon Beam is a member of the Peace and Freedom Party, with all its well-publicized sympathies for the Black Panther Party. Beam said that he had not been active in the PFP's "Free Huey" cause, but of course he knew about the Black Panthers and he didn't mind that they were known to refer to police officers as "pigs." Jensen could not easily challenge Beam "for cause" because he had stated unequivocally that, despite his political affiliation, he was capable of listening impartially to both sides in the case. Never mind that that might not be true. All witnesses are presumed to be telling the truth. Beam also could not be excluded from the jury via the "death penalty" route, for to the key question—"If you were to serve on this particular case, Mr. Beam, and there was a finding of murder in the first degree, would you consider the alternatives, the death penalty and life imprisonment as potential verdicts that you would reach?"—he answered "Yes."

And so against young Gordon Beam, Prosecutor Jensen

was obliged to use the ultimate weapon—the peremptory challenge. No need to explain to the Court why this or that juror is being excluded; no need for a legal peg on which to hang your antipathy for Juror X. All you need say is: "The People excuse Mr. Beam." Whereupon the judge tells Mr. Beam, "Get your slip and go down to the second floor." And that's the end of Gordon Beam.

Naturally, this powerful weapon was also available to the defense. Each side could use the peremptory challenge against potential jurors they, for one reason or another, did not want *twenty times*. But under the peculiar circumstances in the Newton trial, if Lowell Jensen had had only twenty and Charles Garry had had *two hundred* peremptory challenges at his disposal, it still would not have been enough.

Periodically, in the procession of jurors, a black face would appear. In fact, one or two of Huey Newton's "peers," who lived in, of all places, the West Oakland ghetto and who had somehow managed to slip by all the sociological obstructions, turned up in the jury box for potential selection. But that's as far as they got. Those who could not be dealt with by use of the death-penalty challenge were summarily rejected by the prosecution's using the peremptory challenge. In the end when the twelve jurors and four alternates had finally been selected, only one black man remained to besmirch the whiteness of the jury. With an eye toward "future references," the defense stood up each time the prosecution rejected a potential black juror. "Let the record show," Charles Garry would say, that the person then being rejected "is black."

Among the blacks rejected were Mrs. Minnie Thompson, who told an unbelieving Court that she thought she could still be impartial despite the fact that "my family and the Newton family had been friends for years." And then there was old Sylvester James, who in his kindly naïveté probably thought he was helping Huey when he said:

"Well, him and my boys went to school together and they used to come by to my house sometimes, him and his brother. . . . I haven't seen him very much since they got out of high school. . . . As nice as the kid was around me, I could not convict him unlessen somebody proved to me definitely and showed me something mighty good to make me think he done it. He was too nice a kid. Both of the boys was awful nice. . . ."

To repeat, Prosecutor Jensen had a rather easy time picking the jurors. But Charles Garry and his associate "attorney of record," Fay Stender, were stuck in the apple orchard with a taste only for oranges. On hand to help them filter out the more obtrusive bigots was Dr. Robert Blauner, who had testified the day before in support of the motion to quash the entire jury panel. In attempting to elicit from a juror responses that would give some clue to deep-seated attitudes buried beneath the topsoil, Garry ranged far and wide in his questions:

"What newspapers do you read? Have you ever heard of the Kerner Report on violence and civil disorders? Did you read it? What do you think of it? What does white racism mean to you? Do you think any prevails in Alameda County? Is there any of it in you? Do any blacks belong to that labor union you're a member of? How do you feel about state laws which require home owners selling their property to sell to whoever can afford to buy? Do you have any friends who are police officers? Would you give the same credence to an ordinary citizen testifying as you might give to a policeman? Have you ever moved out of a neighborhood because blacks moved in? How do you feel about the Black Panthers? How do you feel about the John Birch Society? Have you ever belonged to an organization which had as one of its principal aims the impeachment of Chief Justice Earl Warren? Do you know anything about what is commonly called 'Black Power'? Do you have a firearm in your home? Do you believe in the citizen's right of self-defense? Do you think it's possible for the police to be guilty of police brutality?"

In his *voir dire* questioning of jurors, Garry was also concerned with what lawyers have come to call the "Perry Mason syndrome." Fans of the Erle Stanley Gardner books and of the television character created from them might expect Garry, like the fictional character, to show the District Attorney to be a complete fool and, absolving his client of guilt, wring a melodramatic confession from the true perpetrator in the closing minutes of the trial. "Now you wouldn't expect Huey Newton to prove who killed Officer Frey, would you?" Garry asked one juror.

As careful as the attorneys were in eliciting juror attitudes, the jurors themselves were just as careful about what they said. As to their views on the Black Panthers and the race question in general, the Huey Newton jury panel tended to be noticeably tight-lipped—at least in open court. There were however, notable exceptions. Mrs. Adrienne (June) Reed, a mother of three and a secretary for Safeway Stores, said quite plainly that she didn't much care for the Black Panthers calling policemen pigs.

"I don't like it any more than I like to hear white people call colored people niggers. . . . I just don't believe it is right."

On the other hand, she claimed that she would not allow the name-calling to prejudice her against the Panthers. "I don't consider that the fact that you call someone what I consider a dirty name is what the man is being tried for. It is entirely different, and I think murder is far more serious than calling someone a pig."

Mrs. Reed also did not like the idea of the Panthers carrying weapons. And again she was explicit in stating her position:

"I am not black and I have never been exposed to the same conditions, but I don't believe that this is the way to settle things. It kind of rubs against the grain. . . . I don't mind seeing a police officer with a gun, but I figure he has a job to do and I don't go for people carrying guns for self-protection. In your home is one thing, but I do not believe any citizen should carry a gun around on the street. I think if this is what our situation is coming to, then we all better worry, black and white."

Under Garry's questioning, Mrs. Reed conceded that, like everyone else, she might be harboring elements of white racism, and, in another frank statement, she ventured to say she did not approve of racial intermarriage.

In the preliminary questioning of prospective juror number nine, Jordan Leandro, a white Hawaiian, told Judge Friedman that he could not be an impartial juror in the Huey Newton trial. It was clear that Mr. Leandro perceived the trial to be a "hang-Huey" venture and, because of his close associations with "colored people," wanted no part in the proceedings.

"I have a son. He is nineteen years old now. He is Chinese-Hawaiian and now he is in Kentucky in the Army and when he was seven years old, his teacher wondered why my son wouldn't play with the white people. So she came over to my house one time and she asked me why. . . . I called my son and asked my son and he told me, 'I *like* to play with them.' Then I told the teacher, 'Look at me and look at my son. My son is brown. I am a white man.'

"There have been a lot of things around my neighborhood that my son has been blamed for which he has never done. Our neighbor across the street one time came to my door and knocked at my door and told me that my son threw a peach at her window and at this time my son was in the house with me for two hours talking about baseball. The next time somebody stole some gasoline from my next-door neighbor. He was also blamed for it. . . .

"I have seen with my own eyes how colored people are treated in California. . . ." Mr. Leandro went on to list interracial couples with whom he had close friendships. "My friends that I work with, they are colored. They are the greatest friends I ever had. . . . So I don't want no part of this. . . .

"You see, I come from the fiftieth state, which is the Hawaiian Islands, and I have never seen anything like this. . . . It's just a small island and everybody is happy. And I can't go against this man. I don't want no part of it."

Jordan Leandro was eventually challenged for cause by the prosecution in that he would not vote for the death penalty, even in the most extreme of cases.

William J. Striplin, a white plastics technician, in the course of explaining his understanding of Black Power and the "Burn, baby, burn" rhetoric, told the Court: "I saw a newscast on television at one of the riots where there were a lot of fire, et cetera, and this was one of the comments that was made at the time. This sort of thing I don't believe in, destroying other people's property and rioting in the streets and total disregard for the law. It just goes against my grain."

Asked by the defense what he thought about the Black Panthers, Mr. Striplin said, "I have mixed emotions on that subject. I suppose, Your Honor, originally I thought it was another organization similar to the NAACP which were trying to better the Negro population. I was a bit disturbed in seeing the things that were around the courthouse and the first thing that came to my mind was Nazi storm troopers when they were standing with their flags and at parade rest. So I really don't know that much about it."

"You don't see any similarity between Huey Newton and Adolf Hitler, do you?" Charles Garry asked. "No, not really," Striplin said.

Striplin was later excluded by defense, using the peremptory challenge.

Mrs. Marian Butler, a drugstore saleswoman and wife of a stockbroker, told the Court that her own First Presbyterian church of Berkeley had once invited a Black Panther representative to address the congregation. The invitation, she said, was extended as part of her church's attempt to understand urban problems. The Panther came, but "he made us all a little mad when he said all white Protestants were racists. But that might have been his opinion only; I don't say that it was the Black Panther Party's opinion."

Mrs. Butler was passed for cause by the defense; she would eventually become one of the final twelve jurors.

Factory worker Milton Hendrickson, a prospective alternate juror, in his absorption with the sports section of the Oakland *Tribune,* had read nothing of the Huey Newton case on the front page. He said that he seldom looked at television or listened to the radio so that he had had no exposure from those media either.

"Have you ever heard of white racism, Mr. Hendrickson?" Charles Garry asked him.

"Well, more or less. To be honest with you, I don't really understand what you mean by white racism."

"Do you think that the black people of Alameda County are being discriminated against?"

"Well, I don't know. I have really had nothing to do with them people."

"In other words, in the area that you live in, San Leandro, there aren't any black people. Isn't that right?"

"No, no, there isn't none."

". . . And are you very happy that there aren't any black people living there?"

"Well, I think more or less most people are, aren't they?"

". . . And you are happy, too, aren't you?"

"Well, I imagine I am."

Understandably, the defense promptly challenged Mr. Hendrickson for cause. The challenge was allowed.

■   ■   ■

Finally, the Huey Newton trial had its jury—after seventeen hundred pages of testimony. There was Ronald L. Andrews, an Iowa-born engineer, forty-five, with a wife and three grown children. "I honestly believe," Mr. Andrews had testified at one point, "that I do not have any racism. If I do, it is something I don't know about."

Thomas R. Hofmann, a bachelor living with his parents, who worked in the trust department of a Berkeley branch of the Wells Fargo Bank. Of the Black Panthers Mr. Hofmann said: "I am not familiar with them. I don't know any individual members. I don't know exactly what their goals and objectives are other than what I have heard here in the courtroom."

Linda M. Aguirre, a junior executive secretary for a San

Francisco paper company. Harvey H. Kokka, of Japanese parentage, a laboratory technician for the Shell Development Company. Regarding capital punishment, Mr. Kokka said: "Generally speaking, I think I do not favor the death penalty. However, I believe in my own mind that there are extreme cases where I would vote for it." And what did Mr. Kokka think of white racism? "I think it is deplorable in every phase," he said.

Jenevie E. Gibbons, bologna slicer in a meat packing plant, wife of a fireman and mother of two daughters. Mrs. Gibbons didn't mind that the Panthers were wont to call policemen pigs. "People used to call them the fuzz," she said, "and that didn't bother me either."

Mrs. Eda Prelli, a widow and mother of two sons and a daughter and an owner of several apartment units. Mrs. Prelli had paid little attention to the news about the Huey Newton case. "I don't like to hear troubles," she said. "I have enough of my own."

Mrs. Mary A. Gallegos, a department store bookkeeper and the wife of a fork lift operator.

Mrs. Helen Hart, a widow, mother of five married children and employee of an airline catering service. She was the last juror to be selected.

Joseph L. Quintana, a Cuban-born immigrant whose travels had taken him to Venezuela, New York and Spain. A machinist and the father of two, Mr. Quintana had promptly told the Court that he did not speak English very well. But that was quite all right, Judge Friedman assured him. "You don't have to be a professor here in order to serve on a jury." Charles Garry asked Mr. Quintana at one point whether he thought Fidel Castro had done "a pretty good job in Cuba." Lowell Jensen objected to the question. "We are really getting pretty far out," he said. Judge Friedman agreed. "We have a lot of problems with the world and we cannot settle them all in this one case," he said. Garry asked Quintana the same question another way: "If the evidence shows that my client Mr. Newton and the Black Panther organization think that Fidel Castro has done a good job in Cuba, would that prejudice you against them?" Mr. Quintana said that it wouldn't.

Mrs. Marian Butler, who had spoken of the Black Panther visiting her church. Mrs. Adrienne Reed, who had been more talkative than most in detailing her feelings.

Finally, there was David B. Harper, the only black man who survived the eliminating process. Harper, thirty-five, a lending officer at the Bank of America in San Francisco, was married and the father of six children. He told the Court that he had not talked about the case very much. "Most of my colleagues refrain from discussing this sort of thing with me . . . for instance when Martin Luther King was killed, it wasn't discussed with me."

"You have heard of the Black Panthers, have you not?" Garry asked Harper. "Oh, yes," he said.

"Do you have any conscientious feelings against the platform of the Black Panther Party?"

"Not at all."

"Is there anything about this case, Mr. Harper, that would lead you to feel that you couldn't be fair and impartial?"

"No. Nothing I can think of."

"Do you believe that Huey Newton killed Officer Frey?"

"I have never been of that opinion."

Four alternate jurors were also chosen: James H. Jackson, a twenty-six-year-old surveyor for the city of Berkeley; Betty Anderson, a bank secretary and mother of two; Richard L. Roberts, an Oakland aircraft maintenance technician; and Edgar A. White, a thirty-six-year-old camera shop salesman from Berkeley. The four alternates took the same oath as the regular jurors, heard all the evidence and were subject to the same restrictions. Judge Friedman outlined their function:

"If at any time, whether before or after the final submission of the case to the jury, a juror dies or becomes ill, or, upon other good cause shown to the Court, is found to be unable to perform his duty; or if a juror requests discharge and good cause appears therefor, the Court may order him to be discharged and draw the name of an alternate juror who shall take his place in the jury box."

But none of these contingencies ever arose, and throughout the trial the four-man body of alternates sat idly by like a Vice President in the shadow of a strong President.

Predictably, the defense rose to protest the composition of the final body of jurors. Not a single juror, not even the lone black man David Harper, could be said to be the "peer" of Huey Newton. Charles Garry asked for a mistrial on these grounds. He also moved that the jury be dismissed and another selected. Both motions were denied.

■   ■   ■

On Monday morning, August 5, 1968, the Huey Newton trial began in earnest. The security valves around the proceedings were twisted a bit tighter. Judge Friedman made the announcement:

"I have taken up with counsel in chambers the fact that various rumors have reached counsel and have reached the Court as to possible harm that may come to the defendant, or that may come to witnesses for the People, or that may come to witnesses for the defendant. It is the duty of the Court to use all reasonable means to see that the defendant is fully protected, and that the witnesses for both the People and the defendant are fully protected. . . .

"It appears reasonable and necessary to this Court, under all the circumstances, that an order be made that with the exception of the jury, who will not be informed of this fact, with the exception of attorneys of record in this case, *all other persons shall be searched for weapons before they enter the courtroom.* . . . [Emphasis added.]

"Now this order will start at one o'clock today. Defendant has objected to the order on the ground that he does not want his friends searched. This order applies to everybody and it includes the defendant's friends, all spectators and all the press, and everyone else who enters this courtroom. There will be no exceptions, includes all persons, black or white or yellow or brown or any other race."

And indeed it did apply to us all: what few Panthers got into court, the radical press, the mass media reporters, the Reverend Earl Neil in full clerical attire, Huey Newton's brothers—one and all were searched. And thoroughly! Empty all pockets of wallets, address books, pocketbooks. You leaned against the wall while sheriff's deputies ran their fat little fingers up and down your pants legs, up around your armpits, in and around the ole crotch. A little screen was set up in the "searching room" so that lady sheriff's deputies could work the women spectators over. I was itching to peek behind the partition to see precisely how the women were handled, but a stern puritan of a deputy told me not to. Still curious though, I asked a lady reporter later how she was searched. "High and inside," she said. "High and inside." David Pryce-Jones, an English reporter who was covering the trial for the London *Telegraph,* said that the security precautions here were at least equal to those the Israelis imposed in Jerusalem during the trial of Adolf Eichmann.

Assistant District Attorney Lowell Jensen made his opening remarks to the jury first. He said that he would produce
witnesses and evidence to reconstruct the events of the night
in question. It was early Saturday morning at the corner of
Seventh and Willow streets in Oakland. On duty at his beat
was Patrolman John Frey. Shortly before 5 A.M. Frey radioed
to police headquarters to make a check on the license number of a vehicle, a "known Black Panther vehicle." The car
was a 1967 beige Volkswagen. Registered owner: LaVerne
Williams. Headquarters radioed back that there were outstanding arrest warrants against the owner of the vehicle.
Frey asked for assistance and then stopped the Volkswagen.
Officer Herbert Heanes arrived on the scene a few minutes
thereafter, parking his car in back of Frey's. There were now
three cars parked in a row on the south side of Seventh
street.

"Now Officer Frey," Jensen continued, "was in the process
of writing a citation to Huey Newton, who had identified
himself as LaVerne Williams. He was a person who was not
known to Officer Frey, but he had produced a registration
for the car in the name of LaVerne Williams and Officer
Frey was writing a citation for no driver's license in possession for a person known to him as LaVerne Williams when
Officer Heanes came up to the car." At this point, Jensen
said, "Mr. Williams" identified himself to Herbert Heanes as
"Huey Newton." The policemen decided then, Jensen's narrative continued, to arrest Newton for falsely identifying himself. Newton got out of the Volkswagen and started walking
toward the police cars. Frey was right in back of him, with
Heanes looking on. Just as Newton got to the back of the
second police car, he spun around, revolver in hand, and
started firing. A struggle ensued between Newton and Frey,
in which Newton obtained Frey's gun and killed him with it.

Meanwhile Officer Heanes, keeping an eye on Newton's companion who had gotten out of the car, drew his weapon from his holster, only to be shot in the arm by Newton. Switching hands, Heanes fired a shot with his left hand. The bullet struck Newton in the abdomen. After the shooting, Newton and a companion ran around the corner to Willow Street and "there, in the wrong place at the wrong time, was a gentleman named Dell Ross, who was sitting in his vehicle." Newton forced Ross at gunpoint to drive him to Kaiser Hospital.

Jensen went on to outline what the prosecution considered to be Huey Newton's motive. Two matchboxes of marijuana, he said, were later found in the Volkswagen. Thus when he was stopped by Frey that night, Huey Newton, a convicted felon still on probation, feared that he would be apprehended in the commission of two additional felonies—namely, possession of marijuana and of a concealable weapon. (Newton was never formally charged, however, with possession of marijuana.) Rather than face these serious charges, he decided to shoot it out with John Frey.

"After the evidence has been adduced," Jensen finished up, "after the law has been outlined to you by the Court, we will ask that as far as the charges are concerned, that you find the defendant guilty of kidnaping, assault on a police officer with knowledge that he was a police officer, and find him guilty of first degree murder."

From Charles Garry, the jury heard what amounted to a capsule biography of Huey Newton and a brief history of the Black Panther Party. He sketched Newton's early life in Oakland and his formation of the Panthers in 1966 and read at full length the Ten Point Program. "The evidence will show, ladies and gentlemen," Garry continued, "that the Black Panther Party for Self-Defense formed patrols to patrol the black community. . . . A group of four men would go and watch the action of the police in the ghetto and wherever the police would resort to any form of brutality, they would step in there at a safe distance from the police and . . . advise a person involved that they had certain legal rights . . . and did not have to be pushed around in a ghetto like dogs. . . .

"The Black Panther Party became a symbol in the eyes of the police department of Oakland and Alameda County to the point where they were enraged at the Black Panthers. The Oakland Police Department made a list of all the Panther automobiles. The evidence will show that they took pictures of the various people who were active and particularly Huey Newton. . . . The result was, ladies and gentlemen, that there wasn't one single person in the Oakland Police Department who did not know the name of Huey Newton, who did not know him by his picture. . . . The police would find any kind of a pretense to stop any Panther automobile to see if there was some violation.

"The evidence will show that the Black Panther Party and its members freely and voluntarily spoke to the press as to their views and their cries against police brutality and the degradation and indignities that a black man in the ghetto has to suffer.

"More and more, the cry in the police department became 'Get Huey Newton.' . . . 'Get rid of him.' . . . The evidence will show, ladies and gentlemen, that this attitude of getting the Black Panthers did not stop upon his arrest on the morning of October 28th. The evidence will show that he was shot in the stomach . . . that he was taken to Kaiser Hospital and after haranguing and trying to get medical attention the police were called before he could get any medical attention.

"The evidence will show that with a man who had been shot in the abdomen, and a bullet right on through with a perforated bowel, this man was placed on a gurney. The police put his hands in handcuffs and pulled him in a manner that I have indicated to you with his stomach being fully stretched at a time when there was a bullet hole in his stomach.

"The evidence will show, ladies and gentlemen, that when he complained to the doctor and to the police he was told to shut up. He was referred to as a nigger and 'Black bastard—you ought to die. . . .'

"After he was taken from Kaiser Hospital to Highland Hospital, where he was fed intravenously and through the nose, the police would stand guard outside of his room and, for whatever pretensions there were, they would go to the bed and deliberately kick the legs of the bed and jar the thing and say, 'We are going to get you; we are going to kill you,' and words that should not be repeated in this courtroom.

"The evidence will show, ladies and gentlemen of the jury, that the Mayor and the Police Chief and the police department were all part and parcel of this move to get Black Panthers and particularly Huey Newton. The evidence will show, ladies and gentlemen of the jury, that Huey Newton did not have a firearm in his possession or in his automobile that he was riding in on the 28th day of October, 1967. The evidence will clearly show that he did not fire a firearm at any time on that date. The evidence will unequivocally show that he did not kill Officer Frey; he did not shoot Officer Heanes and he is completely innocent of any of these charges."

These remarks were made on a Monday morning—August 5, 1968. It was like the Tuesday approaching and the Friday past. There were constant reminders that I was in a courtroom and yet I might have been completely wrong. Perhaps it all happened in a theater. The Alameda County Theater of the Absurd presents a brilliant play entitled *Free Huey* written jointly by LeRoi Jones and Samuel Beckett. Playing the lead—a handsome young black revolutionary named Huey Newton. Mr. Newton is a fine young acting talent and the first Negro to star in a major production—of this kind. Playing the judge will be Monroe Friedman, veteran character actor of forensic stage productions too numerous to name. Mr. Friedman, it is thought, is perfectly cast for a role in which he must portray a man of smiling fair-mindedness, a man scrupulously attentive to teensy-weensy legalities of no apparent significance to reasonable men. In supporting roles, we have Charles Garry playing the cocky, though dedicated defense attorney; Fay Stender as his nervous, hardworking assistant, like her boss passionately in love with lost causes; and Lowell Jensen as the cold, unflappable, rabbit-punching prosecutor.

At this stage of the trial I still had not cultivated that lively sense of the paradoxical required to even begin to understand the Black Panthers. My mind was still therefore throbbing with such circular issues as what "Free Huey" meant. Is it a command, a request or an exhortation—or perhaps all three? Does it mean, examine the evidence, go through the court rituals and *then* free Huey? Does it mean storming the Alameda County Jail and freeing him by force of arms? Or what?

After you stripped away the rhetoric, one man—a single human being, isolated from history—was on trial for his life. If you wanted to, you could reduce all the proceedings to a whodunit. And every so often, I did that.

Huey could never have shot John Frey in cold blood. He's too clever for that. He knew that the police were watching every move he made. He would never have allowed himself to be caught with a gun. Certainly he was too smart to drive around Oakland with pot in his car. No—that was much too stupid to be Huey. Not he who was so careful to study California gun laws before sending armed Black Panthers to march on the state legislature. No, Huey didn't murder John Frey. Some other Panther, maybe, but not Huey Newton. But then on the other hand, he probably did shoot him. Where the hell did all those bullets come from? Tell me that! Four cats standing out there by the cars. One disappears; one gets wounded; Huey gets wounded, and John Frey gets killed. And Huey didn't fire a shot? I don't believe it. The revolutionary face to face with the oppressor—the oppressor spews hatred at the revolutionary and the revolutionary fires nary a shot. Bullshit! I don't believe you, Huey. You shot him, Huey. I know you did. I don't think you should serve one minute in jail for it, but I know you did it. You can bullshit the judge and the jury and the press all you want to, but I'll bet a million dollars you shot John Frey.

Then there were moments when I sat there staring past the press, past the plain-clothesmen and the counsel table to the judge on the bench sitting in front of that enormous flag—bigger than all of America. In these moments I didn't care whether Huey Newton shot John Frey or not.

What does it matter? Do I really give a damn? I hope to God he did shoot him. Shoot him, Huey! Shoot him dead! Kill him for me, Huey. Kill him for us. Revenge is ours, saith the Blacks.

But then the "real" world with its passion for detail would intrude itself again. The procession of prosecution witnesses began. First to take the stand was Dr. George S. Loquvam, who had performed the autopsy on Officer John Frey. The cause of death, Dr. Loquvam said, was "shock and hemorrhage due to multiple gunshot wounds." Five separate bullets entered Frey's body. The fatal one went through his back just below the right shoulder blade, penetrated three lobes of his right lung, causing him to bleed to death "from his lung into his right pleural cavity."

Radio Dispatcher Clarence Lord of the Oakland Police Department was on duty the morning that John Frey was shot. He came to court with a tape-recorded conversation via police radio between himself and Frey. On that October morning Frey called in for a "quick rolling 36 on Adam Zebra Mary 489," which translated meant that a vehicle (the beige Volkswagen), license number AZM 489, should be checked out for outstanding violations. Lord testified that he ran the information through the police department computer system to find that outstanding were two overdue parking tickets. He further confirmed with Frey that the car was "a known Black Panther vehicle" and that the registered owner was a certain LaVerne Williams of 1144 Twelfth Street, Oakland. Under cross-examination Mr. Lord admitted, albeit reluctantly, that, for the convenience of the police staff, a list of some twenty of the infamous Panther cars had been posted on a bulletin board at headquarters.

The first police officer to reach the scene after the shooting that night was Patrolman Gilbert DeHoyos. He was out patrolling in his patrol car, he said, and sometime after 5 A.M. that morning he responded to a "940B"—the Oakland police radio code for "EMERGENCY." DeHoyos arrived at Seventh and Willow, he testified, to find John Frey lying in the street and Herbert Heanes slumped over the front seat of one of the parked patrol cars. DeHoyos sent for an ambulance. At that point Frey was still alive and DeHoyos covered him with a blanket. Frey murmured, "Help me." He said no more.

Herbert Heanes, the first of the prosecution's three "star" witnesses, took the stand on August 6. With a trace of unease, Heanes recounted the events of October 28, 1967. Responding to a radio request, he drove to the designated area of Seventh and Willow to back Officer Frey. When he got there, he parked his car behind Frey's patrol car, which in turn had been parked behind the Volkswagen. Heanes said that he got out of his car "and took up a position to the right rear of the Volkswagen." Two men were seated in the car and Frey was standing near the driver's door. Frey left this spot and went to his car to use the police radio. There followed a conversation between Frey and Heanes. Leaving Frey sitting in the patrol car, Heanes said that he went over to the Volkswagen to talk to the men in the car.

"Can you tell us whether or not the person who was in the driver's seat of that Volkswagen is now present in this courtroom?" Lowell Jensen asked.

"Yes, sir," Heanes said. Judge Friedman asked Heanes to make a specific identification and Heanes left the witness stand, went down to the counsel table and touched Huey Newton on his left shoulder. "This gentleman here," Heanes said.

Continuing his testimony, Heanes said that he addressed Huey as "Mr. Williams" and asked him if he had further identification. Huey volunteered that he was "Huey Newton." Heanes then had another chat with John Frey, after which Heanes asked Huey to get out of the car. A moment later, Frey informed Newton that he was under arrest and told him to get out of the car. Huey got out of the car and started walking "rather briskly" toward the rear of the police cars. Heanes said that Frey was three or four feet and slightly to the right behind Newton. "They continued walking until they reached approximately the rear of my patrol car, which would be the third car. At this point Newton turned around and started shooting."

According to Heanes's narrative, he drew his gun from his holster upon hearing the first shot and was promptly shot through the arm. "I grabbed my arm momentarily," he said, "and then out of the corner of my eye I noticed someone standing on the curb between the Volkswagen and our police car. I turned toward him, aimed my revolver at him. He raised his hands and stated to me he wasn't armed and he had no intentions of harming me. . . . At this point I turned back around, my attention toward where Officer Frey and Newton were, and I noticed them on the trunk lid of my car tussling. . . . They seemed to be wrestling all over the trunk area of my car. . . .

"Next thing I can recall is that I was on my knees looking in that direction. I saw Newton. He was approximately in the same position as earlier, facing me, with Officer Frey facing from the side—from the side of Newton. At this point I aimed my revolver at Newton and fired. . . .

"Next thing I recall is that I was laying in the police car. I picked up the radio and called an emergency 940B."

In his cross-examination, Charles Garry immediately implanted the startling idea that Herbert Heanes in aiming at Huey might have shot John Frey. "Did you shoot and kill Officer Frey?" Garry asked. "No, sir, I did not," Heanes said. (The testimony of a ballistics expert would later show that the bullet which killed Frey could not have come from Heanes's gun.)

Still the defense managed to gain an important point from Herbert Heanes: "*You never at any time saw a gun in the hand of Huey Newton, did you, sir?*"

"No, sir, I did not," Heanes said. (Emphasis added.)

It also became clear under Garry's relentless cross-examination that Heanes was not at all sure where the original shots had come from. Garry asked him about the position of Newton's companion just after the shooting began. ". . . You turned around because you thought that the passenger had shot you; isn't that right?"

"I saw something out of the corner of my eye," Heanes said. "I had no idea who it was or what it was and I turned on it, turned on him, and at this point he raised his hands."

"And you thought he had shot you in the arm; isn't that right?"

"No, I did not."

"You didn't think that?"

"No, sir."

"Then why did you turn around on him?"

"At that point there was gunfire and I was a little nervous about anybody in that area."

"It's a fact, is it not, sir, that you did not know where the gunfire was coming from?"

"I had an opinion as to where it was coming from."

"But you didn't know, did you?"

"I couldn't say for a fact, no."

Garry also cast doubt on the notion that Huey might have misidentified himself or that Heanes and Frey did not know precisely who they were dealing with that morning.

"Did you ask him for his operator's license?" Garry asked.

"No, sir, I did not."

"Why didn't you?"

"I was already under the impression that he didn't have one."

"How did you get that impression?"

"Officer Frey had told me that he had asked for identificaation and all he could produce was a registration card from the vehicle."

". . . Didn't Huey Newton say, 'I have my operator's license if you want to look at it'? Didn't he tell you that?"

"Not to me, he didn't."

"You knew, did you not, that he did have his operator's license with him?"

"No, I did not," Heanes said.

"Why didn't you ask him for it?"

"As I stated before, I was under the impression he didn't even have one."

Remarkably, incredibly, Heanes claimed that neither Newton nor his companion was searched. Why did these crack Oakland policemen forgo what would have been routine ghetto procedure? And more precisely, what policeman arrests a Black Panther—Huey Newton yet—without searching him?

"When was it that you frisked Mr. Newton and the passenger?" Garry asked.

"I didn't frisk either one of them at any time."

"Why didn't you?"

"Well, everything had gone so calmly I didn't feel any need to."

"Are you positive that at no time was Huey Newton and the passenger frisked and examined to see whether they had any weapons upon them?"

"No, sir. They weren't."

■   ■   ■

And the next day there appeared "star" witness number two—number two in sequence, number one in importance. Henry Grier! Henry Grier, father, husband, homeowner, bus driver, "eyewitness" to first degree murder. Mr. Grier was forty years old. He was discharged from the United States Navy in 1965 after twenty years of service. Nowadays he worked for the Bay Area's A. C. Transit Company. And there for all to see: Mr. Grier was black.

No black man, in complete possession of his faculties, as they say, would climb to a rostrum so public as this one and point the accusative finger at another black man, least of all Brother Huey P. Newton. This unspoken fact made our Mr. Grier all the more credible to a jury eleven-twelfths white. No black man, they must have thought, would do such a thing—*in these times, in this place.*

Or would he?

Mr. Grier testified that on Saturday morning, October 28, 1967, he was driving his bus along the "82 express line" extending from Seventh Street in Oakland to Mission Street in neighboring Hayward. It was about 4:58. There were three passengers on board. He was within two blocks of the 82nd line terminal. The street in the area was partially obstructed by the newly constructed pillars of BART—the Bay Area Rapid Transit system. His path was also obstructed by three parked cars—two police cars and a "little Volkswagen I believe the car was," he said.

"As I approached the police cars and, I say, the thing that attracted my attention was the beacon light on top of the police car and I knew something was taking place there so, of course, you slows down."

Grier said he stopped and then navigated his bus around to the left of the police cars. "I had to get out in the middle of the street to get around these cars," he told Lowell Jensen under direct examination.

"Before you stopped your bus, Mr. Grier, did you see any

person on the street near the police cars and the Volkswagen?" Jensen asked.

"I did," Grier said.

"How many persons?"

"Three that I know of."

"Were they facing toward you or away from you?"

"Facing me," Grier said.

". . . Were any of these people police officers?"

"Yes, it was."

"How many?"

"Two."

"And where were the police officers in reference to the
third person?" Jensen asked.

". . . As I approached from Willow, east on Seventh, and
this is in the early part of the morning, the lights was on, I
observed the police officer walking facing me with a man
and he appeared to have him sort of tugged under the arm,
and the other police officer was about ten paces behind the
two people that I first observed."

The scene, at this stage, did not unduly disturb Grier. Still
under direct examination by Jensen he explained: ". . . As
I stated before, the beacon light was working. I sort of
glanced over—I just thought: 'Somebody getting a ticket.'
Never thought any more about it."

Grier further testified that he drove the rest of the short
distance to the end of the bus line, turned around and that's
when the real action started.

And what about the identity of the man who was with the
police officer that morning? "Is he here in the courtroom
now?"

Handsome, cocksure, six foot one, Grier went down to the
counsel table and put his hand on the defendant's shoulder.

Huey yielded nothing by way of emotion that you could see.

The two policemen and Newton were walking toward him, Grier said. "As I approached the officer and the man there, as I say, my lights is directly on him. I could see him very plainly. This man, as I got as close to this table to them, the coach is rolling, I saw this man do this [Grier illustrated the move by tucking his hand into his shirt*]; and just at that split second out with the gun . . . just at that time the police officer that was right along beside the man grabbed him and the arm. The gun was up in a position like this and during the struggle, and twisted like this, the gun went off. . . .

"Immediately I stopped the coach. And at that time I was in this position. I stopped the coach, pulled the brakes, and we have a radio-telephone in the coach. I didn't have time to identify the run, which is required. I just said, 'Get help, police officer is being shot. Shots are flying everywhere; get help. Help quick.' . . .

"After the last shot was fired, which I could see the fire, sort of orange-blue fire from around the muzzle, after that—he fired the last shot, he went diagonally across Seventh and where he went I don't know, sir. . . .

"When the first officer was hit, I was looking at him, and he did draw his gun and fire . . . everything was happening so fast. But the officer that was hit first did fire his gun."

"Was that after he was hit?" Jensen asked.

"Yes; and after he fired his gun, and as I said, I turned to see what was going on among, you know, the tussle, and this

* Although in a statement to the police on the morning of the shooting, Grier said that the murderer had drawn the gun from his jacket pocket.

is when I said, as I stated, the officer was going on down, and being shot, as he was going down."

You'd think that Henry Grier would be afraid that some Black Panther might thrust a bullet up his ass. But no, Henry Grier was not afraid. You would think that at some point itching doubt would creep across his skin and make him unsure—unsure that he might not be Judas kissing Christ—unsure that his eyes might not have failed him on October 28, 1967. Or failing all of this, you might also think that Henry Grier would, at the very least, be hesitant to be the one most immediately responsible for sending another human being to his death. Shouldn't that give him pause? Not that it should necessarily hold back the pointing finger, but shouldn't it make him uncomfortable?

But Henry Grier was not shackled by any of these doubts. He was star witness to murder and he was zealous—nay, gleeful—in his role. Now and then he was smug, cocky. Now and then he wisecracked, he played smart-ass. Now and then, with nasal disdain, he would refer to Charles Garry as "Counselor"—"Counselor" this, "Counselor" that. Did he remember what the weather was like on October 28, 1967? Well, no, he really couldn't say because he wasn't a weatherman, but, he said, it was "sort of hazy" that morning. "What do you mean by 'hazy'?" Garry wanted to know. "Overcast," Grier said. ". . . Your visibility was not impaired; is that what you are saying?" "That's *exactly* what I am saying, sir," Grier said.

Early in the cross-examination it came out that Henry Grier had not been to work the week preceding his appearance in court. "In agreement with the District Attorney's office and the official of the Transit Company, I was asked to leave duty. . . . They told me that the D.A.'s office was taking me in protective custody." While in "custody," Grier was put up at Oakland's sumptuous Lake Merritt Hotel.

"Did you ask why you needed protective custody?" Garry asked.

"I did not."

"Nobody was threatening your life, were they, sir?"

"No."

". . . Were you given a subpoena to be here as a witness today?"

"No, sir," Grier said.

Under cross-examination Grier said that when he first drove up to the scene there were *four* people standing by the parked police cars and Volkswagen. He continued on the two-block distance to the end of the bus line, negotiated his turn and drove up to the scene again—this time on the other side of the street. He estimated that this short round trip took him between four and five minutes. Grier went on to say that the person he saw do the shooting was clean-shaven and wore *"a dark jacket and a light shirt."* (Emphasis added.)

Henry Grier's testimony abounded in discrepancies. Even the Oakland *Tribune* was obliged to say so. In a story on Grier's day in court, the *Trib* spoke softly of Garry hammering relentlessly away at "apparent contradictions" and "inconsistencies" in Grier's testimony. But the *Trib* went on to assure its readers that all was well in the "Hang Huey" trial: "The six-foot-one, 200-lb. bus driver seemed unperturbed by Garry's questions. He stuck to the testimony he gave under direct examination by Jensen and was not rattled by the inconsistencies Garry found between his statement to the police October 28 and his description in court."

But Oakland's *Tribune* did not say what the "apparent contradictions" were. If the testimony of Patrolman Herbert Heanes was to be believed, the shooting occurred almost immediately after Newton got out of his car. Heanes had also said that Newton's companion did not get out of the Volkswagen until the shooting started. But as Grier told the story, he saw *four* people standing outside the cars as he drove by the first time and the shooting didn't start until after he had turned around and returned to the scene "four or five minutes later."

On the morning of October 28, less than two hours after the shooting, Grier told the police that the man who did the shooting was under five feet tall. He was very small, Grier said then, "sort of a pee-wee-type fellow you might call him." He wore a hat, Grier said, and a "light tan color" jacket and a dark shirt—probably a black shirt, Grier thought. That same morning the police showed Henry Grier a photograph of Huey Newton. According to a transcription of the October 28 statement, Grier, while he did have doubts about the identification, went on to say explicitly, "I *did* get a clear picture—clear view of his face. I wouldn't say positive, I wouldn't positive say it was him but they do resemble."

But now in court—almost a year later—Henry Grier was absolutely certain about the identification: "The man that I saw at the scene of the crime is the man in this courtroom this morning."

"You are positive of that?" Garry asked.

"I am positive."

And in the interim between the time Henry Grier made his original statement and the time he appeared in court, whoever it was who had done the shooting had switched clothing and general appearance: from a clean-shaven, "sort of a pee-wee-type fellow," wearing a hat, tan jacket and dark shirt to someone wearing no hat, a dark jacket and a light-colored shirt.

But for all the "apparent contradictions" in Henry Grier's

testimony, the jury did not seem to be moved—it was probably in utter frustration that toward the end of the cross-examination Charles Garry said: "Mr. Grier, you know what an Uncle Tom is, don't you?" Prosecution objected to the question. It was, he said, "incompetent, irrelevant and immaterial."

Judge Friedman said that he could not see the relevancy of the question either.

■   ■   ■

On August 12 we heard from Citizen Ross—Citizen Dell Ross. He had been billed as a very important witness for the prosecution. The entire kidnaping charge against Newton revolved around Ross as the victim. Moreover, his word that Huey Newton had a gun on October 28, 1967, would corroborate the testimony of Henry Grier. The year before, Dell Ross had given the Oakland police a two-page signed statement. In addition, he had appeared before the grand jury to say that on the morning in question he and a friend were sitting in Ross's parked car on Willow Street near Seventh. They heard something that sounded to them like firecrackers. Ross's friend jumped out of the car and ran away leaving the door open. A moment later Huey Newton, gun in hand, and his companion came dashing around the corner and got into Ross's car—Huey in the back seat, his friend up front with Ross. Newton was supposed to have yelled repeatedly that he was "too mean to die," that he had "just shot two dudes" and he would have kept on shooting if his gun hadn't jammed. Ross was an important witness indeed. As in the case of Henry Grier, the unspoken psychological theory would prevail. Would Dell Ross, a black man, tell a deliberate lie against his brother, Huey P. Newton?

Or wouldn't he?

On his day in court, Ross, thirty-fivish, wore dark glasses, a light blue sports jacket, red turtleneck sweater, dark brown slacks and black patent leather shoes. He approached the witness stand with obvious reluctance. His lawyer was with him, and this was perhaps the first sign that something was amiss.

"Were you in the city of Oakland October 28, 1967?" Lowell Jensen asked him.

"Yes, I was in Oakland," Mr. Ross said.

"Do you have an automobile?"

"Not now."

"Did you have a car then?"

"Yes."

"Would you tell us what kind of a car it was?"

" '58 Ford."

"What type of Ford?"

"Convertible."

"What color was it?"

"Black with a white top."

"White-topped black car, 1958 Ford Convertible, is that right?"

"That is right."

"Now on Saturday, October 28, 1967, at about five o'clock in the morning where were you?"

"I was here in Oakland."

"At what place in Oakland?"

"I refuse to answer that question on the grounds it would incriminate. I don't want to say anything wrong."

It may never happen again, but Lowell Jensen was surprised: he was caught completely off guard. He asked the court reporter to read back Ross's answer. The answer was read. Ross slouched in his chair and mumbled, "That is all I have to say."

In short order the jury was whisked from the courtroom so that the attorneys could squabble in relative privacy. Judge Friedman said that he would consider the matter of Dell Ross's self-incrimination overnight. The next morning he was moved to say: "The Court finds it a little difficult to understand exactly where this witness would be incriminating himself. However, the provisions of the Constitution must be very liberally construed in favor of the witness, and therefore, at this posture of the case the Court will *not* direct the witness to answer."

But there was a hitch, a big hitch. Judge Friedman cited Section 1324 of the California Penal Code:

> *In any felony proceeding, if a person refuses to answer a question on the ground that he may be incriminated thereby, and if the District Attorney of the county in writing, requests the superior court in and for that county to order that person to answer the question, the judge of the superior court shall set a time for hearing, and order the person to appear before the court to show cause, if any, why the question should not be answered, and the court shall order the question answered unless it finds that to do so would be clearly contrary to the public interest or if it would subject that person or could subject the witness to a criminal prosecution in another jurisdiction, and that person shall comply with the order. . . .*

Lowell Jensen of course had his petition for a show-cause order all ready. Judge Friedman read the petition aloud and decided the time for the hearing on the matter should be now, right now. Douglas Hill, attorney for Dell Ross, pointed

out that under the law he was entitled to ten days' notice
before the hearing. But there was no turning back the tidal
wave of justice.

Dell Ross was granted immunity from prosecution for
everything except perjury and contempt. But Judge Friedman warned the bewildered Mr. Ross that if he continued
to refuse to answer questions, he would be placed in jail
and would remain there "until you have purged yourself."
Sadly but firmly, Ross said, "You'll have to send me to jail
then."

But the wily Mr. Jensen had another idea. "Mr. Ross, do
you *remember* what happened on the morning of October
28, 1967?" Reassuringly, the judge told Ross, "If you don't
remember what happened that morning, why, you should
say you don't remember. This Court does not desire to force
you into anything."

It looked like an escape hatch to Mr. Ross. "I can't remember anything happened eight or nine months ago," he
said.

This admission cleared the way for the prosecution to
"refresh" the witness' memory. And in order to do this Jensen
would have to read from Ross's grand jury testimony, which
would then become his official statement for this trial.

But Judge Friedman, Lowell Jensen and all the rest of us
were in for another jolt. The next morning Charles Garry
produced a tape recording of a conversation between him
and Dell Ross on July 28. Transcripts were passed around
to the jury and the recording was played in open court. The
taped discussion emphasized that Ross had come to Garry's
office voluntarily and that he had come to tell the truth.
Ross said that at the time he made his original statement to
the police, he was afraid because a warrant had been issued
for his arrest for parking violations. "And you were scared

and you went along with whatever they had you say. Isn't that right?" Garry asked him.

"That's right," Ross said, "because I'm just awful. Everywhere I've been I've been treated kind of cold. I'm not proud about what I said to them." Ross went on to repudiate his earlier statement to the police that "the light-skinned" man in the back seat (Huey Newton) had a gun. "No, I didn't see him with no gun. He was kinda out. . . . He didn't say anything at all that I can remember and I didn't pay no attention to him because I was driving."

"Now he didn't say that 'I just shot two dudes.' Did he?" Garry asked.

"He didn't say anything," Ross said.

During the playing of the tape recording, Dell Ross passed the time twitching and looking at the ceiling. And from there on he played dumb. Questioned by Jensen, he said he didn't remember anything. He didn't remember going to Garry's office; he didn't remember who Huey Newton was; he didn't remember whether he had anything to do with the shooting on the morning of October 28, 1967. Nothing. The final effect was that his statement made to the grand jury and his tape-recorded statement canceled each other out.

Eventually the Court would grant a motion to strike *all* of Ross's testimony from the record and to acquit Huey of the kidnaping charge. Citizen Ross was summarily declared to be a nonperson:

"Ladies and gentlemen of the jury, on motion of the defendant concerning the witness Dell Ross the Court instructs you that the entire testimony of said witness, including papers and recordings and all statements heretofore made by any counsel, or by the Court in connection with said witness are stricken from the record and you are instructed to disregard entirely all of such matters as if you had never heard them."

■   ■   ■

To a degree that no other witness in the Huey Newton trial could match, Mrs. Corinne Leonard brought discredit upon herself and her profession. Mrs. Leonard was the Kaiser Hospital nurse from whom Huey Newton had sought treatment for his bullet wound on the morning of the shooting. In establishing the last few links in the story of October 28 her testimony was necessary to the prosecution, but her appearance largely resulted in her own indictment. For the occasion, Mrs. Leonard, a bleached blonde, wore a thick layer of makeup and a new pair of backless, spike-heeled "mules."

"It was about ten to six when he came in," Mrs. Leonard said. "He said he wanted to see a doctor right now. He said: 'I have been shot in the stomach.' He said: 'As you can see, I am bleeding to death.' He was very belligerent and he wanted a doctor out in the waiting room area and he said: 'Goddamit,' he says, 'get a doctor out here right now.' He says: 'Can't you see I am hemorrhaging?' and I told him he wasn't. He had a very small opening. No blood was coming out from that at the time. . . . I thought at first maybe he had something to drink, or something, for the way he was acting, he didn't act in any acute distress because he was hollering and yelling and jumping about the emergency room and saying 'Get a doctor out here right now,' and I asked him if he belonged to Kaiser and he said, 'Yes, yes. What difference does that make?' He said: 'Get me a doctor out here right now.' I asked him his name. He wouldn't tell me. And I said, 'Well do you have a Kaiser card?' and this did not go over too well. He said yes that he did have one but he wasn't about to give any identification of who he was.

"And I told him to be seen by a doctor he would have to sign a permit, which he refused to do. He said that he didn't have a permit. He said he didn't have to sign anything. He called me a white bitch. He said, 'Get the goddamn doctor out here right now,' and I told him anybody who is in any acute distress could not carry on like this. And then he took his coat and jacket and threw it up on the counter and said, 'Can't you see all this blood?' which was very little on the shirt. I was not impressed at all. . . ."

■   ■   ■

It did not become clear to me until very near the end of the trial that the question of Huey Newton's prior felony was a very critical issue in the case. I also did not understand why the jury should have to determine what seemed to me to be a simple matter of record: Did Huey Newton commit felonious assault in 1964 or didn't he? Was he convicted of that charge or wasn't he? Having been convicted and sentenced to three years' probation, when precisely did his probation begin and end?

Probation Officer Melvin Torley testified that Newton's period of probation extended from October 29, 1964, for three years. But Torley said that he was not sure what date he had told Newton his probation would terminate.

Charles Garry asked him: "When he asked you, Mr. Torley, when the date terminated, you told him it was October 27, 1967, didn't you, sir?"

"I don't know," Torley said. "I don't recall having said the twenty-seventh of October."

"Then your answer is that you don't remember whether you told him that or not, isn't that your answer now?"

"I don't recall that I said it was October twenty-seventh or twenty-eighth, yes."

"But you could have told him it was on October 27 when he asked you, isn't that right, sir?"

"Yes," Torley said.

Torley's admission that he might have told Newton that his probation was over on October 27 immediately cast doubt on what was supposed to be Newton's motive. Prosecutor Jensen had claimed that on the night of the shooting Huey Newton was under the impression that he was *still on probation* when John Frey stopped him. And it was supposedly the fear of being caught with marijuana and a weapon before his probation expired that led Newton to shoot it out with Frey.

There was further significance in Huey Newton's "prior felony." If the prosecution could prove that ex-felon Newton had a concealable weapon on October 28, 1967, then according to California law the defendant would be *automatically guilty of second degree murder*—even if he never fired a shot.

The last witness for the prosecution was Jan Bashinsky, a chemist for the Oakland Police Department. Mrs. Bashinsky told the court that bits of debris taken from the defendant's pants pocket and a vegetable substance taken from two matchboxes discovered under the seat of the Volkswagen had been analyzed and found to be marijuana.

When the prosecution had completed its case, Charles Garry moved for a judgment of acquittal:

". . . The mere showing that the defendant shot Heanes and then shot Frey, accepting Grier and Heanes testimony as true, shows nothing of premeditation, the essential element of first degree murder in either degree. You cannot infer malice unless there is an absence of provocation and evidence of an abandoned and malignant heart. By that, if Your Honor please, if there is showing of provocation, that is, if Officer Frey had provoked Huey Newton by the evidence, then you cannot infer that. You have to have direct testimony in order to be able to maintain the malice and the premeditation. . . . What is the provocation in this case? The length of time between Frey's stopping of the defendant's car and Heaness's calling in of the emergency on the tape, approximately fifteen minutes. The defendant patiently and calmly submitted to all the questioning of Frey and Heanes, and gave his correct address and name; the fact that the witness Lord, police dispatcher, admitted that the P.I.N. [police computer] data showed the magistrate was unknown, thus the ticket was only for parking, and not even for a misdemeanor; and also Lord's testimony that there was no showing that officers had tried to serve this warrant in the daytime; also that Frey knew it was a known Black Panther vehicle and that all officers had a list of Panther licenses and had seen pictures of Panthers and the defendant.

"You cannot infer an absence of provocation from those facts; so you cannot infer malice . . . evidence which raises a mere suspicion of guilt is insufficient to sustain a conviction. . . . The trial court must specifically find that the evidence could support a conviction of first degree murder beyond a reasonable doubt before he can properly deny the motion. . . . Surely the evidence submitted here is insufficient to establish first degree—premeditation, malice, beyond a reasonable doubt. . . .

"With regard to the motive here, which the prosecution

may argue supplies the malice and premeditation, it is contradicted by the fact that the defendant clearly had plenty of time to get rid of both marijuana and gun; by the testimony that the defendant might well have been told by his probation officer that the probation was over the day before, and by the absence of fingerprints on the marijuana boxes, and the fact that the prosecution has either lost, misplaced, thrown away, or concealed the paper bag which the matchboxes came in; raising the inference that this contained—this container could have been favorable in some respects to the defendant. Then the lawbook of defendant found, which the prosecution did not bother to have anyone testify to on direct, and which the prosecution did not even bother to introduce for fingerprints or have a blood analysis done on it, was this because it might have shown the defendant's blood, thus substantiating that the defendant had the book in his hand against his stomach when he was shot?

"This would have appeared, from the placement of the blood on the inner pages of the book, to be the only way the blood could have gotten there. If the book were laying on the ground next to Frey, the way the technician Lusk said it was, it could not have received that blood on the inside pages. You will notice there is none of it on the bound cover, because the blood from Frey was in a pool on the ground and couldn't have gotten up into the inside pages over the heavy binding. If the defendant was carrying the book in his hand, and if you take Grier's testimony that Frey had him by the left arm, then where is the gun? At least the inference is indisputable that the defendant wasn't premeditating anything with the lawbook in his hand. We know the defendant had the lawbook somewhere. He must have carried it out of the car with him. You don't go about premeditating murder with a lawbook in your hand.

"Briefly I want to talk to the Court about provocation. Frey did provoke, because he stopped the car without any basis. That is provocation. When we show provocation we cannot infer malice. . . . There is no evidence of prior ill-feeling between Newton and Frey. This cannot be supplied during the defense case by inferences or otherwise. . . . By the time Newton shot Frey, that is, taking the testimony we have before the Court, taking the evidence at its worst for this purpose only, according to both Heanes and Grier, Heanes was shooting at Newton and Frey was grappling with him and, according to Grier, everything took place in less than one minute. . . .

"Now getting down to the fragments of marijuana which were not shown to have belonged to Newton, or where the pants came from, no fingerprints on the boxes—Huey and the passenger had plenty of time to get rid of the boxes and the fragments, if they knew about them and were worried about them. Where is the motive? Where is the showing of malice? Where is any showing of premeditation, when Huey quietly and calmly obeyed the officers' commands and indeed sat there in a car for at least ten minutes? During part of the time Frey and Heanes were nowhere near him: they were in the automobile listening to the car radio. Why didn't they flee if they had some things to worry about? You cannot infer from the fact that these two boxes of marijuana are in the automobile, he was worried about them—assuming he did know about them; and we don't have any evidence that he had any knowledge of the existence of that. The car was not his; there was another person in the automobile, by the evidence that was submitted. There is an absolute absence of malice or premeditation. . . . Officer Heanes has testified that he did not see a gun in the hands of Huey Newton. He has testified that he did not know for a fact where the gunshots were coming from; he said he had an idea, but he couldn't say so as a matter of fact.

"Henry Grier has identified the defendant in this courtroom. . . . But the statement that he made on a prior occasion is also evidence of equal dignity with the testimony that is here in the courtroom. Grier has testified that he did not know the height of the man. He has testified that the man had a black jacket on, and he is unequivocal about that. And he also testified that he doesn't know whether the man had a hat or anything else on. And yet one hour and thirty-eight minutes after this tragic event took place, this witness made a narration of the following facts: that the person who did it was under five feet; it was a sort of pee-wee fellow; it was a person who had on a light tan jacket. He also made the statement that he could not identify him positively. He also stated at that time that the officer fell on his back and he was shot. And if Your Honor recalls the demonstration here, this witness testified that this officer fell on his face and that he was shot in the back. What I am trying to say . . . is that Grier's testimony has been tailored to fit certain weaknesses in the prosecution's case."

■　　　■　　　■

With customary calm, Prosecutor Lowell Jensen offered argument against the motion for a judgment of acquittal on the murder charge:

"There are two problems, as I see it, with counsel's argument. One is a legal problem. The second is a factual problem. The contention that counsel makes is that this Court at this juncture in a criminal trial has the power under [Section of the California Evidence Code] 1118.1 to decide that the jury may not find a conviction on first degree murder—as I understand counsel's argument. In other words, what he is saying is, 1118.1 empowers a trial court after the production of the People's case to acquit as to a degree of an offense. Now, there is no such case in California law interpreting 1118.1 in such a fashion; and in effect what he is asking this Court to do is to make up a brand-new law. . . . I think he totally misconceives the relation of provocation to malice. . . .

"As far as counsel's argument goes on—he makes various arguments as to the significance of the paper bag. Counsel would argue that the significance is such that the jury may not find the defendant guilty of first degree murder. Now, just on its face, that is a rather startling, illogical conclusion to reach; and it is legally of no merit whatsoever. He makes an argument in reference to Fricke on criminal law [the bloody lawbook found at the scene] that [because] there is a lawbook at the scene, there can be no premeditation. I need hardly point out that the book is not capable of firing 9-millimeter cartridges or .38-caliber cartridges and neither Officer Heanes, who was shot, nor Officer Frey, who lost his life, were injured by that book. The point is simply this . . . there is sufficient evidence that could be used to support a first degree murder conviction on appeal."

Judge Friedman was inclined to agree. The defense motion for a judgment of acquittal on the first degree murder charge against Huey Newton was denied.

And so on Monday, August 19, the defense proceeded with the presentation of its case. Somehow, Charles Garry's assistant, Fay Stender, had managed to turn up one of the passengers who had been aboard Henry Grier's bus the morning of the shooting. He was young, black Tommy Miller, an aircraft cleaner at the naval air station in neighboring Alameda.

Mr. Miller testified that he boarded the bus near the corner of Seventh and Willow streets. He handed the driver a five-dollar bill, and while he was getting his change and the bus was moving, shots rang out. He, along with the other three passengers on the bus, got down low out of range. He said that he could see there was a commotion across the street. He could see the flashing red light from the police cars. He made out two policemen in uniform, one of whom had some fellow up against a car. But he could see no faces. *It was too dark.*

Just before the noon recess that day, Charles Garry asked Judge Friedman to declare a mistrial. "I hate to bring this kind of matter up," Garry said, "but I feel impelled to do so. We received in the morning mail death threats made out to both the defendant Huey Newton and myself, and I want to make it part of the record. . . . I was compelled to call in the Federal Bureau of Investigation, and we have received death threats on the telephone on many occasions, but we felt compelled, since this was written in longhand, to call in the authorities. This is creating a serious handicap on how the defense is proceeding and we have been under this kind of strain for some time. . . . I might explain to Your Honor that my client does not share my views of having security. As a matter of fact, he thoroughly disapproves of the security measures. I disagreed with the security measures during the course of the trial, but I agree with Your Honor's position that some kind of security measures are appropriate because of the circumstances I have already related; the Court itself has heard rumblings of it. But I cannot understand how you can get a fair trial with an area charged so that it is necessary to have security guards and to have the kind of protection that this trial has had to have and still have the jury free from any kind of compunction so they can give this defendant a fair trial. It is for this reason that I have asked for a mistrial on many occasions and at this time . . . we feel compelled that we have to again ask for a mistrial. . . . It is a question of recognizing that we have in our community today, in our state and in our country completely opposing views of the struggles that are going on, and it is utterly impossible to get a fair trial in this atmosphere that is charged with so much hatred. . . ."

The request for mistrial was of course denied. "I do not find in this courtroom that this man is receiving anything but a fair trial," Judge Friedman said. "This room is not charged with anything except the ordinary matter that we have in any trial. . . ."

For whatever it was worth, the hate mail was read into the record:

DEAR SIR:

This is not a threat: we are four retired marines, U.S.A. we are going to say we do not see why any attorney would see fit for a fee to defend Huey P. Newton. We all knew Policeman John Frey. So to make this short and to the point, you or Newton will not be alive ten days after this trial is over. It makes no difference which way the jury decides. . . .

The other letter was addressed:

NIGGER LOVER:

I guess you feel that the murdering coon's gonna get off because the jury and witnesses have all been intimidated to the extent that no one dares convict. I hope he will be gunned down in the streets by some friends of the poor policeman he killed. The Black Panthers parade all over the place and I don't see why the KKK and American Nazi Parties couldn't do the same. It is supposed to be a free country for everybody. It is too bad we ever stopped lynching. At least the dam niggers knew their place in those days and didn't cause any trouble. I remember reading about one time they strung up some coons and pulled out pieces of their flesh with corkscrews. That must have been a lot of fun. I wish I had been there to take part in the good work. I hope this race war that we are having starts right away. We outnumber the blacks ten to one, so we know who will win. And a lot of damn nigger lovers will be laying there right beside them. I wish Hitler had won and then we could have kicked off the shinnies and started in on the coons.

KKK

If seven women and five men were going to convict Huey Newton of murder, it would *not* be because they felt sorry for "poor John Frey," the innocent policeman gunned down in the streets in the simple performance of his duty. Frey had been on the Oakland police force a little over a year when he was killed. He had specifically requested that he be assigned to duty in West Oakland. Ironically, he was scheduled to be transferred a week after the day of his death. A procession of witnesses would show that he was something of a racist—the simple nigger-hating variety—and that he had a propensity for harassing black citizens.

Daniel King, a sixteen-year-old grocery clerk, told the Court of his own weird encounter with Frey. It took place just a few hours before the policeman was killed. King testified that he and his sister were on their way to an all-night restaurant when they ran into Frey accompanied by a white man who had lost—of all things—his pants. The man accused young King of stealing his pants. Calling him a nigger and a pimp "and all sorts of dirty names," Frey held King while the trouserless man gave him a good pounding. Then Frey told King's sister that they were going around the corner for a chat. King was driven instead to another section of town, where Frey left him in the car with the man to get another beating.

Two days before that a Mr. Belford Dunning, a black insurance agent, also had the misfortune of running into John Frey. While driving that night, Dunning was stopped by a policeman, who was in the process of writing him a ticket when another policeman (Frey) pulled up to the scene. The first cop went to his car to send a radio message while Frey stood guard over the "prisoner." Dunning got out of his car to ask Frey why he had been stopped. "It's none of your damn business," Frey said. "Get the hell in the car."

"I asked him," Dunning testified, "why I should get in the car. 'I am only standing here waiting for the officer to tell me why I was stopped. Do you know why?' He said, 'Hell no,' and told me again to get the hell in the car. 'What's the matter with you?'" Dunning said he asked Frey. "You act like you're the Gestapo or something." Dunning said that Frey leaned back, stuck his thumbs into his gun belt and said, "I *am* the Gestapo."

John Frey was a graduate of the Clayton Valley High School. One of his teachers there had been Bruce Byson, an instructor in English and speech. After Frey became a policeman, Byson invited him to speak to one of his classes hoping to counteract what Byson called "the bad image teen-agers tend to have of policemen." "I was hoping," he told the court, "to have the kids accept him as an individual."

Frey accepted the invitation. Speaking to the class, Frey referred to black people in the ghetto as "a lot of bad types." He used the word "nigger." "I grimaced," said Byson, "when he used the word . . . and he saw me and changed and said 'Negro.'"

Until August 21, 1968, the identity and whereabouts of the mysterious passenger who was with Huey Newton in the Volkswagen the night of the shooting were things known only to Newton himself and his attorneys. Had he been found, Gene Alan McKinney might have been charged as an accessory to murder. But the Oakland police were not especially zealous in pressing the search for McKinney; Huey Newton was already in the bag. In the days immediately following the October 28 shooting, the police, in the hope that McKinney would step forward to testify against Newton, let the word circulate that McKinney was not a "suspect." Therefore it was a surprise to many when Gene McKinney took the stand as a witness for the defense.

Charles Garry opened the questioning:

"Calling your attention, Mr. McKinney, to the 28th day of October, 1967, at Seventh and Willow, were you a passenger in the automobile with Huey Newton?"

"Yes, I was," McKinney said.

"How were you dressed on that occasion?"

"Can't remember."

"Now, Mr. McKinney, at the time and place on that morning, did you by chance, or otherwise, shoot at Officer John Frey?"

"I refuse to answer on the ground it may tend to incriminate me."

"Mr. McKinney, did you at that time . . . fire a weapon at Officer Heanes?"

"I refuse to answer on the ground it may tend to incriminate me."

And so the defense had provided the jury with a peg on which to hang their doubts. If the seven women and five men had begun to doubt that Huey Newton committed murder—if they had begun to ask themselves, "Well, if Huey Newton didn't shoot John Frey, who did?"—they could now ease their tension by speculating that this Gene Alan McKinney fellow might have done it.

The prosecution of course objected vigorously to Mc-Kinney's unresponsiveness. "I assume that his attorney," Lowell Jensen said, "told him all the things that he could do and that he could come in and give him advice before he showed up in this courtroom but can't walk in here and say that he was there and . . . start testifying about that transaction and then in the middle of that say, 'I have a privilege against self-incrimination.' There is no such thing. I ask the Court to direct this man to answer."

The Court complied, but McKinney refused to answer any more questions. "The Court finds you in contempt and directs you to go to jail immediately until such time as you consent to answer the question," Judge Friedman said. The bailiff led McKinney from the courtroom and took him upstairs to jail.

The closest that any of us in court would come to a live re-enactment of the events of October 28, 1967, was when we heard a tape-recorded transcription of the police radio broadcasts made the morning of the shooting. Lowell Jensen had played a portion of these recordings before. We had heard John Frey calling into headquarters for a license check on the Volkswagen, the "known Black Panther vehicle." Now Charles Garry wanted to have the rest of the recording played. It would show that on the morning in question the Oakland police, thanks to "eyewitness" Grier, were looking for a man wearing a tan jacket and not Huey Newton, who was dressed in black.

But the recordings were interesting for several other reasons. They demonstrated that there was no mistake about who this suspect Huey Newton was, despite all the police disclaimers. They showed that the Oakland police had a lively fear of the Black Panthers and that *any black man* walking the street might very well be a Panther.

In the following transcription, "Radio" designates the dispatcher speaking from police headquarters. The numbers represent various on-duty policemen speaking from their respective patrol cars. 101B is Officer Herbert Heanes, by now already wounded. It should also be noted that the police originally thought that LaVerne Williams, Huey's fiancée and registered owner of the Volkswagen, was the other "male" Negro in the car.

RADIO: All cars stand by, we've got a 940B [EMERGENCY] working at 7th and Willow. . . .

101B: Please send two Code 3's [ambulances] down here. Uh . . . the . . . Huey Newton has . . . just did it.

RADIO: All cars stay off the air unless you got an emergency. All cars stay off the air . . . Attention all units, Huey Newton is a suspect on the two officers who were shot just a few minutes ago. . . . Attention all units, we had a 940B down at 7th and Willow; two officers are shot. Huey Newton is the suspect, one of the Black Panthers. If you see this subject use caution; he's armed; he shot two officers down. . . .

RADIO: Can anybody give me any description of the vehicle if any used on this?

105A: We can't get any information right now; it's sort of in turmoil.

141: . . . Apparently on foot.

RADIO: All right, check. They're on foot. Attention all units. Also LaVerne Williams, he was also involved. These are known Black Panthers. . . .

RADIO: All cars stay off the air. All cars stay off the air.

181: Give me a resuscitator crew down here; hurry up!

RADIO: Check . . . We have the inhalator en route now. I have some more information on Huey Newton. Be on the lookout for Huey Newton, male Negro, twenty-five, lives at 881 47th Street.

143: Huey Newton has got on a dark hat; he's wearing a beige or tan jacket. He's on foot westbound from the scene across the area of the construction.

RADIO: Check, all cars stand by. Attention all units. On this Huey Newton, he's wearing a dark hat and a light brown jacket. He's last seen westbound through the construction at the new post office. . . . May be in the vicinity of the new post office right now. . . . 29 to 26, head down to the new post office construction at 7th and Willow. Huey Newton may be—he's on foot. . . . Use caution; he's armed. . . .

RADIO: Attention all units. Attention all units. New additional information. Witnesses just now state they see the suspects getting in a '58 Ford convertible. . . . Suspects are holding a driver at gunpoint in a '58 Ford convertible, white over black. Last seen going up 7th Street towards Broadway. . . .

RADIO: . . . One of the suspects may be shot, but the verification of this is unknown at this time.

VOICE: Huey Newton's got a real pile of real fuzzy hair and a real light-complected Negro.

RADIO: Check. Additional information on Huey Newton. He's a light-skinned Negro and he has his hair piled up pretty high on his head.

VOICE: It's real fuzzy and soft but not piled up high. Just a lot of hair.

RADIO: Check. It's one of those fuzzy hair-do's. The latest style.

VOICE: No grease!

RADIO: Check. Original hair style.

VOICE: African style.

29: Any further orders?

RADIO: Negative, 29. Just cruise the area around and . . . I don't know what to tell you. . . . Attention all units. Attention all units in the city of Oakland. *Be on the lookout for two male Negroes of any type riding in any vehicles.* Use caution. [Emphasis added.]

2A: Two male Negroes in a '57 Chevy convertible at 5th and Broadway. Do you want to send a car by?

RADIO: All right. Check. All units at 5th and Broadway, a '57 convertible there. Ford. Two male Negro occupants. Who is responding?

28: I'm rolling.

1B: 1B is rolling.

RADIO: Check, 1B.

4B: I'm stopping a car full [of niggers, that is] at 46th and West. I've got the Emeryville Police Department with me.

RADIO: 46th and West, check.

4B: This looks okay. [The wrong niggers.]

2A: Be advised they are not the suspects mentioned before. [Wrong niggers again.]

RADIO: All right. Check. Attention all units at 5th and Broadway. They are not the suspects. . . .

5A: I have two male Negroes at 18th and Adeline. . . . One is dressed all in black, and the other in white. One seems to be in pain. Do you want to send another car to check them out?

RADIO: All right. Check. All cars stand by. 18th and Adeline. Two male Negroes. One looks like he is in pain and might be the one that was shot.

29: Five blocks away.

43: We're three blocks away, coming in.

111: We've got plenty of help down here.

RADIO: Check. Is this the subjects or not?

111: We don't know yet.

172: . . . These parties are not the suspects at 18th and Adeline. [Wrong niggers again.]

RADIO: All right. Check. Attention all units. The subjects at 18th and Adeline are not the ones. . . .

And then a minute or so later came the superbly ironic fluff. No playwright, however gifted, could have made it believable. But this was no dramatist reaching awkwardly for irony; this was the Oakland police playing out reality.

RADIO: . . . All officers on the beat, circle the area and be on the lookout for these subjects. Stop anybody that might look like the *victims* . . . er . . . the suspects. . . . [Emphasis added.]

If Ralph Bunche and Senator Edward Brooke had just happened to have been riding around West Oakland that morning, they would have been stopped and worked over just like the wrong nigger suspects (or *victims*, if you will) at Eighteenth and Adeline or the wrong niggers at Fifth and Broadway. It wouldn't have made any difference because the Oakland police wouldn't have known who Bunche and Brooke were. And even if they did know, it would not have made any difference because their orders were to stop and work over male niggers *of all types*—greasy-headed niggers, dry-head niggers, niggers in purple pants and red shirts, niggers with portfolios. All types.

> *Up against the wall, Mr. Under Secretary,*
> *Up against the wall, Mr. Senator,*
> *All you niggers—up against the wall . . .*

■   ■   ■

Early in the trial the defense had made a motion that the trial be conducted in a larger courtroom to accommodate the obviously wide public interest. True to his provincial perspectives, Judge Friedman had rejected that motion. His own courtroom was large enough, he said. The proceedings were not, after all, theater, the judge pointed out. But of course he was wrong. They *were* theater, very important theater.

They were especially theater when the audience learned

that Huey P. Newton, the male lead, would be on stage the
next day. Whether I would get a seat to see Huey's performance would depend on the usual variables: how impressive was the day's line-up of witnesses and, in that connection, how big a press and spectators' gallery they would
draw, how early I could get up in the morning to assure
getting a seat.

On that Thursday morning, August 22, I somehow managed to unfasten myself from bed at what I thought to be
a ridiculously early hour. I got to the courthouse about 5:15
A.M., fully confident that for the first time I was going to be
first on line. I scurried around to the Thirteenth Street
entrance, where the reporters who did not have reserved
seats were required to wait until 8:00 A.M. when the courthouse opened for business. (The routine after that was to
troop up to the second-floor sheriff's office, where we would
again wait on line until nine-thirty. Whatever press passes
were not claimed by the local media by that time would be
handed out first-come, first-served to such "other" reporters
as were on line.) If all of the local press people showed up
on any given day, as they were likely to do today, it would
mean that all the rest of us would have to scramble for
three seats.

I wanted to cry when I got to the courthouse steps, but
all I could do was laugh. Huddled in a parked car by the
curb were *five* reporters.

"Want some coffee? You're *sixth* on line," they shouted at
me. I knew most of them; they were the same reporters of
the radical press with whom I had stood on line almost every
day for the past four weeks. This morning they had come to
court as early as midnight.

As we were wont to do when the odds were against our
getting into court on the press line, I dashed around the

corner to the "spectators" line in front of the Twelfth Street entrance. There were five people on line here, too, but the odds were more favorable here because at least fifteen spectators could count on getting a seat.

The numbers grew very quickly. By six o'clock we had become a warm little community sitting on the cold steps. It was a community like many others, with people sixteen and people fifty-six, people barely speaking English, people with neckties, with robes, with sandals, people with hair carefully parted, with hair in great unkempt clumps. But it was a community like few others because here on the stone steps of the Alameda County Courthouse we seemed more compassionate than usual, less savage. There was hot tea for everyone because number eight on line had taken it upon himself to bring a whole mini-busload of tea. Though we could easily "lose" our places on line, though each of us wanted with equal fever to get inside, though we knew it was impossible for *all* of us to get in, we moved about freely —with no desire to cheat, with no fear of being cheated. Some fell asleep, some went away to get something to eat, to buy newspapers, and when they returned, number three on line was still number three; number sixteen, still sixteen. We shared our food, our reading, our politics. The unreality of the little community was intoxicating.

It was also short-lived. The real world began to assemble at seven-thirty. Lawyers and district attorneys and defendants came to court. People came to get licenses to marry or to drive. People came to get new plates for new Buicks. And finally came the officers of peace with their implements of war to take up their positions at the doors.

The unreal compassionate little community began to decay. If it could have entered the courthouse en masse, it might have survived, but it could not. There was not enough room. Number seventeen on line clashed with number three, number five with number four. Number eight was no longer number eight because he had been distributing tea and had no rightful place on line. We all began to move with great stealth—hungry to cheat, afraid of being cheated.

"Wat the fuck are all you white boys doin' in the fronta the line?" someone wanted to know.

"Because we were the first ones to get here," the white boys said.

"That don't mean shit. Tha's *our* brother in jail up there. Tha's *our* brother on trial. Know what I mean?"

"That's true," the white boys conceded with some meekness, "but we were the first ones out of bed this morning; we were first driving over here and that's why we're first on line. Fair is fair."

"*Fuck* fair—we been standing on line for four hundred years. Know what I mean?"

The unsavage little community grew savage. Pushing, shoving, jostling, kicking. The thick plate glass on the courthouse doors shattered from the weight of the hatred. The sheriff's deputies rushed outside with their helmets and billy clubs and big bodies to restore order.

A new line was formed, the broken glass was cleared away; the jostling stopped, but order was never restored.

The Black Panthers arrived—Eldridge Cleaver, Kathleen Cleaver, Bobby Seale, Emory Douglas and then the titular head of the party, Stokely Carmichael. A pathway up the stairs was swiftly cleared for them and they went to the front of the line. No one of course questioned their pre-eminence. Eldridge and I exchanged nods. He asked me if I knew Stokely, who by then was sitting on the steps, encircled by admirers who wanted to know why the Student Nonviolent Coordinating Committee had severed relations with him.

(The news had just that morning come out.) I had never met Carmichael before; I remember trying to think of something sweepingly significant to say to him. I couldn't think of anything, so I backed up a bit and started taking pictures. He wore black leather like Eldridge and the others and glasses—tinted light enough so that you could look into his eyes—tinted just dark enough so that you could not *plainly* see his eyes.

Reporters representing the local mass media began to arrive. Admission for them would be no problem. They didn't have to stand on line; their seats were reserved. Among them, as always, was Rush Greenlee, then of the San Francisco *Examiner*. Rush and I had come to be good friends in the months that I had been in Oakland—bound together immediately by the common need to cope with the contradictions of being a black reporter for white media. Better than most, he knew the Panthers. More than most, he was trying to know them better. This was no simple matter in a community largely unwilling to concede that the likes of Huey Newton might even be *human*, let alone innocent of murder. On the other hand, the Panthers would frequently withhold their trust of him so that he often found himself in the precarious middle. Still, I admired him—though Bobby Seale, half in jest, half-seriously, was wont to dismiss Rush (and me) as the spineless "black bourgeoisie" and say that the Black Panthers "would welcome the opportunity to throw the black bourgeoisie on the trash heap of history." I admired Rush. He was slipping stories sympathetic to the Panthers past editors who still thought of the police as Boy Scouts in blue, helping kiddies get across the street. He was meeting deadlines twice a day on some very complicated material. Chubby, flustered though he always seemed to be,

Rush's dignity was intact—as a human being, as a black man, as a journalist.

"Bet you the celebrated Gil Moore doesn't get into court today," he mocked me as he went up the stairs. "I'll speak to Sheriff Madigan about you. This nonsense of *Life* not having a reserved seat can't go on."

But I *did* get in that day. Sandwiched in somewhere on a phalanx of Black Panthers, I got in. I *had* to get in.

This was Huey's day. He took the stand. He looked like he couldn't wait to get up there.

"Mr. Newton, did you kill Officer John Frey?" Garry asked his client.

"No, I did not," Mr. Newton said, looking straight at the jurors.

"Did you shoot, wound Officer Herbert Heanes?"

"No, I did not," Mr. Newton said.

"Did you on the morning of October 28, 1967, know about any contents of marijuana or any other type of drug in your vehicle?"

"I did not," Mr. Newton said.

And from here on Charles Garry and Huey treated the events of October 28 as mere afterthoughts. They had more important matters they wanted to discuss.

"The black liberation movement," Mr. Newton said, "is a movement to free blacks from exploitation and oppression." And "Black Power," he went on, "is the means by which blacks will free themselves from this oppression of the ruling class here in North America."

He began to go into "the historical context of the black liberation struggle," working his way from twelfth-century Africa up through generations of tribal kingdom wars to the beginnings of the European slave trade.

Clearly the seven women and five men of the jury were, at the very least, engrossed. So, indeed, was the Honorable Monroe Friedman, although not so much with black liberation as with what, to him, must have been an astounding fact. Here he was sitting within three feet of the founder of that mad band, the Black Panthers. Lo and behold, this young man was calm; he had dignity and, perhaps most peculiar of all, he seemed to be literate.

I was sitting directly in back of Stokely and watched the back of his head rocking back and forth; he was dozing. It may have been that he was very tired from his plane trip from the East Coast, or it may simply have been that he was bored.

But Prosecutor Lowell Jensen had had quite enough of Huey Newton's lecturing:

"Your Honor, at this time I am going to object to the continuing narration without any questions."

The lecturing abated somewhat for the moment, but Huey seized every available opportunity thereafter to launch into discourses on his political thinking. The entire Ten Point Program was recited into the record, each point of the program affording him the opportunity to make a lengthy dissertation. He had gotten to point number ten:

> We want land, bread, housing, education, clothing, justice and peace. And as our major political objective, a United Nations–supervised plebiscite to be held throughout the black colony in which only black colonial subjects will be allowed to participate, for the purpose of determining the will of black people as to their national destiny.

Judge Friedman's dormant curiosity was stirred: "Does your party say by what means this should be accomplished?"

"Well," said Huey, "we go along with Thomas Jefferson in

his statement that whenever the institutions of a country no longer serve the people, then it is the right of the people to change the institutions."

"By what means?" the judge persisted.

Clearly Huey Newton enjoyed telling him: "By constitutional means or by revolutionary means. We have adopted Jefferson's program, even though we criticize him as a hypocrite because at the same time that he was writing the Declaration of Independence he had us as slaves."

"Next point," Judge Friedman said abruptly.

Huey continued with point ten of the Panther program, which at considerable length cites the Declaration of Independence:

> . . . That, to secure these rights, governments are instituted among men, deriving their just powers from the consent of the governed; that, whenever any form of government becomes destructive of these ends, it is the right of the people to alter or abolish it, and to institute a new government. . . . But when a long train of abuses and usurpations, pursuing invariably the same object, evinces a design to reduce them under absolute despotism, it is their right, it is their duty, to throw off such government, and to provide new guards for their future security.

Every so often, Huey was reminded that the Court's central concern was what took place on the morning of October 28, 1967. He was at one point about to explain why he thought of black people in America as being "colonized." The prosecution objected to the question as being irrelevant. Judge Friedman sustained the objection: "It may be that if it is established there is some reason to go into this, the Court may allow it, but we don't even know if he was at the scene of the alleged homicide. . . He hasn't even admitted being there. If you wish to go in and show us what happened on that day, then it may be that this may have some relevance or may be admissible. I don't know at this point."

But Charles Garry and his voluble client had other matters to take up first. Huey spoke of his early years in Oakland, the alienation that he and most other nonwhite people experience in American public school systems and the formation of the Black Panther Party in 1966. "We were basically concerned with organizing the community, defending the community and teaching it to defend itself against the oppression that existed. This oppression which I speak of was mostly seen in the relationship between the ghetto with the police authorities. Our view of the police is seen quite different from that of others. In our community the police is seen as the oppressor. When white people see a policeman in their middle-class community, they feel happy and secure."

Huey described reactions after the Panthers began to patrol the police activity in West Oakland: "The police began to stop Panthers, harassing and arresting us for no apparent reason. I have personally been harassed in this fashion, maybe forty or fifty times—where there was no arrest made. They would simply stop, search me and attempt to interrogate me . . . every time they would stop the automobiles they would write down the license number of the automobile, and on many occasions the police would wait outside of my house and if a friend would pick me up he would stop the car and write down the number, and so what was happening was that at any time that the Black Panthers rode in a friend's car, the friend's car was automatically recorded as a Panther car."

Finally, Huey got around to discussing October 28. Dressed in a black beret, black leather jacket, white shirt, black trousers, he had gone to a party that Friday night (or, more specifically, that Saturday morning) to celebrate the end of his probation. He left the party with a friend, Gene McKinney.

"Gene had told me," Huey testified, "that he was hungry. We arrived late at the party. I believe they had food at the party, but it was all gone when we got there. Gene asked me to leave and take him to Seventh Street, because we both knew that there are a couple of after-hours eating places there. . . . I started to drive down Seventh Street. . . . I remember going down Willow Street, and I was looking for a parking space. . . . And as I made a left turn at Seventh and Willow, I noticed a red light in my rear window.

"I pulled over to the curb and came to a stop. The police officer got out of his car, walked over to mine and said, 'Well, well, well, what do we have here? The great, great Huey P. Newton.' . . . He asked me then for my driver's license, which I gave to him. Then he asked me who the car belonged to and I said it belongs to LaVerne Williams and as I said this I took the registration out and handed it to him. At this time he gave me back my driver's license and went to his car with the registration. . . .

"It must have been about two to three minutes later that another officer pulled up behind the first one. . . . He paused at the first officer's car for a second and then walked up to my car and asked me, 'Mr. Williams, do you have any further identification?' And I said, 'What do you mean, Mr. Williams? My name is Huey P. Newton and I have already shown my driver's license to the first officer.'

"The second officer then just looked at me and said, 'Yes, I know who you are.' And then he just stood there, it must have been about three or four minutes. . . . The first officer was still in his car. The first officer then got out of his car, and came over to my door and ordered me out of my car. As I got out of my car, I picked up my lawbook, which was in between the seats, sort of back of the emergency brake. As I was getting out of the car, the second officer walked around the car to the passenger side and the passenger got out of the car, and they started to walk back around to our side, the street side. . . . The first officer opened up the door and I got out of the car with the book in my right hand, and I asked him if I was under arrest. He said no, I wasn't under arrest. I leaned on the car with my hands on top of the book . . . and the officer made a frisk in a very degrading fashion. . . . He took my shirt tail out and made a complete search of my body. He ran his hands on the inside of my pants and searched in between my legs, touching my genitals. . . .

"Right after I was searched, the first officer told me to go back to his car, he wanted to talk to me. . . . And we started to walk back to the car. Actually he was kind of pushing me, because he was walking at a pretty rapid rate, and we passed by the first car and we approached the second car. But he kept going. We stopped at the back door.

"At this time I opened the book up and I said, 'You have no reasonable cause to arrest me.' And at this time, he said, 'You can take that book and stick it up your ass, nigger,' and as he says this he gives me a straight arm in the face. . . . He kind of dazed me. I went down on one knee, and as I was getting up, I saw the first officer draw his service revolver and then I felt the sensation of boiling hot soup being spilled on my stomach. And then I remember hearing a sound, a loud sound, or volley of shots. It was like an explosion.

"I didn't know what it was. It seemed as if it was coming all around, and I can vaguely remember crawling on the ground or moving or being moved. I can vaguely remember being on my hands and knees and things were spinning. And

I don't know whether someone was carrying me or something, but I had a moving sensation. . . . After this I don't know what happened. The next thing that I remember is that I was at the entrance of Kaiser Hospital. . . ."

The first couple of hours of Lowell Jensen's cross-examination were quite mild in tone, almost friendly. He retraced some of Huey's direct testimony about October 28, allowing his quarry to fly freely in answering questions. If you didn't know who was who and you just happened to wander into Department Eight of the Alameda County Superior Court that day, you could easily have gotten the idea that Jensen was Huey's lawyer.

Later on, however, Lowell began to tighten up. He produced a Xerox copy of a back issue of the *Black Panther* newspaper and asked Huey to read a poem from it which had been written by the Minister of Defense. Huey read the poem:

> Guns, Baby, guns;
> Army .45 will stop all jive,

("I am not a very good poet here," Huey interjected.)

> Buckshots will down the cops;
> P-38 will open the prison gates,
> The carbine will stop the war machine;
> A .357 will win us heaven.
> And if you don't believe in playing,
> You are already dead.

The introduction of the poem, of course, immediately raised the specter of bloodthirsty, pistol-packing Panthers roving the streets. It also brought the P-38 automatic pistol into play—a weapon which fires 9-mm cartridges of the sort found at the scene of the shooting.

Naturally Jensen brought up Huey's record—the 1964 assault conviction and the two subsequent clashes with police in neighboring Berkeley and Richmond. Newton was given a free hand to explain the circumstances of each of these incidents, but Jensen could be assured that in the minds of the jurors the collective weight of these old episodes would work against the defendant. Violence was, as Jensen would later put it, "no stranger to Mr. Newton."

Jensen also introduced the July 20, 1967, issue of the *Black Panther* newspaper, and for a while it seemed that this would be, at the very least, embarrassing to the defense. That issue contained the celebrated "Bootlickers Gallery," a roster of black leaders whom the Panthers considered as "catering to the oppressor." Prominent bootlickers included Roy Wilkins, Bayard Rustin and, alas, the late Dr. Martin Luther King, Jr. Jensen thought that he would put Newton in the rather uncomfortable position of publicly assaulting a martyr.

But Huey explained, rather convincingly, that the party's position on King had changed since the "Bootlickers Gallery" was published. What had prompted the Panthers to call King a bootlicker in the first place, Huey said, was King's statement, "If any blood be shed, let it be ours and not our white brothers'." "We thought this was strictly out of order and we disagreed with it and we thought that he didn't have black people at heart, not with a statement like that.

"But after this, there were certain other things Dr. King said. He denounced the war in Vietnam, for instance. He also saw the point of some of the more militant young blacks who were beginning to say that they were going to defend themselves and they were not going to shed blood each time America wanted us to shed blood. Dr. King made a great change in his last days. . . ."

In exploring Newton's activities on the afternoon preceding the shooting, Jensen focused some attention on a speech

Newton had made around two o'clock in the afternoon at San Francisco State College:

"Now, this speech that you gave in the afternoon, what was the topic of the speech?"

"The future of the black liberation movement."

"At that time did you talk about groups of three or four persons arming themselves and acting in the streets of the cities in reference to the black liberation movement?"

"I can't recall."

"Do you recall whether or not at that time you said that the black liberation movement had to overthrow the corrupt institutions of the United States?"

"I probably said we had to revolutionize the corrupt institutions."

"Recall whether or not you told the audience there that groups of three and four persons in guerrilla bands could go out in the streets and take care of business."

". . . No, I didn't say that."

"Taking care of business—what is taking care of business?"

"Organizing the black community in a political context . . ."

"Does it include executing policemen?"

"No, it does not."

"Have you ever talked about taking care of business in the context of shooting policemen?"

"No."

"Did you ever talk to a man by the name of Saul Stern, who works for *Ramparts* magazine, about the black liberation movement?"

"Yes."

"Did you tell him about taking care of business?"

"Yes, I believe I did."

". . . Can you tell me whether or not you told Mr. Stern

that taking care of business included shooting the Gestapo police?"

"I did not say that."

"Or executing the racist cops?"

"No, I didn't say that."

"He just made that up, you didn't tell him that?"

"You don't believe everything you read in the newspapers, do you?"

It was perhaps only on the question of his high school literacy that Huey's credibility on the stand was shaken. Under direct testimony he had told the court that he graduated from the Oakland Technical High School without being able to read or write. It was a rather transparent defense attempt to win juror sympathy for a young man who had surmounted poverty and humble beginnings to reach out for greatness by individual initiative in the classic American tradition.

Certainly Lowell Jensen didn't go for it. He produced a handwritten statement by Newton for his juvenile probation officer in 1958. Newton conceded that it was his handwriting but that the statement had been "copied" rather than written. He claimed that one of his friends had probably written the original and that this version was a "drawing."

It was true that Newton had great academic difficulty in school; it was probably also true that Newton had heard the familiar words "You're not college material" and that he was a "poor reader" when he got out of high school, but it strained credibility too much to say that he graduated without being able to read a word of English.

"You graduated from high school," Judge Friedman asked, "and you didn't know how to spell 'cat,' c–a–t?"

"I couldn't," Newton said.

■   ■   ■

For all the tension surrounding Jensen's cross-examination of Huey Newton, there were moments of humor. Jensen was asking him about his probation officer, Melvin Torley, and whether Torley had instructed him in the rules about carrying weapons:

". . . Isn't it a fact that you carried a shotgun or a rifle; is that right?"

"Yes."

"Because that is not a concealable weapon?"

"That is true."

"And if you had a handgun, a pistol, it would be a felony for you to do that, wouldn't it?"

"I don't know whether it would be a felony or not. It would be against the rules that my probation officer laid down to me."

"Did he tell you that it would be a felony when he gave you this set of rules?"

"No. My probation officer doesn't know too much about the law. . . ."

On another occasion, Jensen was boring in on Newton's 1966 clash with Berkeley police:

"Isn't it a fact that you were in a struggle with the police officer in full uniform, and that you had come up and hit him because he was arresting Bobby Seale?"

"No, that is not a fact."

". . . Isn't it a fact that in the fight with that police officer you tried to take his gun away from him?"

"No, it is not a fact."

"Did you try to take the gun away from the other officer?"

"No. The other officer did not have a gun, as I remember."

"He admitted that he was drunk in Municipal Court; he said that he had had three quarts of beer. . . . That is in their record. *Isn't that a fact?*" (Emphasis added.)

When Huey Newton left the witness stand on Monday evening, August 26, after two full days of testimony, the consensus was that he had made an impressive showing. It didn't matter very much whose side you were on; you had to concede that his appearance had been a plus for the defense. He came across as a reasonable man, a responsible man—a man of calm, of dignity, of conviction. Even the Honorable Monroe Friedman was moved. In his chambers, the good judge said wistfully, of the founder of the Black Panther Party: "He could have been a fine young man. It's really too bad. . . ."

■   ■   ■

Black Sociologist John Herman Blake was precisely the sort of witness the defense would not have needed if Huey Newton had had a jury of his peers. Blake was supposed to act as something of an interpreter. It was his job to "explain the ghetto"—its language patterns, its relationship with movements such as Huey Newton's, its relationship with the police department. Charles Garry had planned to have him testify before Huey Newton, but Judge Friedman could not then see the relevance of his testimony: ". . . If the defendant is trying to explain why he shot somebody, that is one thing. This may be admissible under certain circumstances, but not under the circumstances before us right now."

"At this particular point, Your Honor," Garry replied, "you don't know what the defendant is going to testify to. . . . I think the defense is certainly entitled to put its own defense in its own way without having to be hamstrung to the point where we contend it in good faith that the language of the ghetto is a special language. . . . The ruling body of the community of Alameda County doesn't communicate or understand the people in the black ghetto. . . ."

"Would that be a defense in a murder charge?" Judge Friedman wanted to know.

"Judge, as I understand the evidence so far," Garry continued, "we are told that the reason that we killed Officer Frey and shot Heanes is because we happened to have some marijuana with us and that we were on probation and so we were afraid of all this, so that we snuffed this man's life out.

"Now, to be sure, we are denying all of that, but this jury may or may not accept our theory of the case, and I can't afford to, as a trial lawyer in this case who spent months on it—I can't afford to hang my hat on this particular area. . . .

"When Newton takes that witness stand, his entire life is going to be subject to cross-examination and I for one don't intend to file any objections. What Huey Newton has said, what Huey Newton has believed in, what doctrines he has advocated, are matters on which he is undoubtedly going to be cross-examined, because he is going to testify to that directly, and I want an authoritative source, a sociologist, to be able to lay the groundwork. . . . He will project this man in such a fashion that this jury will undoubtedly come to the conclusion that a man with this kind of view, this kind of belief, would not commit the kind of crime that he is charged with in this courtroom. . . .

"You couldn't try Thomas Jefferson and just say 'Did you do this particular act?' without bringing in Thomas Jefferson's solid beliefs in the revolutionary system of America. . . ."

Lowell Jensen naturally didn't see things that way: "What

we are doing now is not philosophy and not rhetoric and not
sociology. With all due respect to the professor, what we are
doing here is trying to find out the truth of what happened
on October 28, 1967, on these charges of murder, assault and
kidnaping. . . . The professor is not an attorney. He wasn't
there on October 28, 1967. He is not a percipient witness to
any of the events of October 28, 1967. . . . To say that a
sociologist may walk into a court of law and say, 'In my
opinion, Your Honor, this man could not commit a crime,'
is to make a shambles of the whole notion of what trials are
all about.

"I could not bring a sociologist into the courtroom to say,
'In my opinion Huey Newton killed somebody on October
28, 1967,' because the Court would laugh and counsel would
turn blue. . . ."

"I would turn black," Garry interjected.

Eventually Judge Friedman allowed Blake to take the
stand "for the purpose of explaining or stating the meaning
of certain words. He can't tell us what Mr. Newton *thought*
they meant, nor what *he* thinks they mean, but what they
mean in the community in Alameda County."

Blake roamed as far as he could within the strait jacket of
Alameda County, 1967. He explained "oppression" and the
black liberation movement. "It does not," he said, "refer to
any specific organization but to the general pattern of new
social and political consciousness in the black community
which is related to developing self-determination and ac-
countability of those people in positions of power with respect to the community presented . . . it is the attempt to
remove any form of oppression in the black community—
political, economic, social or psychological."

He explained to the bewildered jurors that a bootlicker

was not quite the same thing as an Uncle Tom. They both behave "in a demeaning fashion," but bootlickers "with respect to the black community have a lot of influence and power and sometimes control. In relationship to the general society, however, bootlickers do not manifest the integrity of their community. . . . They prostrate themselves before the power structure."

Then it was on to such expressions as "chuckin' an' jivin'," "signifyin'" and, as Blake put it in a burst of scholarship: "the concept of takin' care o' business."

Blake should have been given a special award for dealing with all of this with a straight face. The language of poor black people in America (that same language that some misguided analysts think originated with hippies) has never been able to sit still for scholarly study. As soon as you try to explain in academic terms—"Well, 'rapping' means this or 'takin' care o' business' means that"—you incur the immediate risk of sounding truly ridiculous to those who already know what the expression means.

But Blake bore up admirably under the strain of the absurdities. Yet for all the impact he was having upon His Honor and the jurors, he might as well have been addressing his remarks to a garden bed of lettuce.

■   ■   ■

The last witness for the defense was Dr. Bernard Diamond, who had testified early in the trial on the motion to quash the master panel of jurors. Charles Garry was obliged to extract "expert" testimony from this witness by dint of the "hypothetical question"—a legal acrobatic technique by which an attorney does a somersault trying to ask a question using "hypothetical" facts that everyone present knows damn well are not the least bit hypothetical.

"Suppose a person is shot in the abdomen," Garry asked Dr. Diamond, "with such a force that the bullet penetrates through the bowels and makes an exit wound in the back. The bullet is not found; it has disappeared. . . . Upon receiving this shot, the person felt a hot steam or flash and then thereafter he said he felt like he was crawling, or felt like he heard a volley of shots; then he felt as though he was swimming or he was being carried, doesn't recall what happened and thereafter about half an hour or so later he finds himself at a hospital entrance where he sees a platform and it is the only thing he remembers up to this time, except the fact that he feels as though he may have been carried or been swimming or floating. . . . He recalls perhaps talking to somebody who is asking him a lot of irrelevant questions, and he notices that he has a memory that she is talking to the police. . . . He has a vague recollection of going into the emergency room. He has a vague recollection of being on the gurney. Thereafter he has a definite recollection of the police putting handcuffs on him and he has a definite recollection of the police beating him. . . . Dr. Diamond, based upon your experiences in the field of medical science and as a psychiatrist familiar with the nature of emotion and trauma, is this compatible with the type of abdominal wound I describe?"

Dr. Diamond was also called upon to stick out his tongue at discrepancies in Henry Grier's two statements. Again, the style of questioning was "hypothetical": "Is a person's memory better immediately after an event takes place, or does it become better ten months thereafter?"

"An individual's memory," Dr. Diamond said, "is almost

always better the closer to the event that the recollection is, so that the earlier recollection is likely to be a more faithful memory than a later recollection."

■　　■　　■

Obsessed with the trial as I clearly was, hanging out in "radical" circles each day as I was, I became cordoned off from the rest of the world. To be sure, everyone around me spoke in universal terms—they spoke of the Third World, of Africa, of Asia and Latin America; they spoke of the incipient decline of Western civilization. And what with all this universal talk, what with all the books and leaflets and posters, one might easily persuade himself that he was plugged into everything of importance—that he knew "wat was happenin'," that he knew "wat was goin' down."

But surely I was insulated from anything that had no immediate connection with the Huey Newton trial or the Students for a Democratic Society or the "fascist pigs" or the Peace and Freedom Party. And while I was busy buzzing about the periphery of the Alameda County "struggle," the world was going about its business in typically perfunctory fashion: taxi drivers in New York complaining about tiny tips; Procter & Gamble giving birth to a new soap; Egypt attacking Israel; Israel attacking Egypt; America dropping another load of democratic bombs on Asia. And at the end of August, 1968, while no one consulted me on the matter, while the event occupied only the tiniest of crevices in my consciousness, America was well on its way to picking Richard Nixon to be President.

It was only because I thought some San Francisco commentator might have something to say about the Newton trial that I turned on the television set in my hotel room that Wednesday night.

Channel 2: Democratic Convention. Channel 4: Democratic Convention. Channel everywhere: Democratic Convention. I had forgotten all about it! And what about all the weighty political questions? Did Humphrey have it all wrapped up? Did McCarthy ever really have a chance? Would mighty Lester Maddox slay ten thousand Philistine liberals with the jawbone of a fried chicken?

But the big story, you'll remember, was outdoors. Tear gas and bleeding heads and flying wedges of law and order. *"The whole world's watching/The whole world's watching."* More gas, more blood. I lay there on the bed, peeking at Chicago over my naked toes. And I thought, "Well, here it comes— revolution or civil war or something. The Panthers were right after all. Here it comes—live and in color on NBC. America done gone and popped her crotch." I remembered a sign I saw on the street in Berkeley the day before. Some funky white hippie was carrying it:

> Let's get our shit together,
> so it all hits the fan at the same time.

The next morning my body bluntly refused to go outdoors. I could feel death sitting at the base of my throat, making me cough loud and dry. But I went to court anyway. How could I not go now? We were getting down to the wire, to the grits. In a few days Huey would be free or he would be on his way to the gas chamber. If nothing else forced you, your sense of theater would demand that you be there for the last act.

For we are all of us enamored of beginnings and endings, artificially carved from an amorphous marble slab. We grab at this or that chunk, hold it up to the sun, examine it in all its exquisite detail. And then we proclaim our findings: "This chunk of marble begins here, ends there, and the study of this carefully selected sample makes the study of the rest of the slab unnecessary. This chunk of marble is where it's at!" . . . Or is it?

But I went back to court with my hacking body to feast on yet another "ending," on yet another sample of marble. I went to devour delicious minutiae—to watch the quiver on the defendant's lips when the verdict came down, to see if the unflappable prosecutor would flap if the verdict was not to his liking. I wanted to watch Oakland explode with tension. I wanted to explode with it.

> *Free Huey! Hang Huey!*
> *Hang Huey! Free Huey!*

For precision, for persuasive effect, for emotional detachment, the prosecution's final argument was superb. When Lowell Jensen was finished, you could feel the noose tightening around Huey Newton's neck; you could well-nigh sniff the gas chamber fumes seeping up through the floorboards.

He took the jury by the collective hand and led them quietly, peacefully up the historical path of the development of English common law and the basic need for civilized societies to protect their citizens: "When man banded together for economic and social advancement and for his own protection against his enemies, it was apparent that . . . within any community there are killers and spoilers.

"Unfortunately, one of man's worst enemies is himself. And so it becomes necessary for any organized society to draw up codes of criminal conduct, to draw up situations where the society itself imposes sanctions upon those persons who refuse to abide by the basic rules of organized living. . . . When man got together, he gave up the right to take the law into his own hands. He gave it to society, and society then acted in his stead. . . . The right to human existence is the thing that must be protected, and the law of murder is simply an outgrowth of the notion that in civilization there must be protection against the very real and unfortunate fact one man may kill another."

With all the care of a physician reaching for surgical instruments, Jensen explained to the jury what murder was, what the law meant by "express malice" and "implied malice," the difference between murder and manslaughter, between first degree and second degree murder. He explained the "felony murder rule": "If an individual is in the process of the commission of a felony, and that felony is one that is inherently dangerous to life, then you are deemed to have malice, regardless of your specific frame of mind . . . regardless of whether or not you intend that another life should be taken, you are held to have that intent in terms of malice because of your commission of the felony."

And then there was the crime of "assault" to deal with. Jensen took pains to explain that as well: "Assault in legal terminology has three components. There must be an unlawful attempt with a present ability to commit a violent injury upon another. . . . You are responsible for an assault with a deadly weapon, assuming you use a gun, even though you don't hit the person with the bullet. . . . And we impose sanctions on people who try to shoot other people."

Jensen reminded the jurors that they would also have to decide whether in fact Huey Newton was guilty of a prior felony: "The prior conviction alleges that in October of 1964 the defendant Huey Newton, was convicted of the crime of assault with a deadly weapon here in Alameda County in the Superior Court, and in this instance we are not involved in any determination of that case. . . .

"You heard his description in terms of what happened. A man with a scar with his hand in his pocket is at a party. He [Newton] stabbed him. But we are not involved in deciding that case. We are not involved in retrying that case. That case has been decided. What we are involved with is deciding whether or not there was a conviction, and whether or not it was a felony."

And what if the jury in its wisdom *did* decide that the defendant had in fact suffered a prior felony conviction? Well, Huey Newton would really be in for it, that's what. Because as Prosecutor Jensen hastened to explain: "Under Section 1201 of the California Penal Code, a person who has a previous felony conviction and who possesses a specific kind of weapon, is guilty on that basis alone of a felony. . . . And if a person is in violation of that section and if as a result of his violation, a death occurs—regardless of his frame of mind—he fits within the concept of malice for second degree murder."

Having set up the legal framework for the jury, Jensen then proceeded with the particulars in the case. Summoning all the passion his basic cool would yield, the prosecution pleaded with the jury to remember the murder victim:

"We have heard the testimony of a lot of people, seen a lot of exhibits and we reflected upon these people and made emotional judgments about them. They sat there on the witness stand and we heard them, but in a murder trial, in this as in every other trial, there is the forgotten man who nevertheless is a part of what we must do in the ascertainment of truth. There is a forgotten man in John Frey. Unfortunately, we tend to do this as people, we tend to forget; we tend to forget that there was a living, breathing John Frey who didn't appear on the witness stand. . . .

"To us, what is John Frey? John Frey is a picture on the

street dying; he is a picture in the morgue dead. He is a mannequin. . . . But don't forget that those were lead bullets that went through his body and snuffed out his life. We must not forget. . . . He had an existence; he was a young man and had a future. He is no longer here. . . ."

Then there was the memory of the gallant Henry Grier to preserve. Jensen asked the jury to bestow on Sir Henry the black knighthood he so clearly deserved: "He is a man who saw the truth and he declared it. . . . If you have a relationship with your fellow man, you don't forget. You stand up. Henry Grier stood up and he said what he saw. And what he saw marks the truth, and unless we can accept the proposition that Henry Grier represents the relationship that should exist between man and woman, adult and child, black and white, unless the relationship of that man can be declared as the truth in this courtroom, we are lost. Henry Grier said you don't forget. Let us not forget. Let us not forget the meaning of that."

Lowell Jensen went on to do a thorough review of all the evidence—the ballistics tests, the medical examinations and of course the eyewitness testimony of Heanes and Grier. He also offered his insights into the character of the defendant:

"What about Mr. Newton? . . . We are saying, aren't we, that Mr. Newton there on the street turned upon a police officer, another officer, opened fire, ultimately took his gun and killed him. That is a rare and unique human being. I mean that takes a special kind of individual, doesn't it? It just isn't a situation which happens frequently or is the kind of thing you see all the time. This is a rare, a unique kind of thing.

"Well, let's ask ourselves about Mr. Newton. 'What about Mr. Newton?' Violence is no stranger to Mr. Newton. . . . Physical conflict with the police is no stranger to Mr. Newton. Is this a rare kind of individual? How many persons who were there embodied within them the experiences and the mind and the mentality of Mr. Newton?

"And you might say this also: How many of us have in our waking moments and in our discussion considered and reflected upon the problem of killing police officers? How many of us have that as a part of our conscious inquiries? How many of us go through that?

"Did Mr. Newton? What is his mind? And isn't it a unique mind?"

And with all the appropriate solemnity, Jensen urged the jury in the last of his summation to face up to their grim responsibility:

"In a courtroom, just as there must be a duty to implement a right, a courtroom must exist on the basis of the declaration of truth. . . . You find yourself in a position where it is your responsibility now to take on this task. I said a long time ago in *voir dire* examination that there was a long and tedious and arduous task before you, and I asked you to take care of this task all the way through. I am asking you to do that now. . . . This is the fundamental thing that is before us—to declare and to implement the truth in this courtroom.

"If it takes time, so be it. Take the time. If it takes perseverance, so be it. Let us persevere. If it takes courage, so be it. Let us have courage. But by all means, ladies and gentlemen, let us have a court of law where we can repair our controversies, where we can go, where we can declare the truth.

"*It is a sad and melancholy truth . . . that Huey Newton, the man in this courtroom, is a murderer. . . .*" (Emphasis added.)

■   ■   ■

The courtroom demeanor of Charles Garry was in constant contrast with that of his adversary. Seldom if ever did the emotion of any given moment in the proceedings register on the face of Lowell Jensen. But in moments when Garry was fearful for the life of his client, you knew it. You had only to glance at his brow, at his eyes, and you would see the despair. And at another time when a hostile witness would begin to wilt under the heat of his cross-examination, you knew that Garry was gleeful because you could see it—in his quickened pacing before the witness, in the higher timbre of his voice, in the cockrobin swing of his broad shoulders.

The differences in the final arguments to the jury reflected their differences in temperament. Garry's summation lacked the rapier precision, the cohesiveness, of Jensen's. And where Jensen was controlled, Garry was expansive. Where Jensen was trying one man for first degree murder, Garry was trying a city, a police force, a nation, a world:

"As I have sat in this courtroom for days like you have, at first picking a jury, asking you questions that probably infuriated you—I hope that your fury stopped as the evidence unfolded—I hope that it got you to thinking about the things that are going on in my beloved America and your beloved America. I hope that you remember the things that we asked you in the *voir dire*.

"Mr. Newton and I feel as though we have a pact with you, and that pact is that you be able to decipher this evidence, evaluate this evidence without prejudgments and without any exterior feelings about what's going on in our cradle of freedom, so called. I hope you can divorce from your minds the conventions that you saw, the two conventions, the spectacle that was made in them of democracy. The candidates today are talking about safety in the streets against violence, but this is nothing but a camouflage for curtailing civil liberties.

"When Mr. Jensen was telling you about Mr. Grier, I was wondering which Mr. Grier he was talking about. The Mr. Grier who stated at 6:38 in the morning what he saw and didn't see? Or are we talking about the Henry Grier who blithely brought forth things in this courtroom that did not occur to him until ten months later? . . .

"The thing that bothered me more than anything else in this case was the fact that the District Attorney's office permitted this man to change his entire testimony and did absolutely nothing about it, and for two and a half or three hours you heard the representative of the District Attorney's office in this county talk to you about truth and veracity, and did not once mention the diabolical changes in this man's testimony. . . .

"I want to show you ladies and gentlemen of the jury a gun. This is supposed to be Officer Heanes's gun. This is a .38. It's a police weapon. Assuming that the nine-millimeter gun is also a .38, it can't be much smaller than this one. This is his [Henry Grier's] statement on October 28, 1967. He stated that this man reached into his jacket or his coat— I am using the hesitation because that is the way he used it—his jacket or coat and took out something and whipped it around. The reason that that had to be changed, ladies and gentlemen of the jury, is obvious. You can't put this in this pocket and have it stay there. . . . That's the reason the testimony was changed [in court] from coat to shirt. This is a shallow pocket. This is the only pocket there is. . . . That's why the testimony was changed, and it was changed with the condonation and the knowledge of the prosecution in this case, to get a conviction. . . .

"Do you believe for one minute that Officer Frey did not know who Huey P. Newton was? Do you believe that? Do you believe that? Do you believe that a man like Officer Frey, who from all the evidence we have had disliked black people . . . wouldn't know Huey Newton, the man who had been in the light of publicity? Could you believe that Officer Frey did not know Huey Newton when he saw him? Of course not. . . .

"You know, since the day that I got into this case, one thing has bothered me. Why in tarnation was Officer Frey so headstrong about stopping Huey Newton's automobile? . . . There is just something about it that is not part of due process of law. It is not part of any understanding of justice. Frankly, it is not the type of police action that I have personally witnessed—but then again, I am not a black man. I am not a Black Panther. I am part of the accepted society. I can pass. I don't think any officer would stop me unless I was actually, openly, overtly violating the law. . . . I hate to keep referring to what I told you in the opening statement. I told you that this is a plan, a concerted plan, by the Oakland Police Department, together with other police departments in this area in Alameda County, to get Huey Newton, to get the Black Panther Party and Huey Newton, above all. . . .

"It bothers me that a twenty-three-year-old young man is dead. It bothers Huey Newton that he is dead. But I wonder how many more people are going to die before we wake up and accept our responsibilities. I wonder how many more people are going to die before we recognize the brotherhood of man. I wonder how many more people are going to die before the police departments of our nation, the mayors of our nation, the leaders of our nation, recognize that you can't have a society in a country that is 66 percent white racist ignoring the role of the black man, the brown man, the red man, the yellow man. . . .

"Officer Frey bothers me. His death bothers me and the things that caused his death bother me. I could see this young man going through high school . . . joining the police force and without proper orientation, without proper attitudes and without proper training, without proper psychological training, thrown into the ghetto, and in a year and a half's time he becomes a rank and outright racist. . . . I just wonder how many more Officer Freys there are. His death bothers me, but Huey Newton is not responsible for his death. . . .

"Huey Newton doesn't ask very much for himself. Huey Newton, in my opinion, is a selfless man . . . a man who is not interested in himself as a person; he is a devoted man; he is a rare man. Mr. Jensen tried to make this man out to be a liar. He says he talks about love and preaches violence. I am reminded of the Book of Matthew, Chapter 10, Verse 34: 'Think not that I am come to send peace on earth: I came not to send peace, but a sword.' I am sure that most of you never heard that version of Christ. He was talking to the twelve disciples shortly before his arrest. You heard Christ say time and time again: 'Turn your swords into plowshares.' He was talking to the multitudes then. But in talking to the twelve disciples he told them to sell and buy swords. This is again found in Luke 22:36: 'Then he said unto them, But now, he that hath a purse, let him take it, and likewise his scrip; and he that hath no sword, let him sell his garment, and buy one.'

"What is Huey Newton saying? What was Christ saying? Christ wasn't saying get out the sword and destroy people.

He was saying that the twelve disciples in order to be able to carry out their mandate would also at a time have to resort to the sword for self-defense.

"Huey Newton is saying to the black community and the black ghetto there has got to be a time when you will defend yourself by political means and other means for your survival. . . .

"The black community today, the black ghetto is fighting for the right of survival. The white community, is sitting smug and saying, 'Let's have more police; let's have more guns; let's arm ourselves against the blacks.' That is not the answer. If you think that is the answer, we are all destroyed. If you think that Mayor Daley has the answer, we are all destroyed. If you think that this nation with all its power and all of its strength can eliminate violence on the street with more violence, you have got another think coming.

"My client and his party are not for destruction; they want to build. They want a better America for black people. They want the police out of their neighborhoods. They want them off their streets. . . .

"I spent ten months on this case. I had to start learning. I thought I knew something about Negro America, because some of my most intimate friends are Negro professionals who have been accepted partially in our great white society. I thought I knew them and we exchanged visits back and forth and we were buddies. It wasn't a week after I got into this case that I came to the conclusion that I knew absolutely nothing about black America. . . .

"White America, listen; white America, listen. The answer is not to put Huey Newton in the gas chamber; the answer is not to put Huey Newton and his organization in jail. The answer is not more police. The answer is to wipe out the condition of the ghetto so that black brothers and sisters can live with dignity. . . ."

■   ■   ■

On Thursday morning, September 5, the seven women and five men of the jury were formally saddled with their impossible duties. Each was asked to disassociate himself from all the frailties of mere mortals. The moral arrogance of the courts requires this of all juries, but few have had it asked of them with so little hope of fulfillment.

But Judge Friedman told them of their responsibility in a relentless monotone—in a voice so free from emotion as to suggest that the twelve Alameda County human beings before him would have no particular difficulty in discharging their duty. Surely these men and women, in determining the guilt or innocence of Huey Newton, would be governed solely by the evidence introduced in the trial and by the law as stated to them by the Court. Surely they would do that. Surely they would not allow themselves to be seduced by such trivial things as mere sentiment, conjecture, sympathy, passion, prejudice, public opinion or public feeling. Surely not.

And why would they have any trouble grasping the legal subtleties of murder, first and second degree, of manslaughter, of malice, of premeditation, of provocation, of reasonable doubt?

The jury sat there meekly as His Honor, adhering to the dictates of legal procedure, bombarded them with definitions. Now and then tense, now and then doodling, now and then bored with the ponderous exactness of the law, I sat squirming in my place in the gallery. Occasionally a classic legal phrase would jar me—like "base antisocial motive," or "abandoned and malignant heart," or "wanton disregard for human life." And sometimes it pleased me to hear the law wax poetic: "If there was provocation, but of slight and trifling character, of a nature not calculated to naturally arouse the passion, or if sufficient time elapsed between the provocation and the fatal blow *for passion to subside and reason resume its empire . . .*"

By ten-thirty that morning the jury had received all its instructions. The bailiff was sworn, the jury placed in his charge. They all filed out of the courtroom.

There was nothing else for the rest of us to do but wait. The judge, the lawyers, the press, the policemen, the people, the immediate family, the distant family, the curious, the idle—we waited. We weighed the evidence, debated points of law, guessed at the verdict, and there were some of us so callous as to bet upon the outcome.

My cough had grown much worse, and I resigned myself to the certainty that some unheard-of malignancy was nibbling away at my lungs. (I didn't know it then, but actually I was experiencing the first symptoms of pneumonia.) I wanted to leave the courtroom to go to a doctor or get cough syrup or anything to stop the hacking, but I was afraid that the jury would return with a verdict as soon as I had left. So I stayed.

I spent the day walking up and down the corridors, in and out of the press room, staring at Huey Newton's sister crying, staring at the Reverend Earl Neil trying to comfort her, staring at Charles Garry, straining himself to be cheerful, at "ace" reporters who had covered a thousand "sensational trials" before, who when the time came would phone in the verdict to their city editors, add a descriptive line here and there for "color" and then go home to the little woman.

The word trickled down from upstairs at about six o'clock

that court would shortly be in session; the jury was returning. Had they reached a verdict so quickly?

No, not yet, as it turned out. The jury wanted to hear a
reading of Henry Grier's statement taken by the police on
October 28, 1967, shortly after the shooting. They also asked
that Officer Heanes's testimony be read in its entirety.
Curiously enough, they further asked to see Huey Newton's
bullet wound.

With no hesitation, the defendant walked over to the jury
box railing, unbuttoned his jacket and raised his sweater.
Then Huey turned around to display the exit wound and returned to his seat at the counsel table.

On Friday, the second day of waiting, paranoia began to
crawl among us. We suspected Reporter X of not being a
reporter at all but a right-wing fanatic bent upon some
mysterious sabotage. And there was a lady spectator who
had been present almost every day of the trial—the whispered word was that she had been hired by the District
Attorney "to pick up stray information." Very soon each of
us had a designated position and you were either *for* Huey
or *against* Huey. You couldn't take any jive-ass middle-of-
the-road position like "I'm for whatever the jury decides."

Later in the day we scrambled back into the courtroom.
Still no verdict! The defense, however, had a motion to
make. Charles Garry told the Court that he had finally obtained from Lowell Jensen's office a recorded copy of the
police Dictabelt recording of Henry Grier's original statement. Lo and behold, the transcription of that recording,
which the prosecution had furnished the defense and the
jury, was incorrect. What was more, it was incorrect at a
very critical point. Bus driver Grier's statement should
read: ". . . I *didn't* get a clear picture—clear view of his
face . . ."—not ". . . I did."

The defense was therefore now moving that the trial be reopened to receive this important, newly discovered evidence.

Motion denied!

"Did," said Lowell Jensen.

"Didn't," said Charles Garry.

"Did!" . . . "Didn't!" . . . "Did!" . . . "Didn't!"

Eventually, His Honor listened to the recording and satisfied himself that the transcribed copy of Grier's statement which had been read to the jury was, in fact, incorrect.

But what would he now do about it?

Judge Friedman ordered Henry Grier's statement retyped, introduced into evidence and submitted to the jury but, astonishingly, *without any indication that the change had been made and in no way drawing any attention to the document.*

And at that point I decided that the Alameda County Theater was not presenting a Samuel Beckett–LeRoi Jones play after all. No, it was a special adaptation of a Lewis Carroll work:

1ST VOICE: Who stole the Queen's tarts?

2ND VOICE: The Knave of Hearts did it.

3RD VOICE: Try him! Try him!

KING: Consider your verdict!

RABBIT: Not yet, not yet! There's a great deal to come before that.

KING: Let the jury consider the verdict.

QUEEN: No, no! Sentence first, verdict afterward.
(Charles Garry plays the March Hare; Lowell Jensen plays the Mad Hatter.)

MAD HATTER: Did.

MARCH HARE: Didn't!

MAD HATTER: Did!

MARCH HARE: Didn't! . . .

We, who could only sit and wait, learned eventually that the jury had chosen its foreman. It was David B. Harper, the only black man on the jury.

I laughed. I laughed hysterically. "Sham," I thought. "Monstrous sham! Blackwash. Tokenism stretched to ludicrous proportions."

The Panthers of course had long since put Harper down without knowing very much about him except that he was well educated, had a frightfully responsible job as a loan officer at Bank of America and that he lived with his wife and six kids in a cute little house in the suburbs. Middle-class nigger wrapped in pretty pink ribbon and you *know*, you just *know*, the nigger's gonna get up on that jury and lay down and let whitey shit all up in his face. Now you *know* tha's wat he's gonna do.

. . . Or would he?

Harper, in the course of the trial, had done things that bootlickers are not generally supposed to do. Like walking into the courthouse through the main entrance—past the demonstrators, past the spectators, past the Panthers, any one of whom might just pounce on him and tear him to pieces. He could easily sidestep these risks by taking the underground entrance, avoiding the crowds.

But here he was waltzing into court every day past the predators and *smiling*, too. The folks would tighten up in the mornings when he came through.

"Don't talk to him—he's on the jury." Cats would whisper and say, "Wonder where his head is at?"

But now the trial was just about over, and David B. Harper was the foreman whether we liked it or not. And on second thought, it did not seem like such an absurd choice. Come to think of it, he appeared to be in charge from the very beginning by the way he used to shepherd the other jurors in and out of the courtroom. Maybe, just maybe, he was the logical choice after all.

Wonder where David Harper's head is at?

For the answer to that, too, we would just have to wait.

On Saturday evening at about seven-forty-five, court was again called to order. But still no verdict. Judge Friedman made the announcement:

"The Court has received a request from the foreman of the jury for further instructions. I have taken it up with counsel and they have agreed as to the instruction that should be given."

His Honor donned his now familiar monotone and reread to the jury the Court's instruction on first and second degree murder and manslaughter:

> *Murder is the unlawful killing of a human being with malice aforethought. The word aforethought means only that the intent must precede the act as distinguished from afterthought . . . as used in connection with murder, malice and varying circumstances. . . .*
>
> *All murder which is perpetrated by means of poison, or lying in wait, torture, or by any other kind of willful, deliberate, and premeditated killing, or which is committed, in the perpetration or attempt to perpetrate arson, rape, robbery, mayhem . . . is murder of the first degree; and all other kinds are murder of the second degree. . . .*

Having been reinstructed, the seven women and five men of the jury left the courtroom.

Judge Friedman raised another matter: "I have consulted with both counsel as to the subject of whether any juror should be excused tomorrow morning if they do not decide on a verdict tonight, about going to church."

But both attorneys had told His Honor that they did not

want the jury to be separated to go to church or anywhere else for that matter.

And so Sunday, September 8, came and the jury did not go to church. Court reconvened at 10:15 A.M. But still no verdict. Judge Friedman had received yet another note from the foreman, asking for further instructions on murder and manslaughter. The judge said that Mr. Harper had specifically asked that the instructions be read slowly. Friedman said that he would oblige: "If you find that I am giving it too fast," he told the reassembled jurors, "why, just raise your hand and I will try to correct it."

The same instructions that were read yesterday were repeated, and the jury retired for further deliberation.

General gloom settled now on the "Free Huey" ranks because it began to appear that the only thing delaying a verdict was that the jury could not decide whether Huey Newton was guilty of first degree murder or second degree murder. We had come full circle.

In the beginning of the trial, the consensus was that, given the climate of Oakland, given the kind of jury that would be chosen, Huey Newton didn't stand the slightest chance of an acquittal, and if ever he were freed, some higher court would have to do it. But somewhere along the way—perhaps when Newton himself did so well on the stand—there suddenly seemed to be justified hope for an acquittal. But not now. Not any more.

It was almost over now. They would reach a verdict today or they would not reach one at all.

There was scarcely a moment all that day that I wasn't coughing—all through the chess games I played sitting on the floor, all through the secret sessions in the courthouse corners listening to theories and rumors. "They'll never let him go," someone said. "And even if they did, someone would blow his head off right afterward." "Hung jury," others said. "Hung jury, sure as shit." "No, second degree murder," came the countertheory. "And soon as they convict him, the Panthers are gonna burn the town down. Just wait."

At least one theory was later confirmed. Extraordinary security precautions had been taken and there were cops everywhere—across the street in unseen places by the lake, across the other street by the library, on the roof—everywhere. Furthermore the National Guard had been alerted and they were all set to take off from Alameda Station in helicopters.

Sunday 9:30 P.M. the word trickled down. The jury was returning to the courtroom. It was *not* that it was growing late and the judge wanted to lock things up for the night; it was *not* that the jury wanted further instructions on the law. No, none of that. *The jury had reached a verdict.*

We rushed upstairs and into the anteroom to be searched. No one objected to this indignity any more. It was routine. It was the daily price of admission to the Alameda County Theater. So we did not object to throwing our hands up against the wall, emptying our pockets and pocketbooks as alien hands probed about in unlikely places.

"Everybody rise! Superior Court, State of California, Honorable Monroe Friedman, presiding. Court is now in session."

His Honor entered, looking very much the same as always —short, gray, quick-stepping, deadpan. He had something he wanted to say before the jury was brought down. He said that as soon as they were brought in, the courtroom doors would be closed and locked and that no one would be allowed to leave the courtroom until the jury had left the courtroom.

In all the six weeks of security and paranoia, this had not been done before.

"Bailiff, please lock the doors."

Suddenly the room seemed to shrink to a third of its size. It was as though we had all been stuffed into some malodorous bottle. The stench of death was everywhere.

The side door opened and the jury marched into the courtroom and took their places. And then the ceremony of the law assumed command. The foreman of the jury handed the verdict to the bailiff, who in turn handed it to the judge, who read it, revealed nothing and handed it to the court clerk. Huey Newton stood still and erect and perhaps unafraid.

As to the first count, the jury found the defendant *guilty of voluntary manslaughter*.

As to the second, *not guilty* of assault with a deadly weapon upon a peace officer.

As to the third: "We the jury, in the above entitled cause find that the charge of previous conviction as set forth in the indictment *is true*."

My senses were numb. I wanted to see Huey's face. Had his eyes betrayed his fear of dying; did they now betray his joy? But of course his back was turned to us in the gallery. But even had he been facing us, I would not have been able to see because a glaze had settled over my eyes. For a full moment, I could hear nothing, feel nothing.

The judge thanked the jury and, scarcely able to conceal their jubilance, they left by the side door.

Those who hated Huey Newton were angry because they had expected the best and the best had not come. Those who loved Huey Newton were relieved because they had expected the worst and the worst had not come.

Still, Huey was not free. Tonight he would sleep in the same cell in which he had slept the night before. And there was now the clear probability that in one cell or another, in one prison or another, he would spend the next *fifteen years of his life*.

Against all the forecasts, Oakland, that gateway to vacation land, did not explode that night. The Black Panthers did nothing. The Alameda County sheriff's deputies came out of their hiding places, the alerted National Guard returned their helicopters to the hangars and Oakland police put their guns away and came down off the roof.

There was, however, a minor blow-up the day after. At about 1:30 A.M. (twenty-seven hours after Newton's verdict) two Oakland policemen—on duty, in uniform and thoroughly drunk—cruised past the Panther office on Grove Street and fired a barrage of .30-caliber rifle bullets into the empty office. Witnesses said the policemen turned around, made another pass and fired another volley. The shots smashed through the glass of the soul-food shop next door and completely shattered the front window of the party office. Pasted to the window had been a huge poster of Huey Newton.

It was an act of rage:

> *Goddamit, we had him! Finally we had him!*
> *We had the gas all ready for that nigger*
> *And that chicken-shit jury let him go. . . .*

The manslaughter verdict in the trial caused great confusion in the San Francisco–Oakland Bay Area in the days immediately following the decision. So many, black and white, were not sure which side had "won." For those who wanted to "hang Huey," the San Francisco *Examiner's* Monday banner headline was, at first glance, reassuring.

Your eyes were automatically drawn to the bold headline "NEWTON FOUND GUILTY"; only secondarily would you see the kicker headline above it: "MANSLAUGHTER VERDICT."

At a press conference held moments after the verdict Charles Garry said with a straight face that he was "keenly and absolutely disappointed in the verdict. It makes no sense on legal or evidentiary grounds."

Typically, Lowell Jensen was less outspoken. He declined to say whether he was happy or disappointed with the verdict. "It's not our job to second-guess them," he said. Jensen also rejected the notion that the trial was a political one: "If you have a political motive to kill entering into a homicide case, you have a very sorry state of affairs. . . . We may very well have a sorry state of affairs."

When the press conference was over, "keenly disappointed" Charles Garry nudged me in the ribs and whispered, "We got 'em. We got 'em." We were heading for the elevators when a giant of a plain-clothesman, whose "keen disappointment" with the verdict was obviously very real, began to order the noisy crowd to disperse. His voice was hoarse with anger. Garry turned on him: "You have no right to talk to people like that. Who do you think you are? You've been shoving people around like this ever since this trial began, and I just want you to know I'm not going to put up with it any more."

The policeman's eyes narrowed; his brick shoulders tensed for battle. "Well, just don't you get tough with me, Counselor," he said. His voice was just barely audible. "Just clear the hallway," he said.

"Now look," Garry said, "don't fuck *with me.*" Clearly, Garry was taunting him. He would have liked nothing better than to have an outraged cop hit him in front of so many witnesses. Clearly, the burly detective would have loved to oblige. Standing before him, after all, was the very son of a bitch who had helped Huey Newton get off the hook.

But the policeman restrained himself, and Garry stepped onto the elevator and went down.

■   ■   ■

Meanwhile the communities buzzed with the news of the verdict. All manner of decoding devices were brought into play in an effort to decipher the manslaughter decision. Partisans on the right and left thought that the jury had attempted to appease both sides and that the manslaughter verdict was a compromise—a middle-of-the-road position between incurring the wrath of the right by letting Huey go and incurring the wrath of the left by finding him guilty of first degree murder.

Another "thesis" was that the decision made no "legal sense." How could the jury find that Newton had shot Frey in a "heat of passion" and had *not* shot Herbert Heanes? And if, as the jury claimed, Huey Newton shot and killed Frey, was not Huey (a convicted felon with a gun) automatically guilty of second degree murder?

No jury, of course, is obliged to explain its decisions. With good reason, the Huey Newton jury agreed among themselves that they would not discuss the verdict with the press immediately after the trial, for to talk about it publicly would be to keep the story alive. One newspaper or magazine might play up one juror's version, another paper would counter with another, and the enormous pressure they had been under would continue long after the trial.

One juror, however, Mrs. Eda Prelli, broke the agreed-upon silence one week after the verdict. (She was the widowed landlady who had paid little attention to the early news about the case. "I don't like to hear troubles," she had said then. "I have enough of my own.")

As scared as those seven women and five men were, I'll never understand how Rush Greenlee managed to get Mrs. Prelli to discuss the verdict; but he did.

Mrs. Prelli told Rush that she had a "premonition" that someone else was involved, that a still unnamed fifth person was present at the shooting scene. She did not believe that the jury had the entire story when it retired to deliberate. "That's what made our task so difficult," she said. "We had to fit those bits and pieces of testimony together. If Huey isn't satisfied with this verdict, he ought to talk to his friend Gene McKinney. He's the key to this whole thing. . . .

"I believe there was someone else there, someone who did some shooting. I just feel it. I had a premonition. I didn't want to be hard on Huey. At first I was for acquittal, but I quickly saw that couldn't work because of the evidence we had. When we first went in Thursday, there was some talk about first degree murder, but we never seriously considered it. . . . It was really a choice between second degree murder and manslaughter. David [David Harper, the black Bank of America loan officer and foreman of the jury] was for acquittal at the very beginning, too, and so was Tom, but they changed for manslaughter," Mrs. Prelli said. (Tom, another juror, was Thomas R. Hofmann, an officer in the trust department of a Wells Fargo Bank.)

Mrs. Prelli thought very highly of Mr. Harper. "David was wonderful," she said. "He led us through the whole testimony. He took all the parts. When one of us asked a question, he clarified it. And he clarified the answers. He's so intelligent."

Mrs. Prelli also praised Henry Grier, the bus driver. "It took a lot of courage to get up there, since he was black, and tell everything. I think he saw Huey shoot that Officer Frey in the back after he fell. I believed Officer Herbert Heanes, too. But I thought Huey told some small lies, like that he couldn't read or write when he got out of high school.

"He's too intelligent. He talked so well on the stand and told us a lot about the Panthers. I didn't know anything about them. It was very interesting. But it didn't tell us who did the shooting.

"And I liked that black professor, Mr. Blake. He really told me a lot about the ghetto and what it's like. And, you know, I was surprised at him, because with that beard and all over his face, he looked like a bum."

Mrs. Prelli said that two of the women on the jury held out for a second degree murder verdict. One, she said, "thought she knew everything because she had been in a murder trial before," and the other "talked all the time—she was the one who had Heanes's and Grier's testimony reread to us.

"She wanted it read again and I said, 'If you didn't get it the last time, you're never going to get it.' She was always taking pills. I told her if she threw them away she'd be able to think. . . .

"Oh, I was so proud to be a part of that trial. It is something to remember. I just hope we did the right thing. We certainly tried. I prayed several times. Don't you think we did the right thing?"

■   ■   ■

David B. Harper, the man who became the foreman of the Huey Newton jury, was born in Indianapolis in 1933. When he was ten years old, the Harper family of five

(David had two brothers—one older, one younger, than he) moved to Arizona, where the senior Mr. Harper set up his own shoe repair business in the small town of Casa Grande.

David, who originally wanted to be a priest, went to a Catholic seminary in Mississippi. Five years later, however, he changed his mind and took a year of medicine at Arizona State University. He spent four years as a noncommissioned officer in the Air Force, leaving the service a staff sergeant. After a brief stint as a salesman in Houston, Texas, Harper returned to Arizona State and graduated with a degree in accounting. He went on to Golden Gate College in San Francisco, where he earned a master's degree in business administration. In 1963 he settled in Oakland with his wife Cora and six children and got a job as a loan officer in the Bank of America's main office in San Francisco.

Like anyone living in the Bay Area in the late 1960's, Harper could not fail to hear of the Black Panthers; his suburban home was far removed from the center of their activities, but like everyone else he read of their exploits. Nevertheless, at the time that the Huey Newton trial began he knew very little about the Panthers, although not *so* little that he didn't realize that they identified blacks like himself as "part of the problem."

David Harper had served as a juror before on at least three other trials. The last one, an armed-robbery case, had been concluded as recently as three weeks before the Newton trial.

I went to see Harper, a year after the Newton trial was over. He had resigned from the Bank of America and moved with his family to Detroit to become president of the First Independence National Bank, a new black bank operating in the city. As he talked to me about the trial, he lit up a cigar, exuding the same self-assurance he had seemed to have the summer before. The episode was as fresh in his consciousness as though it had happened yesterday.

He remembered some of his thinking before the trial started:

"The way I saw things building up in Oakland, the whole town could blow up at any time. All we could do was buy ourselves a little time. The only thing we had for our protection—poor as it was—was the law. And I thought that if I could execute the law, if I could prove that a black guy could be part of the legal system and come out with something fair, applying the law, then maybe, just maybe, we've made some progress. If not, we've bought some time. It might not have worked, but it was worth trying. I had a lot at stake—I could have gotten killed, after all, though I doubted somebody black would shoot me; I was worried about my neighbors."

During the trial the Oakland police called his home to say that threats against his wife's life had come into headquarters and they were going to furnish the Harper home with a twenty-four-hour guard. But Mrs. Harper was as much afraid of the police as she was of anyone who might want to kill her.

For all the dangers inherent in serving as a juror on the Newton trial, Harper welcomed the chance. Not only that; he wanted to be foreman. He *engineered* his selection. Very likely, Ronald Andrews, the engineer, would have been chosen foreman, Harper said, had the jury voted at the beginning of the trial. For Mr. Andrews, tall, slender, graying at the temples, had all the superficial characteristics of a leader. "He was the white middle-class image of what a leader is supposed to look like," Harper said.

But by the time the trial was over—by the time the jury

was ready to begin deliberation—there was no other choice for foreman but Harper. He knew a little about how people react in groups, how leaders emerge from groups, and his selection was assured. Furthermore, no one else wanted the responsibility.

In the very beginning they had been patronizing with our Mr. Harper—patronizing in that familiar way that some white people are when they are suddenly thrust into a social situation with niggers; they don't know what to say to the strange creatures and so they patronize. But this had long passed; that had been seven weeks earlier. They had grown accustomed to him being around. They had seen him smile, heard him laugh. They had come to learn that he was a "responsible" man, with a responsible job, living in a responsible community. By golly, if you didn't look too closely, you'd swear he was a white boy.

But now that the trial was over there was so much more to be concerned with than how to be comfortable with a Neegrow in the room.

They had to wade through all the sociology, all the history, the polemics, the philosophy, the ballistics tests, the contradictory testimony, and water it down to that monstrous oversimplification that the legal system calls a verdict.

And having made up their minds, they had to worry about whether someone would be so displeased with the decision as to want to shoot them. Obviously they needed a leader to point the way through the morass.

Enter David Harper.

"We realize we're putting you on the spot," they said, proposing that he be foreman. "And it's perfectly all right with us if you decide that you don't want the job, but . . ."

I wasn't there to see and David can't be expected to remember so trivial a detail, but surely the irony did not escape him. Surely he must have grinned with devilment when, with mock reluctance, he accepted his unanimous appointment.

One small though important step had now been taken, but most of their work was still before them; they were nervous, bewildered. They lit cigarettes; the talkative woman juror began to take her pills; Harper lit up a cigar.

The jury room, like most, was too small. There was no space to wander afar and have private thoughts. So they paced about in their cell—by the window, by the blackboard, in and around the two little rectangular tables.

But the early listlessness faded and soon they were eager to compare notes. After all, they had been together for some seven weeks and had been asked to suppress what would otherwise have been a natural impulse—to talk about things. Did Henry Grier tell the truth; did Heanes? Did Huey Newton commit murder in the first degree? And what of the bigger questions: Were things as bad as some black people kept saying they were? Was the city, the county, the country falling apart? And no less fascinating: What did David Harper think about all this?

Yes, it was true that he was almost as emotionally distant from Huey Newton as they were. It was also true that seldom in his lifetime had he suffered the psychic, the economic oppression that most black people in America are obliged to suffer. Still, for all there present in the room to see, he was black, and to be black "for all to see" is to know a special rage. What was more, he was not so out of tune with the masses of his people that he was unaware of their plight.

And for their information, he had not forgotten the recent "good ole days" in Casa Grande, Arizona, when black lives were as cheap as desert sand. And just incidentally, from his own teaching experience at a local junior college, he could testify there was an excellent chance that Huey Newton *did* emerge from high school "a functional illiterate."

They *did* agree that Huey Newton had done very well on the witness stand, that he had been a model of calm and reason. There was also general agreement that John Davis, the ballistics expert, was a paragon of professional grace and precision, and that he had been fair to both sides.

And then the jurywomen went to work on Corinne Leonard, the nurse who had admitted Newton to Kaiser Hospital. "What a little bitch she was," one of the ladies said. "And did you see her with all of that dye in her hair—oh, and that cheap little dress she had on. Did you see her?"

When it came to an appraisal of Henry Grier, David Harper and his fellow jurors parted company. They, like the press, saw Mr. Grier, the black bus driver who dared to put the finger on Huey Newton, as brave, truly brave. It took genuine courage, after all, to face the defendant in open court and accuse him of first degree murder. Was it not admirable that Grier did not allow his blackness to divert him from shouldering the burden of civic responsibility? Most assuredly, Henry Grier was a brave man.

David Harper could not muster up one sliver of respect for the "brave man." "Henry Grier," he said, "was *their* image of what black men are supposed to be. Henry Grier made a fool of himself. If ever there was an Uncle Tom, *he* was. Then he tried to be so righteous in it. He galled me—I got the impression that he did not consider himself black because he was living in a suburb. He wasn't black; he was a nigger. . . ."

But Harper knew these sentiments could not be voiced then and there. They were volatile. They would unleash a whole chain of racial hostilities, and the next thing you knew it would be eleven against one.

Nor would it be wise for him to say something like: "Let's bring it down front—I think Huey Newton is innocent and I will not be moved. I don't give a shit what you say; I say, 'Free Huey.'" That kind of rigidity would ensure a hung jury, whereupon Newton would be tried once again for murder, and who knows what sort of hangmen would be brought together for that trial?

The strategy here had to be low-keyed. He could *not* let the deliberations disintegrate into a racial slug fest; they could, so easily. He could *not* march around the room saying, "This is a political trial"—even if it *was* a political trial. He had to keep as relaxed as possible, as unemotional as possible. And that could best be done not with salt but with honey. David Harper charmed them. He *hustled* them into the "proper administration of justice."

Harper assumed his position of authority, standing by the blackboard in front of "the class." The other jurors, the four men and seven women, took their seats in front of the tables:

Ronald Andrews, the gray-haired engineer.

Linda Aguirre, the junior executive secretary.

Marian Butler, the drugstore saleswoman and wife of a stockbroker. It was she who had been told in church by a Black Panther that all white Protestants were racists.

Mary Gallegos, the bookkeeper and wife of a fork lift operator.

Jenevie Gibbons, the bologna slicer.

Helen Hart, widow, mother of five married children, who worked for an airline catering service.

Thomas R. Hofmann, bachelor and trust officer in the Berkeley branch of the Wells Fargo.

Harvey H. Kokka, laboratory technician for Shell Oil.

Eda Prelli.

Joseph Quintana, the Cuban machinist who didn't speak English very well.

Adrienne (June) Reed, the secretary for Safeway Stores—the lady who didn't like to hear "white people calling colored people niggers" or "Black Panthers calling policemen pigs." She was also the lady who did not approve of racial intermarriage.

Most of the ladies and gentlemen of the jury wanted to vote right away, but the foreman disagreed. "There's nothing to vote on yet," Harper said. "We haven't examined any of the evidence; we haven't compared any of the testimony; we haven't done any of the things that juries are supposed to do, so how can we vote?

"Let's have some basic understandings. Let's agree on what is important testimony; let's review that testimony and having reviewed it let's act it out. Let's assume that every important witness told the truth until such time as we can show that he did *not* tell the truth. Let's take October 28, 1967, and come up with a series of events—'a theory of action'—for that morning. *Then* we can vote. . . ."

All that sounded reasonable enough, and so the ladies and gentlemen of the jury agreed that the important testimony was that of the people who were at the scene of the shooting: Huey Newton himself, Henry Grier and Patrolman Herbert Heanes.

The foreman sent notes to the judge asking that Heanes's testimony and both of Grier's statements be reread. Linda Aguirre was assigned to take notes during the reading.

On that first afternoon of deliberations, a dispute arose over the location of Huey Newton's abdominal wound. Newton had claimed that Frey struck him, he fell to one knee and that while he was down he felt in his stomach the sensation of "hot soup" being poured upon him.

It was inconceivable to some of the jurors that Newton might be telling the truth. Harper pointed out that if Huey was telling the truth, if only just this once, the entrance wound near Newton's navel would be higher than the exit wound in his back.

The foreman sent a note to the judge asking that the jury come back into court and be allowed to see Newton's wounds. The judge obliged; the jurors craned their necks to see Newton's scars and, sure enough, the entrance wound was higher than the exit. And so it was not inconceivable, after all, that Huey Newton, Minister of Defense of the Black Panther Party, might tell the truth. He *had* been shot while he was down, and he had been shot by someone who was on his feet.

On that first night, Thursday, the jury recessed for supper at about nine-thirty. Sheriff's deputies armed with machine guns escorted them from the courthouse to Oakland's Jack London Inn where they would spend the night. They finally got to bed at about one o'clock in the morning.

On Friday and Saturday, the second and third day of deliberations, a "theory of action" began to evolve. The key to the theory was Henry Grier's testimony, and what Grier had to say was the most important testimony *in Newton's favor*. They retraced bullet trajectories; they used three jury-room chairs to represent the two police cars and the infamous "beige Volkswagen"; they acted out the lead roles: John Frey, Herbert Heanes, Gene McKinney and Huey Newton.

Grier had testified that he drove past the scene, saw the four men standing outside the cars. Four or five minutes later, after he had turned around and was passing by the scene again, the shooting began. This statement collided head on with what Herbert Heanes said—that the shooting began *almost immediately* after Newton and Frey began walking toward the rear of the cars. And in terms of the time sequence Grier's testimony *jibed with Newton's*.

Huey claimed that when he and McKinney got out of the Volkswagen, they were thoroughly searched. Then Frey separated Newton from McKinney and directed Newton to start walking to the back of the cars. And as Huey's story continued, he confronted John Frey with his lawbook to say that Frey had no reasonable cause to arrest him; whereupon Frey struck him.

The jury figured that all of this action—the searching, the walking to the rear of the cars, the interchanges between Newton and Frey, Frey's striking him, Newton's falling down —took up the "four or five minutes" before the shooting that Henry Grier was talking about.

The jury came to the conclusion that Herbert Heanes was lying. He was lying when he said that they did not search Newton and McKinney, and he was lying when he said that Newton fired the first shot. *Heanes himself fired the first shot.* He was very jittery that October 28 morning. He was afraid of Newton; he was afraid of what John Frey might do to Newton.

He reached the peak of his terror when the scuffling ensued and Frey pushed Newton to one knee. It was still dark and Heanes probably could not see clearly what was going on, but in his panic he drew his service revolver and fired, hitting Newton in his abdomen. ("We understood," Harper said, "why Heanes could not or *would not* remember what happened to one of his shots. It was a bad dream to him—a nightmare. He probably couldn't even admit it to himself, much less to open court.")

As the jury's theory of the action continues, Frey, hearing a shot from behind him, spun around, his gun drawn, and fired in Heanes's direction. A bullet struck Heanes in the right arm. In the meantime, the dazed and wounded Huey Newton got to his feet and, seeing Frey's gun drawn, probably thought that Frey had shot him. Newton began to wrestle with Frey, and in this tussle Frey's gun went off. A bullet from Frey's gun ricocheted from the pavement and struck Heanes in his arm. Heanes switched his revolver to his other hand and, from a kneeling position, fired a shot the impact of which disarmed Frey and spun him around. This gave Newton the opportunity to pick up Frey's gun and empty it into his back. The jury further speculated that Huey was probably not even aware that any of the shots fired had come from Heanes.

The foundation of the jury's theory rested upon the testimony of the ballistics expert, who, from powder burns left on their clothing, determined that Frey's bullets were loaded with ball powder and Heanes's with flake powder. But for this distinction, there might be no way to tell readily which bullets had been fired from which gun.

"Newton's clothing did not have any ball powder on it. Officer Frey's clothing had ball powder on it," John Davis had testified. "Let's assume, just for the sake of argument . . . that Officer Frey's gun was used by somebody else to shoot Officer Frey. If the gun was at that time close enough to put ball powder on Officer Frey's clothing, I think it would be fair to assume if Officer Frey had shot the defendant he would have been close enough to have put ball powder on the defendant's clothing. This being the case, I would be inclined to believe that the bullet which struck the defendant was *not* fired by Officer Frey's gun with ball powder on it. . . ."

The jury further theorized that while all the shooting was going on, Gene McKinney did what most people might have done—took cover lying on the sidewalk.

On Saturday afternoon the voting as to guilt or innocence began. The bailiff had supplied scratch paper. The paper was torn up into small bits for the balloting. An old cigar carton, apparently left in the jury room for that purpose, became the ballot box. On the first ballot five voted for first degree murder, four for voluntary manslaughter and three for acquittal.

At this point the objectivity that had marked the preceding two days began to disintegrate. As soon as it came to applying the law, emotions began to creep in. They had voted carefully every step of the way up until that point—on various theories of action, on what was important testimony, on what a given witness had said. They had agreed finally on a "series of events." And according to that agreed "scenario" Newton was fired upon first (by Heanes), but at no time did Newton fire a shot at Heanes.

Again according to the action theory the jury had worked out, it would seem that Newton's shooting of Officer Frey entailed no "premeditation, no malice aforethought." And yet there were *five jurors voting Newton guilty of first degree murder*.

My own guess is that it was simply that these men and women had come to a wall they could not penetrate. Beyond the barrier lay Huey Newton's innocence, and no powers of logic, of reasoning, could get them to the other side. Their minds, their hearts were shackled by the powerful certainty that whoever this Huey P. Newton was, whatever this Huey P. Newton was all about, he was *guilty of something*. Call it "first degree murder" if you will. Call it "voluntary manslaughter" if you like that name better. Call it any goddamn thing you please, *but Huey P. Newton is guilty of something*.

"I was astounded," Harper said, "by how they could ignore

facts—facts that were staring them in the face—facts that we all had agreed upon."

On Saturday night and Sunday morning petty animosities began to creep in. Alliances formed. Linda Aguirre, one of the more outspoken women, tended to vote "against" Eda Prelli, taking the opposite position of whatever stance Mrs. Prelli took. In addition, Miss Aguirre accused Mrs. Prelli of voting for acquittal only because she was a slumlord and therefore afraid that her black tenants might try to avenge Huey Newton's conviction. Mrs. Prelli, meanwhile, was still shaking her head and bemoaning the fact that she had gotten trapped on the jury and was thus cornered into an onerous civic responsibility she wanted no part of. "I've never been in trouble in all my life," she kept saying. "How did I get into this? What did I do wrong?"

Then there was the obstreperous Mrs. Jenevie Gibbons, the bologna slicer. "She," Harper said, "was the hardest to manage, the most difficult to get along with. She irritated just about everyone on the jury. Someone would be expounding a theory and suddenly Mrs. Gibbons would interject with something like 'And then he did the dirty deed.'" Mary Gallegos, who had the misfortune to be arbitrarily chosen Mrs. Gibbons' roommate at night at the hotel, was nearly driven out of her mind by her talkative companion.

Joseph Quintana, the Cuban immigrant, Harper said, perfectly matched the classical stereotype of the hot-tempered Latino. "Vocally, Quintana was the strongest juror for acquittal." It was his contention that Huey Newton had shot John Frey in self-defense and should therefore not be held responsible for the policeman's death. But Quintana's short temper, combined with his uncertain command of the English language, made him ineffective in converting any of the others to his point of view.

At the opposite end of the spectrum from Quintana was June Reed. "Except for her disapproval of racial intermarriage, she seemed to consider herself quite the Liberal," Harper said. "She was the strongest woman on the jury and the strongest voter for first degree murder." When the trial was over, the short grapevine among the few jurors who kept contact had it that Mrs. Reed got into considerable difficulty with her neighbors and her own conscience because she had, in effect, "gone soft on Newton" by finally voting for manslaughter with the majority. The word also had it that Mrs. Reed was going to report to the authorities what to her was a near-certainty: Charles Garry, Huey Newton's lawyer, was a Communist.

Amid the irrationality, however, were pockets of reason. Harvey Kokka, for example, the Japanese technician, tended to stimulate calm thinking; during the trial he kept good notes; during the deliberations he kept reminding everyone that they had a job to do and that they could not afford to let themselves get emotional. But every so often he had to throw up his arms in despair. "I just don't understand Caucasian thinking," he said once.

By Sunday evening whatever dispassionate analysis had existed originally was completely lost. Some of the jurors began to murmur that it didn't matter whether the prerequisites for first degree murder were present or not. So what was all the squabbling about when, underneath it all, they knew that Huey Newton had murdered John Frey?

Someone suggested that perhaps Newton was *too* good on the stand—that he was an accomplished liar and was now close to getting away with it. So probably he had murdered John Frey after all.

On still another tangent, another juror brought up Huey's prior convictions as a way of persuading fellow jurors that he was probably guilty once again. After all, as Jensen had pointed out, this young man was "no stranger to violence." But Harper hastened to say that "It didn't matter if Huey Newton had killed five other guys; it doesn't prove that he killed this one. We're only trying this one. All the things he may or may not have done in his past life may tell us something about the man, but it does not prove to us that he killed John Frey. Let's stick to the facts. Whether the guy's *capable* of doing something or not is not the question. We are not trying his philosophy or his capability."

But the flight from reason continued. And then Ronald Andrews said something—flippant on its surface, startling in its implications: "One of these days we may be in Huey Newton's shoes and we're gonna want a fair shake."

It was as though the unspoken understanding all along was that Huey Newton was to be hanged without proper cause, but now maybe on second thought he should be tried justly— not so much in the interests of justice as in the cause of enlightened self-interest.

If you are a Black Panther or black anything, your basic cynicism would already have told you that what Ronald Andrews said was so. If you were like David Harper, black and cynical, but not so blinded by your cynicism that you didn't have one last whisper of hope that black men and white men could still come together and function within a system of law, then Andrews' statement jolted you and caused you to revert to your instinctive black doubt. If you had, like Harper, tried to make the law work for you—if you had, like Harper, momentarily slipped up but still had hopes that you were succeeding—Ronald Andrews' statement could only bring on despair.

But to return from the cosmos to the work at hand: the seven women and five men began to freeze into stationary

positions. And such unity as they had developed in the beginning was now shattered into emotional splinters. No one
could agree on what the law was—what first degree murder
was, what second degree murder was, what manslaughter
really was.

The bloc of jurors which was holding out for a murder
conviction began to use the California felony rule to say that
when Huey Newton finally picked up John Frey's gun, he became a felon with a dangerous weapon. The homicide re-
sulting from that act would normally be judged "justifiable"
or at worst manslaughter, but in this instance of a "prior
felon" committing another felony Huey Newton's action constituted second degree murder.

With the ugly vision of a hung jury swimming in his head,
Harper began to alter his position from acquittal to voluntary
manslaughter. But it was still going to be difficult to steer
the jury to this more moderate course. And it seemed clear
that if they didn't reach a verdict Sunday night, they were
not going to reach one at all.

They had to be brought back together. Harper thought
that if they all attacked him, they would have to be unified.
And so he did something calculated to unite them. He wrote
a note to Judge Friedman:

> We've reviewed the facts; we've attempted to follow the
> law. We have been logical up until this point. And now it ap-
> pears that emotions are taking over. Is there something you can
> do to remind the jury that they are required to be dispassion-
> ate in the proper administration of justice?

Harper read the note to his fellow jurors. They were
furious. Mrs. Butler, who had had almost nothing to say up
until that point, suddenly became quite vocal. Of all the
things to do, the foreman was going "to tell the judge on
them." Some of the jurors said that they were going to write

their own note to the judge. Harper told them: "You can write it if you want to, but if you write it, I won't sign it, and if I don't sign it, it doesn't go to the judge."

But the foreman's note never went to the judge either; it was no longer necessary to send it. They began to argue points of law again with some semblance of rationality.

At about nine-fifteen Sunday night another ballot was taken. The vote came out ten for manslaughter, two for first degree murder. Tom Hofmann, whom no one guessed to be one of the holdouts, finally changed his vote. June Reed, the last holdout for first degree murder, simply could not stomach the course the jury seemed to be taking and went to the bathroom while the balloting was going on. Finally she yielded, casting her oral vote from the toilet, and it was twelve to nothing for voluntary manslaughter.

Everyone was jubilant now. Their terrible task had finally been set to rest. Mrs. Hart was so happy she began to cry. The men all came over to the blackboard to shake David Harper's hand for the masterful job he had done. Each of the women rewarded him with a big kiss.

IV

Alert Now in Limbo

The frightful paradox that is the indictment of modern civilization and the cause of its moral collapse is that a blameless, cultured, beautiful young woman in a London suburb may be the foundation on which is built the poverty and degradation of the world. For this someone is guilty as hell. Who?

This is the modern paradox of Sin before which the Puritan stands open-mouthed and mute. A group, a nation, or a race commits murder and rape, steals and destroys, yet no individual is guilty, no one is to blame, no one can be punished!

—W. E. BURGHARDT DU BOIS

To look at the record of the murder trial of Huey P. Newton with the naked eye is to imagine that the defendant received a fair and impartial trial. For all the trappings of a fair trial are there—the prosecution on the one side, the defense on the other; the judge, the carefully selected jury in the middle.

But if you sat through those seven weeks, you could not fail to get the crawling sensation that the entire proceedings were rigged. And they were rigged as recently or as far back as one cared to delve. If I thought myself to be "revolutionary," I might simply declare Monroe Friedman to be a fascist pig, thereby achieving a political orgasm and ending the discussion. But Monroe Friedman is not a fascist pig, and while calling him one might provide me with momentary gratification, the name-calling exercise would be, at best simplistic, at worst inaccurate.

His Honor did not rig the Huey Newton trial, nor did Lowell Jensen nor the Oakland Police Department. They were all part of the rigging, to be sure, but no one of them nor even all of them collectively can be said to have been master of the situation. They are small; the rigging is big.

They are so small as to be pawns. They are historical puppets. American history wrote their scripts, manipulates their strings, controls their movements. Such a puppet was John Frey, the policeman. He was effectively conditioned by history to imagine that his omnipotent whiteness combined with the brass badge of authority pinned to his chest extended him the right to tread upon the dignity of people he thought manifestly inferior to himself. He could have nothing but contempt for Huey Newton, who in his youthful arrogance had imagined that he might be the one to stop men like John Frey (with guns if it came to that) from acting out their historical conditioning.

Huey Newton, too, it can be said, was conditioned by history—more recent perhaps, but history nevertheless. And if you insist upon using dates, you might say that his conditioning began in 1959 when a young NAACP organizer named Robert F. Williams decided to parry the violent thrusts of the Ku Klux Klan—not with moral suasion, not with Christian humility, but with old-fashioned American-made rifles.

And if, for one reason or another, you did not like Robert Williams or the year 1959, you might explain Huey's conditioning by looking to Malcolm X in 1964:

It is criminal to teach a man not to defend himself when he is the constant victim of brutal attacks. . . .

I myself would go for non-violence if everybody was going to be non-violent all the time. I'd say okay, let's go with it, we'll all be non-violent. But I don't go along with any kind of non-violence unless everybody's going to be non-violent. If they make the Ku Klux Klan non-violent, I'll be non-violent. If they make the White Citizens Council non-violent, I'll be non-violent. But as long as you've got somebody else being violent, I don't want anybody coming to me talking any non-violent talk. . . .

Now, I'm not criticizing those here who are non-violent. I think everybody should do it the way they feel is best and I congratulate anybody who can be non-violent in the face of all that kind of action in that part of the world. I don't think that in 1965 you will find the upcoming generation of our people, especially those who have been doing some thinking, who will go along with any form of non-violence unless non-violence is practiced all the way around. . . .

It was stones yesterday, Molotov cocktails today; it will be hand grenades tomorrow and whatever else is available the next day. The seriousness of this situation must be faced up to. You should not feel that I am inciting someone to violence. I am only warning of a powder-keg situation. You can take it or leave it. You can take the warning, perhaps you can still save yourself. But if you ignore it or ridicule it, well, death is already at your doorstep. There are 22 million African-Americans who are ready to fight for independence right here. When I say fight for independence right here, I don't mean any non-violent or turn-the-other-cheek fight. Those days are gone. Those days are over.

If George Washington didn't get independence for this country non-violently, and if Patrick Henry didn't come up with a non-violent statement, and you taught me to look upon them as patriots and heroes, then it's time for you to realize that I have studied your books well.

But perhaps the names Robert F. Williams and Malcolm X cause you discomfort so that your reckoning of history prefers to leave them out. Use the date April 4, 1968, then and say that the historical conditioning of Huey P. Newton was reaffirmed the moment that 30.06 rifle slug penetrated Dr. Martin Luther King's neck, tore through the flesh and blood of his right jaw and went on to sever his spinal cord.

Whichever date one chooses, the result is the same. And history having created its John Freys, its Huey Newtons—history having placed them in the same arena—forced the collision.

There was an inevitability about the Huey Newton trial which fairly drove me insane. The smell of manifest destiny was everywhere. A giant ferris wheel, spinning, controlled by a conspiracy of faceless robots. In its path lay Huey Newton—Langston Hughes's "Black Panther":

> Pushed into the corner
> Of the hobnailed boot,
> Pushed into the corner of the
> "I don't-want-to-die" cry,
> Pushed into the corner of
> "I don't want to study war no more,"
> Changed into "Eye for eye,"
> The Panther in his desperate boldness
> Wears no disguise,
> Motivated by the truest of the oldest lies.

In this bountiful era of misinformation, it is commonly supposed that the Black Panthers are strange mutations which somehow suddenly sprang up, weedlike, amidst a nation of gentle people. If, indeed, there were ever "mutations" among us, they were not your Rap Browns, your Stokely Carmichaels, your Huey Newtons; it was Martin Luther King. The true wonderment should be: how could so compassionate a heart as his have survived for so long in so violent a climate as America's? Truly, Martin Luther King was "un-American."

The Black Panthers, on the other hand, are American to the core—in their lifelong romance with guns, in their inherent disdain for intellectualism, in their haste to solve big problems with simple solutions. Quite rightly, that reporter from the San Francisco *Chronicle* saw early in Huey Newton and Bobby Seale a dash of Hollywood. His reactions to one of the Panthers' first press conferences bear repetition:

> If a Hollywood director were to choose them as stars of a movie melodrama of revolution, he would be accused of type-casting. . . .
> But these two are not actors and this is not Hollywood. . . .

It is still commonly supposed, also, that the Black Panthers have taken up arms for the systematic slaughter of policemen and the random slaughter of whites—all this for reasons for which the most astute observers cannot account. I am continuously amazed at the number of people who think of the Panthers as bloodthirsty terrorists, peculiarly liable to lunge through bedroom windows in the middle of the night. The people who imagine that this might happen don't seem to be made more comfortable by the simple, the immutable fact that the Black Panthers, for all their bombast, have never been proven guilty of murder.

Four policemen have died in "confrontations" with Black Panthers in four years (including Officer John Frey, if you still want to count him). None of these instances suggests the sort of mindless slaughter of which the Panthers are supposed to be so capable. All of them involve "questionable circumstances," the details of which we will probably never know. The only case that even remotely resembles a "slaughter" involves not a policemen in the holy performance of his duty, not some white suburban flower rocking her baby to sleep, *but another Black Panther.*

The Black Panthers, as of this date, claim that twenty-eight of their ranks have been killed by policemen. Very quickly you might say, "Bullshit! Some of those niggers were killed by other niggers." And that's true. Some of them were.

But after you subtract those from the twenty-eight and after you subtract a few more "questionable" cases, you end up with at least *fifteen* positive instances of Panthers slain at the hands of policemen. The police claim that *five*, not four, of their men have been "murdered" by Panthers. Accepting the police at their word, we end up with a score of fifteen to five. That means that for every policeman killed in Panther incidents *three* Black Panthers die. By my reckoning, that is indeed a slaughter—but who is slaughtering whom?

The three-to-one ratio causes no national alarm because that's about what the score has always been. And, as we all perfectly well know, nonwhite lives come much cheaper than white ones—one-third as cheap.

The image of the Black Panthers as "mad killers" had its origins partly in the excesses of their own rhetoric. When Huey Newton and Bobby Seale shouldered their first rifles, they wanted, among other things, to be feared. They succeeded in that regard—beyond their wildest reckoning, they succeeded. But the myth was picked up and perpetuated by a nearsighted press which could not see past Huey's bandoliers. White readers could readily believe the mass circulation of half-truths: given their long, bloody record of inhumanity to nonwhite peoples, they knew that "revenge" was certainly in order—and long overdue.

When Huey Newton shouted "self-defense" in 1966, it sounded to Bay Area citizens just like "reprisals," just like "an eye for an eye." From the very beginning the Oakland *Tribune*, the San Francisco *Chronicle*, the San Francisco *Examiner* busied themselves with assuring their nervous readership that the isolated bit of madness calling itself "Black Panther" had no connection whatever with the "responsible" Negroes of the community and with America at large. No, the Black Panthers, a fascinating but poisonous exotic plant, had sprung up in a vacuum. Isolated as it was, the poison would be easily controlled. It would wither and die before very long. Comforting news, indeed.

The comforting news is now of course circulated on a national scale:

Maybe you've heard about those crazy folks they call Black Panthers. You know, the ones that talk tough and carry guns. They started in Oakland; then they kind of spread out a little bit, and now they're in big cities all over the country. Yes, them! I wouldn't worry your pretty pink head about them though, because even the most generous Justice Department estimate says that there're only twelve hundred of 'em. Less than that, actually; two of them were "justifiably" killed by police just yesterday.

None of the media will address itself to the fundamental questions: "*Why* are there Black Panthers? Why, in this time, in this place, are there Black Panthers?" Are those questions *so* complex? Are the answers?

The disquieting news never gets on the air: *Every non-white man, woman and child in America is a Black Panther.* We do not all wear black leather; we do not all boast "Free Huey" buttons, but every one of us is a Black Panther. Some of us are not even aware that this is so, but every one of us is a Black Panther—every grinning elevator man, every white-uniformed nanny who "has been a real part of the family for twenty-five years," every not-so-black Harvard graduate, every nigger so high he can't stand up straight—we're all Black Panthers. The "uniformed" Black Panthers proclaim the same rage the rest of us feel but, for one cop-out or another, do not show. Eldridge Cleaver is skilled in exhibiting that rage; I, for one, am skilled in suppressing it.

In their own blundering way, the Oakland Police Department touched on the heart of the matter when they were looking for Huey Newton on October 28, 1967:

"Be on the lookout for two male Negroes of any type riding in any vehicles."

The Federal Bureau of Investigation is also quite right when it describes the Black Panthers as one of several major threats to national security. What nation is secure while the wrath of better than one-tenth of its people festers? But the FBI should carry its reasoning a step further, because the *real* threat to national security rests not with the Black Panthers or the masses of black people, or with the Students for a Democratic Society, or even with the omnipresent "Commies," but with America itself. America—in its blindness—in the enormity of its hypocrisy.

So much hysteria has attended all discussion of the Panther movement that one finds it constantly necessary to remind oneself that when the guns, the threats and the counterthreats are set aside, we are talking about human beings—American human beings. And as such they embody all the contradictions you might expect. Believe it or not, there are Black Panthers who have wives and children. They make love to their wives; they send their children to school. And like many American parents, they're careful about what school their children go to. The Chief of Staff of the Black Panther Party, for all his skill in handling a .357 Magnum, is afraid of dogs—of police dogs, of Chihuahuas. Occasionally Black Panther wives suffer a lapse in "revolutionary fervor" and want to go off to Reno for swingin' weekends. Three doors down the street from the national headquarters of the Black Panther Party in Berkeley is a men's "beauty parlor" called A.J.'s Artistic Fingers. Here the preoccupation of young, broad-shouldered black men is not with radical social change but with being first on line under the hair drier.

In the early Oakland days there were as many reasons for joining the Black Panthers as there were people who wanted to join. There were those who thought of them as just another street gang. The party office was a good place to "hang out" for young cats who had no place to go and nothing to do. Some were enamored of guns and saw in the party a good chance to be men instead of boys, to be "bad mother-fuckers" whom whitey and "simple niggers" wouldn't mess with. Others got swept up in the rakish glamour of black leather and boots, and it was not so much that they wanted to be Panthers as that they wanted to be Lash LaRue. Many, of course, joined in earnest. The Black Panthers were going to change the quality of their lives—"by any means necessary." In among that first wave of joiners, and indeed in all the succeeding waves, were infiltrators and *agents provocateurs* who saw in the Black Panthers a burgeoning threat to "national security."

It was also possible for young men in cities across the country to don leather jackets and berets, call themselves "Black Panthers" and have no connection whatever with the national organization.

With the usual luxury that hindsight affords, one can now say that the Black Panthers were never the tightly woven organization they should have been. For too long, joining the party was much too simple a procedure, and many an unscreened member would later show himself to be destructive of party ends, whether by blunder or by design.

Every "Panther incident" has to be viewed with the sort of healthy skepticism that most citizens abandon when the accused turn out to be linked with that band of madmen our newspapers have come to call "black militants." On April 2, 1969, twenty-one Black Panthers were indicted in New York City and variously charged with conspiracy to murder, arson, reckless endangerment and possession of weapons and explosives. Alerted in advance of the dramatic haul, all the local media were on hand to film the early-morning arrests of eleven of the accused. District Attorney Frank Hogan said that there was "a general plan to destroy elements of society which the defendants regarded as part of the power structure." Those "power structure" elements were supposed to have included five department stores—Macy's, Alexander's, Bloomingdales, Korvette and Abercrombie & Fitch.

No one but the most loyal of Panther sympathizers could have read the newspaper accounts, heard the television reports of the apprehension of the "New York 21" and come away with a "healthy skepticism" as to the guilt of the accused. In much the same way as in the Huey Newton case, as in hundreds of other lesser "Panther incidents," the news of an indictment read like news of a conviction.

Having no privileged information on this latest Panther plot, I could weigh the newspaper accounts only against my broad impressions of the movement—against a series of probabilities. It seemed to me wildly improbable that the national Black Panther leadership as I knew them would give their blessings to a plot that would result in the pointless deaths of thousands of *their own people*. That speculation had to be weighed against the distinct possibility that there might be "crazy niggers" involved who might have had a "revolutionary seizure" and come to the conclusion that the revolution was too long in coming, that it was time to "get the shit on" and start destroying all the symbols of the "capitalist pig power structure."

There was a third consideration: What was the probability that national police paranoia about the Black Panthers had stretched to such lengths that nothing to eliminate them was too ruthless? Not even the complete fabrication of a "plot" to blow up five department stores, three police stations and one botanical garden. Having seen in Oakland a policeman so feverish about "putting away" at least *one* of the black devils that he arrested him for the willful, malicious spitting of a grape seed on an Oakland pavement, I had long since decided that police across the country had reached the conclusion that the Black Panther Party had to be eliminated. And to borrow a Panther phrase—"by whatever means necessary."

Unhappily, a host of American minds are so locked into immovable positions that they cannot admit of two very real possibilities: (a) there *are* Black Panthers who largely conduct themselves as rational human beings; and (b) conversely, there *are* law enforcement officials who largely conduct themselves as pigs.

The most cursory examination of the fate of the "New York 21" following their imprisonment should outrage anyone who thought there was substance to the long-hollow proposition that "the accused are presumed to be innocent until proven guilty." Bail for twelve of the fourteen defendants was set at $100,000 each, a figure so monstrously high as to amount to what a federal judge called "a euphemism for the denial of bail." Effectively denied bail, the defendants were in jail for close to ten months without having been tried on charges.

During this time defense attorneys were obliged to get a court order for one of the prisoners to see his wife. The Department of Corrections took the extraordinary step of placing the defendants in as many as seven different jails. Each time defense counsel wanted to see his clients together, he had to notify the Department at least two days in advance. After a fight with his guard, Richard Moore, one of the prisoners, was placed in a solitary punishment cell, without shoes, blankets, soap, toothbrush or more than one meal a day. No formal presentation of charges against him was made; no hearing was held. Lawyers learned of his punishment a week after the event.

The torrent of abuses continued even as the pre-trial hearings began the following February.

Should anyone have been surprised that the defendants were by this time very close to being the madmen they were deemed to be ten months before? What possible regard could they have for the "calmness and solemnity" befitting a courtroom? Which epithets should they have chosen to adequately convey their fury? Was it enough for them to declare His Honor to be "full of shit"?

It would be outrage enough if these travesties with which the "Panther 21" are so painfully familiar were reserved for "radicals, Commies and Kooks." Far more frightening is the realization that the injustices they incur are commonplace and that a thousand uncelebrated defendants a day are quietly trampled to death by "the administration of justice."

It really wasn't so very long ago that Huey Newton sat Bobby Seale down and said, "Let's have a Black Panther Party." If, in late 1966 or early 1967, some black pundit had been asked to make a guess about their future, he would probably have made all the wrong projections. How could he have guessed that in less than four years the very mention of the party name would generate such widespread fear and anger? How could he have foreseen that the time would come when no television or newspaper day would be complete unless it had included a report on the latest Panther confrontation with established authority?

They were not, after all, what a consensus would call "great men." Neither of them was a spellbinding speaker. Neither of them overwhelmed you with the power of his vision. They had read economics and history and philosophy, but their studies were hurried. They had no time; they had to *act*, "seize the time." Mostly, Huey Newton and Bobby Seale had raw nerve. Either of them would walk into the mouth of a cannon without flinching.

Yet the not-so-great men did great things; not the least of them was the fact they managed to get a sizable number of black men and women scattered in cities across the country *to think collectively*. This is no small accomplishment when one considers how very deeply American individualism is ingrained in all of us, black and white. None of the Panthers, the *real Panthers*, had any individual hustle. Whenever one of their numbers put the squeeze on you, it was almost always for "the breakfast-for-children program" or the "liberation school program" or the "Huey Newton defense fund." And if you listened carefully to them bellowing "Power to the people!" it sounded quite simply that they meant just that.

The true adherents to the movement came to be puritans, idealists, romanticists, fanatics—all tightly interwoven. They were the vanguard and as such completely ready to die at any time, in any place. But off in the distance was heaven— the revolution. And that would make everything all right. The precise path to revolution, to heaven, was not always clearly in focus, but never mind, it was out there—somewhere. There was nothing that could happen in their lives, nothing so trivial, that it was not intimately connected to the "revolution." Every decision, every act was "revolutionary." ("It may not be right, but it's revolutionary," Eldridge Cleaver was always fond of saying.) They had revolutionary barbecues, revolutionary dance parties, revolutionary weddings, revolutionary funerals. They were so easily romanticized. Huey Newton, Peasant Revolutionary, versus the

System. But Huey Newton is not Emiliano Zapata, and America, 1971, is not Mexico, 1912.

They carried the art of the cliché to new heights. The whole world was conveniently divided up into sections labeled "fascist pigs," "racist dogs," cowardly snakes, avaricious businessmen, the demagogic ruling class.

They grew too fast. They had the good luck and the misfortune to be creatures of the age of television. In a single stroke, television made them and destroyed them. The Black welfare mothers and the "cats on the corner," who should have learned about them firsthand, got lessons on the Panthers filtered through the distorted sensibilities of network TV. The plain black folks—"the people"—came to be afraid of them, as much as any white middle-class housewife.

They were thus effectively isolated. Black people, high and low, belatedly, powerlessly springing to their defense, can do little more than ask their assassins to conduct "thorough investigations." Murmuring our vigorous living room protests, we watch our TV screens in impotence as an Eldridge Cleaver flees to Algiers, as a Fred Hampton is shot to death in his Chicago bed.

And all the while America imagines that in decimating the Black Panthers it can decimate "the problem." There will be more of them. They will dress differently; they will have a different name. The threat to "national security" will be greater. Underneath all these differences they will still be Black Panthers.

Counting "real" Panthers, stragglers and informers, counting ex-Panthers and part-time Panthers and assorted infiltrators, the Black Panthers by the most generous estimates probably never exceeded six thousand. But it did not take numbers to spot America's raw nerve ending. And once it was spotted, it did not require numbers to step on the exposed nerve:

> Negroes,
> Sweet and docile,
> Meek, humble and kind:
> Beware the day
> They change their mind!

Hence the terror! It seemed to all that the day was fast at hand—niggers were changing their minds. Now at long last, after begging and pleading and whimpering and cajoling, the niggers were stretched beyond all human capacity to stretch. They would now cleanse themselves in blood and fire. Or so it seemed.

The black masses were too busy surviving to join them in the streets; the welfare mothers didn't give a shit about what Marx said or what Mao and Che said, but quietly cheered on the Black Panthers even while they were sometimes afraid of them. For here now before them were black men who seemed not to be afraid, men who could not be quieted by money or threats. And they were not whispering subversive little things in bars the way black men used to. These Black Panthers were saying it out loud everywhere they went—in the courthouses, outside the courthouses, in the prisons, at Yale, on Channel 2: *We just don't care any more; we mean to say we don't give a good goddamn any more. Nobody gets out of this life alive anyway, so FUCK YOU, AMERICA. You can beat us to death with your bullets and your dollars, but fuck you anyway.*

God, but it was sweet to hear black men standing up like that. It didn't pay the rent and feed the babies, but *God* it was sweet to hear it.

And as for me, I am awake now, but to what end? To

drag my blackness on upward to higher fallacies? When, where can I rest my woolly head and be peaceful with it? Which grave shall I choose? I am Jamaican, but not really; English, but not really; American, but not hardly; African, but not lately. I stand therefore alert in limbo—part me, part Panther, part nothing.

Even assuming that they would have me I could not join the Black Panthers. I am afraid, I flinch. And there is no room in the party for fear and flinching. The party is certain about almost everything. I am certain about nothing but my own uncertainty. My language is strewn with doubt, with "howevers," with "yes, buts." The language of the party brooks no long-windedness: *Right on!*

Right on when? Right on how? Right on where? And with whom?

I curse them for raising ten thousand questions and answering none of them. I thank them for wrenching me from political slumber when I was scheduled to die quietly, ineffectually, in my sleep.

Epilogue

I̲N̲ AUGUST, 1970, the State of California opened the gates of the California Men's Colony at Los Padres and let Huey P. Newton go free. The Court of Appeal had found that the trial court erred when it failed to inform the jury of Mr. Newton's contention that he was unconscious at the time of the October 28, 1967, shooting. The Court pointed out that it was "reasonably probable" that had proper instructions been given, the result would have been a more favorable decision to Newton. "The judgment of conviction is reversed."

And so the revolution's handsomest martyr had been resurrected. Women inside the movement, on the fringes of it, and women no closer to the movement than the Huey Newton posters hanging in their bedrooms squealed with apolitical delight. Indeed, he did look all-powerful, all-knowing on the day of his release as he stood bare-chested on top of a car to address his cheering followers. But as usual there was no immediate way to separate followers from fans.

America has this unerring faculty for coopting dissenters, not always by shooting them, but by transforming them into entertainers, into "stars."

But what exactly would the Minister of Defense now do? Certainly not flee the country to avoid retrial. "They should be so lucky," he said. "What has happened is that I've been transferred from maximum security to medium security for institutional convenience."

The speculation on Mr. Newton's plans brought to mind an earlier evaluation made by a dutiful probation officer. No irony was intended:

"His tendency to overreact in stressful, unstructured situations was first noted ten years ago and has become increasingly evident in recent years. That he has chosen to commit himself to a life pattern likely to involve him in repeated stress situations is particularly foreboding."

Afterword

"JUST TO SEE WHAT THE END WILL BE"
by Ekwueme Michael Thelwell

■———————————————————

Lord, I must go, I will go, I shall go
Just to see what the end will be."
—NEGRO SPIRITUAL—TRADITIONAL

"Young man, young man, Best don't make yo' mouth
write no checks yo' ass cain't cash."
—JUNEBUG JABBO JONES
Address "On Revolutionary Practice"
Spruell Hall, Berkeley, October 1967

Warring Ideals in One Black Body

If the Panther phenomenon appeared contradictory, defying in its practice and results both logic and reasonable expectation, it was, compared to the complex personality of Huey, its principal architect, a monument to order and clarity.

Born in Monroe, Louisiana, the youngest child and seventh son of a preacher man, Huey came to Oakland a child and thus grew up urban.

"I spent my first fifteen years in the church," he was to say, and in truth, there would always be something preacherly and strangely religious in his makeup. But, always a war between the highest values of the black tradition—dignity, self- and race respect, kindness to children, politeness to elders, communal responsibility, uplift—in conflict with the most nihilistic street code of urban hustler life, that flashy, violent, predatory, mean-spirited "I'm badder than you, motherfucker," player ethic.

Even in elementary school these contradictions were evident. Delicately handsome, sweet-faced, almost pretty, the baby of the family (but don't ever, *ever* call him Baby Huey), he is doted on in the family, even indulged if not by the stern father, then by the gentle mother. But in the playground he is a terror. A poor reader who is marvelously verbal, loving language and reciting long poems from memory. Though a slow learner and very indifferent student, he is extremely bright, brimming with ideas. He is a great and constant rapper, inveterate "dozens" poet, but his voice is high, reedy, thin: major reason for the playground fights. But the willing brawler is able to dominate all groups with quick intelligence and an attractive magnetism. He is always clean, almost narcissistically so, even as a child.

As a teenager he is lover and "player"; yet also a reflective, compassionate, sensitive youth, spontaneously generous and loyal—"sweet Huey"—one second, and the sudden, unpredictable frightening outburst of violence—"crazy Huey"—the next.

David Hilliard Remembers:

Santa Fe elementary school . . . There is no one like Huey. He always has something to say, something interesting. He won't let anything go. . . . He was always a fighter and a talker, known for his high-pitched, rapid-fire voice. . . . Always immaculate, clean, sparkling . . . He used Dixie Peach—the best cream you can buy he tells me—to slick his hair down into handsome, soft waves . . . He washes his face so well his cheeks look polished. . . . Teeth sparkle—some mornings he brushes them fifteen times.

Huey hurries around the corner. Every morning we go to school together. I wait on the porch. He approaches quick stepping, well washed. I jump off the porch for Huey doesn't stop. He is going to school rapping one idea after another.

He is not a good reader. Nor does he try to improve his reading, believing adulthood will bestow an instant ability to read . . . His IQ score is somewhere down below dull-normal. But he does possess a powerful memory, reciting 'The Bells' and 'The Raven.' This morning it is The Rubáiyát of Omar Khayyam . . ."

And later in the streets it's the light-skinned, good-looking son of the preacher man, clearly narcissistic but ever ready to go down, duke it out. Smart, quick, articulate, but undersized and prettyish with that thin, girlish voice; still not to be messed with. Challenge him and "Crazy Huey" emerges, quite ready to take it on out beyond the limits of reason or self-preservation. (In Louisiana, his daddy didn't take no white folks' shit, either, perhaps another reason he found it advisable to leave.)

That was the complex, baffling personality who had in 1968 entered prison.

Sunday, September 8, 1968

The jury returned its verdict to an aroused, sharply divided community and considerable confusion. Neither side nor its partisans were quite able to decide whether the verdict represented victory or defeat. Political necessity dictated that each loudly proclaim the first while privately brooding over the nagging possibility of the second. However, the carload of allegedly drunk police officers who shot up the Oakland party office that night left no doubt as to their reading of the verdict.

The trial's anticlimactic result left the book's principals— journalist, defendant, and party—writhing in the throes of their own particular crises.

For Gilbert Moore, the first thing to go was that distancing shield, the comfortable myth of journalistic objectivity. Against his will and best professional judgment he had found himself being drawn into the story. Yet he did not feel professionally compromised. Quite the opposite. Now he had a story—one that he wanted, needed, indeed, *had* to tell fully and fairly. He was certain he was still capable of doing so, in fact, that he was now far better prepared to do it than before. But he worried that that particular telling must inevitably involve him in the narrative in ways almost certain to be unacceptable to his employers. The sensitive young man, very proper Negro, correct professional sent to California, was returning to New York a troubled black man, but a better reporter. Rather than merely file a story, he could now bear witness. But witness to precisely what, and to whom would this witness be directed?

He could not quite see how it would be possible to render all he had seen, felt, and understood in California in language palatable to his editors and their readers. And what was possibly worse, it was even less likely to please the Panthers and their stridently ideological supporters. The more it tilted to one, the more certain was the other's displeasure. On the one hand, the stone; on the other, the hard place. Waall, as Mr. Mohammed says, "go for self." The irony made him smile. He ordered another Scotch and leafed through the journal which he had kept sporadically during the trial.

What's this from Camus? He could not remember when he had copied it into the pad. But reading it now as if for the first time, he understood why.

"Any publication is an act. And that act exposes one to the passions of an age that forgives nothing." Let the church say Ahmen! It was odd but something in him dreaded the writing while something else could not wait to begin.

His colleague Richard Hall remembers.

"The brother was, was . . . strange when he came back to New York, changed, really quite different. At first, for at least two weeks, he would not come into the office. When I went to see him he hadn't even unpacked. The suitcase was still on the table and next to it, a bottle of Scotch. 'Here, man, have a drink!' he said. And all he wanted to do was talk. Talk all night, language in torrents, and even his language was changed. In fact, so had his entire personality. I finally unpacked the suitcase for him. I remember he kept saying, 'I can't go back, man. I can't fucking go back.' " [to *Life*]

Of course Moore not only went back, he filed his Panther story. In fact, he did so six times. Too long. Rewrite. Too abrasive. Rewrite. The story was never carried in the magazine. Moore took a leave to write this book and never returned.

Moore wrote and published this book. It was a catharsis of the spirit, but at the end he locates himself "alert, now in limbo." He thanks the Panthers for breaking his slumber. He is now awake but to what end? "Jamaican but not really; American but not hardly; African but not lately," he knows he can never again be comfortable in corporate white America.

Making a living free-lancing is easy for no writer. It is perhaps harder for Blacks, and quite impossible for a Black with principled reservations about which assignments he can and should accept and how he will address the ones he does undertake. A free black mind is, after all, a concealed weapon. It is not difficult, therefore, to understand why Gilbert Moore disappeared from the professional scene, and almost out of the "safety net."

So it is a pleasure now to be able to report that the brother has reemerged with a powerful novel, *The Flight of the Black Swan*. A love story, set in the turmoil of the sixties, the novel revisits the scene of political struggles—Vietnam, the Panthers, and so on—through the presence of a black journalist who covers the decade for a journal much like *Life*. Moore's extraordinary novel will make some fortunate publisher very happy indeed.

And Huey . . .

The defendant also faced crises both personal and professional in nature. Huey's name was now an international cause célèbre of the Left, yet he faced the isolation and obscurity of the cell block for what might prove some long time. It was the ultimate contradiction: twenty-six years old and growing more famous daily, while gut-shot, isolated, in a cell and facing the hardest time a black man could do, cop-killer time. Compounding which, he was not entirely sure that he approved of all that had been happening in the Party since his arrest—and for that matter, with his name.

The vacuum created by his imprisonment was increasingly being filled by Eldridge. His literary visibility, flair for dramatic rhetoric, and his white radical associations were enabling him to place his ideological and psychological stamp on the Party's operations and image.

He was reported to be investing much of his royalties in the purchase of guns while recruiting numbers of his prison buddies whom nobody but he really knew. Accompanying this was increased talk about "setting a revolutionary example by moving on the system," beginning of course with the police.

Only recently, at 4:00 A.M. a couple of Panthers had come roaring up to the house where David Hilliard and his family lay asleep. The men were fleeing from a shootout which they had themselves initiated because, as they explained, "Eldridge say we gotta start moving on the Pigs." Confronted by an understandably annoyed Hilliard, Cleaver had defended the attitude, and, by implication, the action. Such men, he explained, "were the soul of the Party . . . the vanguard . . . good fighters for the first day of the revolution."

Huey wanted to ask him exactly who the revolutionary example was for . . . the Berkeley radicals? And, on the revolution's second day, were *they* going to be the fighters? Unable to do much else, he retrieved the term "Jackanapes" to describe precisely that kind of irresponsible adventurism. Also, he appeared to be increasingly ambivalent about the public definition of the Party being created largely by Eldridge and *Ramparts,* and uneasy about his own role therein.

First there had been that picture, entirely Eldridge's inspiration. But there he was grim-faced, in leather jacket and beret, posed in an enormous thronelike wicker chair brandishing a rifle in one hand and a spear in the other. He'd never liked the damn picture. He thought it looked silly and emphasized the wrong shit. "That picture isn't me," he protested.

But after *Ramparts* ran it in full color and it was blown up into a poster to be sold nationwide to fund the defense, it became him, at least in the minds of new converts in the college dorms and culture centers across the nation.

The magazine was, in the argot of the time, a head trip. It now began to devote space in each issue to pronouncing the Panthers the "new revolutionary vanguard." If that vocabulary seemed remote from American political experience and discourse, the accompanying iconography was even more so. Each Panther story featured a formal full-page color portrait of one of the leaders. He was usually seated, solemnly and stiffly posed against a shiny background of a surpassingly deep red fabric, like the depictions of Chairman Mao said to be prized by Chinese workers. These portraits, in their highly stylized proletarian kitsch were, seen, in the Maoist enthusiasm of the editors, as revolutionary mass art. But to Western eyes, it was indeed an odd combination: inner city blacks presented as revolutionary royalty in the manner of the Chinese proletariat by the white children of American privilege.

Unfortunately, the style carried over to the Party newspaper being edited by Cleaver. Huey in abstentia became the focus of what can most charitably be called a personality cult, Mao-style. As if to demonstrate his loyalty, the editor made sure that each issue prominently displayed the poster, as well as smaller shots of the founder in heroic poses scattered throughout each issue . . . as were, too, inspirational gems of revolutionary wisdom from the Comrade Minister. This also was when the annual mass rally in celebration of Huey's birthday became a Party institution. Although in prison, Brother Huey was not going to be forgotten. But it is not clear just how seriously Huey took all this homage.

Mike Thelwell remembers:

Throughout the book Gilbert Moore is often stumped, unable to decide whether the Panthers are putting him on. Back then we had no doubt: they could not possibly expect to be taken seriously. For example, my first encounter with the political persona of Huey P. Newton: this was by way of a phone call from Ed Brown, a serious brother who was developing economic programs for black farmers in the Mississippli Delta.

"Boy, is yo' awl niggers up there done gone crazy or what?" Ed drawled.

"My man, so what is your problem?"

"Y'awl stone crazy, bro. I'm a looking at this here picture . . . A blood call hisself the 'Minister of Defense.' "

"What *are* you talking 'bout, bro?"

"Thass what I'm a-telling you. Here's this here brother, young dude, militant looking, too. The Brother be sitting on a, a *throne*, man, must be . . . I dunno, African or somethin'."

"Yeah?"

"An' he wearing a scowl, an' he got him a big Afro with a little beret perched on top, man."

"You making this up, man?"

"No, I ain't making this up, man, an' he got him a leather jacket too and dig, he holding what look like a spear . . ."

"A what?"

"A *spear,* man or maybe it could be a . . . a *harpoon?* And in the other hand he got him a gun, look like a beat up ol' shot gun. An' he the Minister of De-fence."

"Of what . . . a government?"

"No, man, of a Party, the Black Panther Party for Self-Defense."

"Never heard of it. You sure you ain't bin drinking that ol' stump liquor again?"

"No, man, this is for real. It say here it's from California."

"California, huh? Well, that explains it."

We concluded it was perhaps a joke, in any case certainly nothing to take seriously. But it did not, as we expected, dissipate and float off into the ether. And the next time we encountered Huey's name, it was not his picture but his prose. But that was no easier to decode. It was the executive mandate drafting our close friend Stokely Carmichael into the Party . . . in particular, the operative clause, the bottom line, so to say.

After a few preliminary whereases, more or less true of the young Carmichael, "because you have . . . distinguished yourself in the struggle . . . acted courageously . . . shown great fortitude . . . a great feeling of love for our people," etc., etc., it got to the nitty gritty:

> *"You are drafted into the Black Panther Party; invested with the rank of Field Marshall, and delegated the following authority, power and responsibility:*
>
> *To establish revolutionary law, order and justice in the territory lying between the Continental Divide, east to the Atlantic Ocean, north of the Mason-Dixon Line to the Canadian Border; and south of the Mason-Dixon Line to the Gulf of Mexico.*
>
> *So let it be done."*

Happily for Stokely, no deadline was attached. But we teased him mercilessly. "Man, you need any help? I got me a week free. We could do it then."

And the Party: Even before Huey's absence, the organization had begun to be beset by an onrush of events which advanced with the escalating up-and-down velocity of a runaway roller coaster. Their "armed propaganda" had succeeded in gaining the media's attention, but that same media was rapidly becoming a double-edged sword, since the Party now had to cope with an ongoing crisis of identity in its unforgiving glare. Add to that, the increasingly fuzzy distinction between friend and foe. There were, on the enemy side, constant rumors of police assassination plots about to come down, and while they did not yet know it, various thug elements of the federal government were preparing their own illegal initiatives of a truly vicious nature. And then there was the kindness of friends, the entangling, distracting, hardly disinterested embrace of the *Ramparts* editors and the new orgiastic white Left.

In the year between the shooting and the trial's ending, an unbelievable amount had happened. The shooting had generated much national press and Bobby and Eldridge, working closely with *Ramparts*, had generated even more. In rapid succession new chapters mushroomed, one a month. Seattle, Des Moines, Los Angeles, New York, Detroit, New Jersey, Chicago.

So much so fast, it must have been hard to contemplate it all, and especially for Huey, from his solitary confinement. In December, just about when Huey is coming out of the hospital, the Party announces a coalition with the Peace and Freedom Party, an almost completely white radical group committed to electoral politics. Does or can a revolutionary "vanguard party" do bourgeois elections? (Ultimately Eldridge will run for President on this ticket, but by the time of the election in November 1968, he is already in exile. Other Panthers—Seale, Kathleen Cleaver, and Newton himself—will also be candidates for local offices in this alliance.)

But as though to balance that ideologically puzzling "coalition" with the white left, a merger is announced two months later, this one with the opposite, with SNCC, the architects and apostles of "revolutionary" Black Power. You go figure. In any event, three SNCC leaders are commissioned into the Party and a central committee established to give unified national leadership and direction in Huey's absence. This central committee (given their official titles Cabinet may have been a more appropriate term) was comprised as follows: Bobby Seale, Chairman; David Hilliard, Chief of Staff, and the Ministries: Newton, Defense; Cleaver, Information; Emory Douglas, Culture; Kathleen Cleaver, Secretary of Communication; and Huey's older brother Melvin, Minister Without Portfolio. The SNCC ministers are: James Forman, Foreign Affairs; Stokely Carmichael, Prime Minister, and H. Rap Brown, Justice.

But what sat underneath this glittery array of "national" leadership? One immediate consequence of the two, so apparently incompatible "alliances," was that just about all public radical political activity in the Bay Area, and on most college campuses, *not* directed against the Vietnam War, was directed into the "Free Huey" campaign. The Party's visibility and its membership grew, but with very few controls and negligible screening. There simply was no mechanism that could do this, so the Party chapters tended to take on a characteristic essentially local and reflective of their community's recent political history and experience. Chicago was very different from New York, New York from Los Angeles, etc.

But a general profile of the national membership had certain commonalities indicative of the distressing social experience of too many young black men in all urban centers. Precisely because the recruits represented the "militant" and defiant elements of the male community, the vast majority of them had some unfortunate prior relationship with the criminal justice system: juvenile or adult records, parole, probation, cases pending, etc. (True in 1968, and more so now, of some sixty percent of black males between the age of fifteen and twenty-five in any given urban center.) Besides which, many younger Panthers were the product of gangs, many were high school dropouts, and a significant number of the older ones had seen military service—The draft then being very much in effect in America's ghettoes.

Then, too, the Party's Eighth Point (freedom for all black men in jails) had two effects. The first had been the Party's second, and most popular community activity, the prison visitation program. They had sponsored regularly scheduled buses going from the Bay Area communities to various correctional facilities around the state, enabling families to visit their members in jail, often for the first time. This led also to what critics called a "romanticization of the lumpen," the notion of the black inmate as political prisoner. Previous incarceration, rather than an impediment to membership, was then a badge of honor.

■   ■   ■

With many of their numbers being already in the toils of "the authorities," the constituency was particularly vulnerable to being "turned" and the organization almost defenseless against the infiltration that was sure to follow on the heels of its heightened visibility. In fact, by the trial's opening in July of 1968, that infiltration was in process. A field report from one of what the FBI was pleased to call its "Racial Intelligence" units was puzzled that the Party seemed "unaware or unconcerned with the possibility of infiltration." The author appeared personally insulted that, on the contrary, they baldly "announced their activity and intentions on television programs and in their

Black Panther newspaper." Hey, the Bureau were not the only ones puzzled by this cavalier attitude. So were a lot of us.

Mike Thelwell remembers:

My first "real" encounter with "West Coast" Panthers came in the spring of 1968 at the New York SNCC office.

There I spent a day rapping politics with four young brothers from the Bay Area who made an indelible impression on me. As I recall one was recently out of jail, another, a reformed small-time dealer on probation, worried whether he should call his probation officer to explain his absence. Clearly up til now their lives had been dead end. Once seeing themselves as losers on the margins of the community, facing futures as burdens if not predators on that community, they were now its warriors and its defenders. They carried themselves with respect and a new sense of manhood. One could not help but be as touched by this—obviously new—self-pride, as by their sincerity in their sense of mission. They would now serve the people, and from that purpose their life took meaning, clearly for the first time.

The longer we talked, the more I liked them. They must have liked me, too, because before I left they tried to recruit me. "It's brothers like you we need to edit the paper, man." For a second, but only a brief second and only because of them, I was tempted. They seemed so young, so earnest, so excited. That was why I could not share with them certain deep reservations I harbored about the crazy political irresponsibility of the paper's editorial posture. Wanting no part of it, I made a lame excuse and we parted.

It could not have been a week later that my worst fears were confirmed. I observed two grim-faced head-breakers of the paramilitary tactical police force which New York had created to prevent or suppress ghetto uprisings, sitting in a parked patrol car on 125th Street most intently reading a newspaper. Even for TPF types their expressions were uncommonly bellicose. So much so, that I bought the paper to see just what could have so exercised the two. It wasn't at all hard to find—the Minister of Defense's Executive Mandate #3, in all the imperious grandiloquence of its prose, and the demented logic of its legalism:

"So let this be heard:

Because of the St. Valentine's Day Massacre of February 14, 1926, in which outlaws donned the uniforms of police and gained entrance to locked doors . . . history teaches us that a man in uniform may or may not be a policeman authorized to enter the houses of people."

It then describes midnight raids on the Cleaver and Seales homes by "uniformed gestapos and white men in plain clothes bearing an assortment of shotguns, rifles and service revolvers" but no search warrants. Therefore, "they had no authority to enter, what they did have was the power of the gun."

"On the basis of these two incidents we are convinced the situation is critical. Our organization has received serious threats. . . . We must be alert to the danger at all times. Therefore, those who approach our doors in the manner of outlaws; who seek to enter our houses illegally, unlawfully and in a rowdy fashion; those who kick our doors down will henceforth be treated as outlaws, as gangsters, as evil doers.

"We draw the line at the threshold of our doors. It is therefore mandated as a general order that all members must acquire the technical equipment to defend their homes and their dependents and shall do so. *Any member having such equipment and who fails to defend his threshold shall be expelled from the Party for life.*

So let this be done."

I read it in amazement with a shrinking spirit and a growing despair that turned into fury. The characterization of police behavior as arrogant and illegal was almost certainly accurate. But so what? What crazed megalomania could possess leaders to jeopardize their followers by publishing that order where it was certain to be read by those same "pigs?" And what about the four political naifs who had been so proud of their new vision? They had impressed me as being willing to do anything rather than be expelled from that newfound community of respect. And whether or not they obeyed the order to "acquire the technical equipment," the police would—if those TPF faces were any indication—henceforth be acting as if they had. In their place I know I certainly would. As an act of political judgment and leadership the publication of Executive Mandate #3 struck me as criminally irresponsible.

We cannot ignore the Panther's contributions to the vocabulary of popular political discourse. Most observers agree that it is undistinguished, their poetic inclinations tending heavily toward street invective directed to the "Pig power structure," an early version of the contemporary rap artist.

But some of their populist exhortatory verse did achieve a certain expressiveness:

> "Seize the Time! Power to the People, cause
> the power of the people is greater
> than the man's technology."

Or sometimes even an allusive poetic ambiguity, as in:

> "Land to the landless
> Industry to the worker
> Blood to the horse's brow
> and death to the oppressor."

Blood to the Horse's brow? Well now, never you mind. The panthers of wrath are indeed wiser than the horses of instruction.

But their most original contributions to the language of political disparagement were reserved for internal consumption. On the right pole, the term of choice needs no interpretation. "running dog comprador bourgeois opportunist motherfucker" is pretty explicit. The originality came in the phrasing, the style. It had to be said just right, in one breath like a single word, and with the right cadence, thus: Runnin-dowg-comprador-bourgeoise-opportunis-*motha-fuckah*." The type this term discribed was rare, however, because the Party's image, posture, and program did not afford fertile ground for anyone seeking to hustle a movement for personal or professional advancement in the wider society.

The other pole, the political type known as the Jackanape, was unfortunately much more common. This term, more correctly the "renegade Jackanape," was Huey's, retrieval to describe the source of a recurring problem: the custeristic undisciplined, adventuristic "gorilla" whose antics endangered everyone. The "nape" saw himself as a "true" revolutionary but came on as an intimidator, always trying to "bogart" down the brothers or "gorilla" a sister for some pussy.

The classic Jackanape action: four Panthers pull a clearly marked Party van into a service station. As they gas up, one leaves ostensibly for the men's room and fails to return. His three unsuspecting companions are astonished to see the dude sticking up the attendant. As are the cops who arrest all of them.

All the key elements of Jackanape attitude and rhetoric are neatly captured in the following from the Panther newspaper of August 1969.

"A dead Pig is desirable, but a paralyzed Pig is preferable to a mobile Pig. And a determined revolutionary doesn't require any authorization from a Central Committee before offing a Pig. . . .

[In fact] when the need arises, a true revolutionary will off the Central Committee.

The inspirational words of Eldridge Leroy Cleaver, soon-to-be diplomat, writing in 1969 from the security of exile.

■　　　■　　　■

There was no way all or any of this could possibly end well, or so it seemed to us. It was as predictable as tragedy. The only question was cost: how bloody, how destructive? And why could not the Panther leadership see the signs? Or did they? At times they seemed to court, even welcome, apocalypse, what with their almost gleeful evocations of urban warfare and later the curious notion of "revolutionary suicide."

But this is not to suggest that the story turns simply on character, or human frailty. Had the leaders only been wiser and more experienced, more prudent in action and restrained in utterance, less macho and doom-eager—in a word, more *political*—then the end would have been otherwise. Not so. It is clear that by the time Gil Moore got off the plane, the terms had been set, the script written, roles cast, and the players, lines committed to memory, were in their places awaiting their cues.

■　　　■　　　■

Even though Moore's book remains the single most valuable record we have of the dynamics of the trial, there is beyond those walls an enveloping national context which bears heavily on the courtroom events, and on the Party's subsequent fate. In fact, outside of which, this incredible tale would have been not only impossible, but quite inconceivable.

1968, truly an *annus horribilis,* had opened with a rapid succession of psychic shocks to the national spirit. Abomination followed atrocity in the media as toxins long festering beneath society's skin erupted into visible stinking ulcers on the body politic. This engendered a mood of national trauma which will be suggested by just a few of the events in the six months preceding the trial's opening. What is most important to remember about this surrealistic sequence is that each succeeding event became, in the new electronic intimacy of television's global village, a collective experience assaulting the nation's sense of reality. Americans were bombarded daily with images of disaster, and moral disorder. The national sense of reality was skewered. The center, which seemed to be shifting, could not hold, or so it appeared.

It began in Vietnam, on the eve of Tet, at daybreak, when thousands of little brown men in black pajamas wrote a symbolic end to the technological arrogance represented by the United States' intervention in their country. They materialized as if by magic, everywhere and anywhere, without the slightest warning, inside U.S. bases, on airport runways, inside the U.S. embassy grounds, in hundreds of short, fierce, bloody, dramatic firefights, and then they were gone. The Tet Offensive took not an inch of territory, but was the most final of statements: this war, massive deployment of U.S. military technology notwithstanding, was not winnable. Little brown indomitable Victor Charlie proved that in his country, he could go where he wanted, when he wanted, and the greatest armed force the world had ever seen could not prevent him. After Tet, the war was psychologically over, all the rest was bombast, compensation, and face-saving. So we escalated the military effort with predictable results.

Thus, on March sixteenth in a hamlet call My Lai, a platoon of young, spiritually exhausted American fighting men shot and killed 504 unarmed villagers without reference to age, sex, or noncombatant status. The dead included 182 women, 173 children, 60 elderly folk, and 89 men. Attempts by the military command to cover up the massacre failed. That May, American students, outraged by the escalation in response to Tet, closed campuses across the nation.

But even before that, in Memphis, Tennessee, on April fourth, the murder of Martin Luther King, Jr., had marked for black youth, a bitter and ironic punctuation to the end of the nonviolent era, and, nation-wide, cities erupted. But Oakland did not.

Bobby Seale, who had gone to ground after persistent rumors of a planned police assassination had seemingly been confirmed by an ex-cop, came in from the cold. In a dramatic press conference from, of all places, police headquarters, he detailed the alleged plot against the Panthers while appealing to the community not to riot but to organize. Oakland does not erupt and Seale and the Party are credited by the Mayor's Office and the press with maintaining calm in the city.

Yet, the next day, on the morning of April sixth, the disputed shootout in which three cars full of Panthers are outnumbered and engaged by a heavily armed police detail takes place. Cleaver is wounded and arrested, and brave, faithful Lil Bobby Hutton, the first recruit, becomes the first martyr. He was seventeen, still not old enough to own a handgun, legally.

Responding to news of King's murder, a visibly horrified Bobby Kennedy had challenged the nation to "ask ourselves just what kind of people are we?" To the day, two months later, live on national television, apparently en route to his party's nomination after a crucial primary victory in California, Kennedy would receive, in a burst of handgun fire, an answer with the brutal finality of murder.

The effect of this rapid-fire sequence of "historical" events dispensed by the media on the atmosphere of the times can scarcely be exaggerated, and needs to be understood. It is common now to hear that "the Panthers were a creation of the media." Which is of course true, and at the same time so glib and facile as to be almost meaningless. First, the Black Panthers existed on two planes, and on their most important—or at least most public—plane of existence, *everything* was a creation of the media. Then also, there are two mediums involved here, that of the establishment and its antithesis, the media of the rebellion, or "counterculture." The second was the consequence, and ironic mirror, of the first, and the Panthers the creature and victim of both.

But more important, it was not only the Black Panthers, but also a countervailing national reality—or wholesale perception of reality—that was being *constructed* by this new electronic presence in ways never previously thought possible, except perhaps in the pages of science fiction. Something fundamental and unprecedented had entered the equation.

And what was different for this generation was quite simply the omnipresence of television. American youth from all regions, races, and classes, whatever their particular circumstances in city, hamlet, or suburb, were the first American generation to share equally, to participate with an intimacy and immediacy never before possible, in a secondary and ultimately superseding level of reality. There was, for the first time, a truly national "experience," the *only* experience in which they *all* shared equally.

Having cut its teeth in social reporting on the Army—McCarthy hearings—"Have you no decency at all, Senator?"—and having its adolescent education in the Southern Civil Rights Movement, television, now grown to adulthood, could deploy its newly acquired technical proficiency to "the Nam." By that time it was no longer merely relaying back unfolding events, it was, by its simple presence, *changing* them, and by its selection and emphases conditioning the audience's perception of social "reality."

Naturally it wasn't long before the subjects—the military, the politicians, the activists—sensing the power of this new presence, learned to design actions and situations almost entirely for the purpose of enlisting that power to their own ends.

The political media event was born: an ostensibly "real" occurrence, but one which anticipated and required the presence of the medium for the realization of its meaning and purpose.

On one level the March on Washington was conceived as a media event, and became a "national experience." So, improbably enough, were the Tet Offensive and the Kennedy assassinations. And later, the entire public persona (perhaps his private one, too) and the presidency of Ronald Reagan—as with (to borrow a phrase, the Mother of all Media Events) Mr. Bush's Desert Storm—was scripted, directed and performed, entirely made for television.

(Later, on the other hand, something like Mr. Reagan's Star Wars, (as with some aspects of Panther behavior,) represented precisely the opposite: the absurd, impossible attempt to reverse the process and impose media values—the technologically synthesized "reality" of the video arcade—on the real world.)

Huey P. Newton, belonging to the first generation of Americans so conditioned, thought instinctively in those terms, as did the other activists of the "youth" movements of the late sixties. But what of the other white kids, the more passive recipients of this new dispensation? They were shocked out of the complacency of the Eisenhower years by the images of turmoil, domestic poverty, racial oppression, being transmitted nightly by the media. Suddenly the great myths of the mainstream, with their unifying homilies of national identity, seemed bankrupt.

Their parents' warm cocoon of avoidance denied them, feeling naked and abandoned, they retreated into a tantrum of public rejection of adult political culture that was, in its stridency and outrage, the exact measure of their previous condition of ignorance and innocence.

The media was not helpful in this generational trauma. You can't trust anyone over thirty, after all. With its insatiable appetite for novelty and sensation, the media contributed to the prevailing confusion by proceeding to proclaim a bewildering succession of "revolutions," "cultures," and "movements," each more unsubstantial and faddist than the last. They enunciated drug, rock, hippie, youth, and a generic counter "culture." They gave us sexual, ecological, moral, and spiritual "revolutions," and "speech" movements—free as well as filthy, as well as the peace and ubiquitous youth "movements." You can supply those I must have forgotten.

The truth is that none were revolutions, nor could they have been, nor were they, in any sense previously consecrated by human use, *cultures*, and only a few were movements. They were in the media's projection, instant and disposable, the stuff of packaging, consumerism, and fashion, and of the medium's pernicious and promiscuous debasement of language, and ultimately of reality.

Unless we understand, or at least are able to visualize this psychic environment of debased reality, the fecund growth culture in which the Party took root, then the American tragedy of the Panthers is both unbelievable and meaningless.

But the event with the most sinister and far-reaching implications for our story was not public, but had to be, by its very nature, secret.

In august of '67, John Edgar Hoover had initiated within the FBI a clandestine program to "expose, disrupt, misdirect, discredit or *otherwise neutralize* . . . (emphasis added) Black nationalist hate-type organizations . . . their leadership, spokesmen, membership and supporters." The targets had included among the usual suspects even the very churchly Southern Christian Leadership Conference of Dr. King. But, in a March 1968 directive, these would be updated to include prominently the now very visible Black Panther Party, mentioning by name Newton, Seale, and Cleaver.

The directive's language is revealing in what it suggests about the preoccupations and sensibility of its author, presumably the director. In other less lethal circumstances, there would be an aspect of low comedy in the following from a pederast of Hoover's widely reported propensities:

> *"In seeking effective counter-intelligence, it should be borne in mind that the two things foremost in the militant Negro's mind are sex and money. The first is promiscuous and frequently shared. White moral standards do not apply among this type of Negro. You do not embarrass many Negroes by exposing their sexual activity or low morals."*

On the other hand, the director discloses:

> *"Money is not as frequently shared* [so much for their socialist rhetoric] *. . . and this offers a continuing opportunity to sow seeds of distrust and suspicion."*

The document concludes with a rhetorical militance worthy of a Cleaver.

> *"Negro youth and moderates must be made to understand that if they succumb to revolutionary teaching they will be dead revolutionaries."* (Later, picking up on the directorial insight on black cupidity, the New Orleans FBI would suggest that a *"fictitious bank account record"* in Newton's name be created with the help

of a *"cooperative"* bank. Then a statement showing *"regular, sub-stantial deposits over years and a large balance"* be anonymously mailed to Panther headquarters. There is no indication of whether or not this suggestion was ever implemented.)

Thereafter, on the evidence of their own files, the Bureau's behavior was a curious combination of adolescent cruelty and excess, stupidity and a viciousness that seemed designed to validate even the most extreme Panther rhetoric. Indeed, given the government's subsequent actions, Panther evocations of "white racist Gestapo police" and the "low-lifed swinishness" of the "Pig power structure," hardly appear the exaggerations they at first seemed.

The Bureau's counterintelligence program—CO-INTEL-PRO—was massive, ruthless, and lawless, and by July of 1969, the Black Panther Party had become its prime target among Blacks. The program was coordinated with local police, and one result was that from March of 1967 to December of 1969, seven hundred and thirty-nine party members—more than one a day—were arrested on various charges. The cumulative bail would amount to four and one-half million dollars. Coincidence? The original directive of 1967 boasts an example of this strategy. Since it is impossible to identify the organization or city we cannot evaluate their claims of having averted "violence."

> *"The X group was active in* <u>BLACKED OUT.</u> *in the Summer of 67. _____ alerted local police, who put X leaders under close scrutiny. They were arrested on every possible charge until they cold no longer make bail. As a result X's leaders spent the summer in jail and no violence traceable to X took place."*

Of the thousands of disruptive suggestions generated internally, the Bureau admits to having initiated two hundred and ninety-five against "black nationalist" groups. Of this number, two hundred and thirty-three were directed against the Panthers, and these are only the ones to which the Bureau has admitted. The full extent to which they ultimately descended in this ugly little domestic war may never be known.

While bemoaning the inadequacy of their funding—*"The problems facing the country demand a much greater concentration of talent, time and money than one agency with its efforts spread so thin can afford [and] the Bureau does not have enough agents, enough concentration . . . or enough money to ensure foreknowledge of what is likely to occur"*— the document still managed to project a very ambitious program. This called for the formation of "squads" specifically targeted at the Black Panther Party in thirty of its field offices. Each squad was to develop a minimum of five informants within the Party.*

Whether or not their straitened circumstances permitted an intervention on the grandiose scale the Director envisioned isn't clear, but what they were able to stretch their impoverished resources to achieve was shameful enough.

Years later a Senate Committee on intelligence activity—the Church Committee—was to find it:

> "deplorable that officials of the United States Government should engage in the activities discussed. . . . Equally disturbing is the pride which those officials took in the bloodshed that occurred.
>
> The committee also found that "many of the techniques used would be intolerable in a democratic society *even if* all targets had been engaged in violent activity. But COINTELPRO went far beyond that."

* (Researchers have identified sixty informants in Panther offices nation-wide.)

I am not aware that any of the officials whose "intolerable" techniques so offended senatorial sensibilities were ever called to account for any of the crimes committed in the name of this government.

And, what was the nature of the "bloodshed" of which these government agents were so prideful? Well, in one instance, two Panthers—John Huggins and Alprentice "Bunchy" Carter— were shot to death in a cafeteria on the UCLA campus. Three young black men—the Stiner brothers and Claude Hubert, all members of US, a cultural nationalist group—were charged with their murders. Simply, as the press suggested, another ghetto turf war between youthful gangsters under cloak of nationalist politics, right? Dead wrong.

US was, of course, the cultural nationalist grouping under the domination of one Malauna Ron Karenga. The Panthers say that the UCLA students had requested their support in preventing US taking over the Black Studies program being established, hence the Campbell Hall meeting.* What neither the Panthers, the UCLA students, or US could have known was the content of certain FBI correspondences in the two months preceding that meeting.

On October 31, the Director had telegraphed the Los Angeles office: *"Your suggestion to capitalize on Black Panther Party differences with Karenga are appealing and could result in a US and Black Panther Party vendetta."* On November 25, the Director informs certain field offices that *"a serious struggle is taking place between the Black Panther Party and the US organization. The struggle has reached such proportions that it is taking on the aura of gang warfare with the attendant threat of murder and reprisal. . . . In order to fully capitalize on these*

---

* After this inordinately melancholy beginning, the UCLA Africana Studies Program has developed into one of the more productive and academically distinguished of such programs in the country.

differences," the Director solicits *"imaginative and hard-hitting counterintelligence measures . . ."* With what effect, we shall soon see.

Also, in December of 1969 there appears to have been a coordinated FBI plan to decimate the leadership in at least three cities we know about—Oakland, Los Angeles, and Chicago.

On December 3, a Chicago apartment was raided, hundreds of shots were poured in and two young men slain in their sleep. On December 8, the Los Angeles Party office and four apartments occupied by members were simultaneously raided. Alerted by the Chicago killings and led by Geronimo Pratt, the L.A. offices resisted and a lengthy, fierce firefight ensued. There were wounded on both sides but only one fatality, that of a police officer, before the Panthers—in the presence of the media and community, which likely saved their lives—were able to surrender. Eighteen of them were arrested.

On December 10th, the Party lawyer, Charles R. Garry, warned by an anonymous caller of an impending raid on the Oakland office, called a press conference, thereby, or so said an FBI "intelligence gatherer" in the Party, preventing that assault.

In Los Angeles, one Darthard Perry, a man with four aka's, an inmate i.d. number, and an FBI code name of Othello, claims to be able to shed some light on these events.

In a sworn deposition he claims to have been recruited as an "intelligence gatherer" in the fall of 1968, with duties "to observe and inform on" the Party's activities in Los Angeles. He names his controllers in the Bureau: Special Agent Brendan Cleary, who must have been "squad" chief because he is identified as being "in charge of black radicals" in the L.A. office and the other agents who directed "Othello," Michael Quinn and William Otto Heaton, are identified as reporting to Cleary.

For his services "Othello" was paid one hundred dollars in cash every fortnight, but he reports that *"by 1975, I was receiving approximately $2,400 per month. Customarily, I would call Cleary using the name Othello and would arrange to meet in an arbitrary location."*

On his role in the Los Angeles raids, Othello contributes this account:

> *"I participated in gathering the layout of the Panther office in L.A., located at 4115-1/2 Central Avenue, plus for three simultaneous raids on three or four apartments. These raids occurred on December 8 and resulted in the trial known as the Los Angeles 18 Trial. It was my work, and the work of known informer Melvin "Cotton" Smith, which caused the raid to happen."*

However, it is his deposition concerning the killing of Huggins and Carter in the UCLA cafeteria that is most interesting. He recounts in telling detail that:

> *"On or about the seventeenth of January, 1969, I was told to go to the University of California campus at Los Angeles and observe the activities in the cafeteria at Campbell Hall.*
>
> *I arrived there in the late morning and observed many members of the Black Panther Party and the US organization present in the room as well as other people not identified with either organization.*
>
> *I observed the situation in the cafeteria, which seemed to be nothing more than a meeting, and left for a short time to go to a parking lot located near the building. The parking lot is reached by proceeding down a pathway, across a street, and then to the parking lot.*
>
> *Shortly after my arrival in the parking lot I heard shots from the direction of Campbell Hall.*
>
> *Within a few minutes I observed George Stiner, Larry Stiner, and Claude Hubert, also known as Chuchessa, jump into a 1967 or 1968*

light tan or white four-door Chevrolet driven by Brandon Cleary of the Federal Bureau of Investigation.

I recognized George Stiner, Larry Stiner, and Claude Hubert from seeing them prior to this date on the fourteenth floor of the Federal Bureau of Investigation building on several occasions in the company of Brandon Cleary, the man I had seen drive them away from the Campbell Hall area.

I had been told to give a report within twenty-four hours of the incident to my supervising agent, Will Heaton, on the fourteenth floor of the Wilshire Boulevard Federal Bureau of Investigation building.

A few hours later I went to the building and met with my supervising agent, Will Heaton. While in his company I observed George Stiner, Larry Stiner, and George Hubert in the company of Brandon Cleary on the fourteenth floor of the Federal Bureau of Investigation Building. I asked Cleary "what was happening" and was told that there had been a "fuck-up—no one was to be killed by 'our' people . . .

Through information and belief, I have knowledge that George Stiner, Larry Stiner, and Claude Hubert were Intelligence Gatherers for the Federal Bureau of Investigation and were working for Brandon Cleary and others when John Jerome Huggins and Alprentice "Bunchy" Carter were murdered."

The two Stiners and Hubert were convicted. At their trial, they say nothing to implicate the Bureau. Shortly after their incarceration, California penal authorities claim not to be able to protect them from Panther partisans in the prison population, which could well have been true. What follows, though, is . . . well, thought-provoking. The three are transferred out of maximum security San Quentin to a minimum security prison camp from which they "walk away"; they have never been seen since. Echoes of the old witness protection program and new government supplied identities? Or shades of poor "disappeared" Jimmy Hoffa?

■   ■   ■

From all accounts, the most promising and impressive of the
Panther field generals was a young man in Chicago named Fred
Hampton. This twenty-year-old seems to have had an uncom-
monly inspiring effect on ordinary people, young and old.

A former NAACP youth leader, Hampton was smart, disciplined, politically clear, highly articulate, and deeply, deeply
committed. His personal magnetism was such that he was able
to build in Chicago the Party's only mass-based organization
that was deeply rooted in the community. (Their Secretary of
Defense Bobby Rush is now a United States Congressman.)

He was skillful enough to negotiate his way around an early
FBI trap intended to incite a war between the fledgling Panther organization and the heavily armed, two-thousand-soldier
strong, Blackstone Rangers. It was later revealed by an ex-cop
that the police feared the Party's political direction of that
youthful army. "They didn't want that head to hook up with
that body."

Indeed, Hampton and Rush displayed remarkable diplomatic talent, putting together a nascent "rainbow coalition" out
of Chicago's ethnic enclaves, at least among the young people.
They had established warm, functioning alliances with the
Young Lords, an organization of Hispanic youth, a white Appa-
lachian group called the Young Patriots, and even had correct
to cordial relationships with the by now fiercely ideological
young middle-class radicals of SDS, even though in Hampton's
memorable phrase, he found them somewhat too "Custeristic."
They celebrated their "rainbow" with buttons displaying its
various colors and one slogan in particular that evokes the later
poetic style of Jacksonian "political doggerel." The Panthers
say,

"White power to white people
Black power to black people
Brown power to brown people
and Panther power to the People's Vanguard."

Under Hampton's leadership the organization's membership grew and its influence expanded—and not only among the young people. They engaged problems of housing, ran a free-breakfast-for-schoolchildren program, a medical clinic, and even encouraged voter registration. Hampton was increasingly trusted and admired, and, in fact, beloved, across lines of age and class within the community in a way that no other Panther figure ever was.

On December 3, after an early-morning police raid on their apartment which was orchestrated by the FBI, Fred Hampton —aged twenty, shot in the arm, shoulder and twice in the head —and Mark Clark, leader of the Peoria chapter—shot through the heart and lungs—were pronounced dead on arrival at the hospital.

The fifth member recruited had been a nineteen-year-old named William O'Neal. A slightly built youth with a sensitive face and thoughtful manner of speaking, O'Neal's militancy and commitment sufficiently impressed his colleagues so that he was named Chief of Security. However, O'Neal had been instructed by the FBI to join and was one of several informants in the Chicago Panthers. He presents himself as having been naive, impressionable, and with a poor self-image.

"I grew up wanting to be a policeman, admiring and respecting policemen, although I'd always thought it was outside my reach." At eighteen he had stolen a car for joyriding, been traced and faced the prospect of jail for "grand theft, auto." But Special Agent Ray Mitchell assured him that it "could be worked out." And suddenly "I was working undercover for the

FBI, doing something good for the finest police organization in America. So I felt pretty proud. . . . We had very few role models back then—Malcolm X . . . Martin Luther King . . . Mohammed Ali, and I had an FBI agent."

So when his "role model" asked him (like Othello in Los Angeles) to diagram the floor plan of Hampton's apartment, the young security captain was pleased to comply. After the murders he felt "betrayed," not having thought that "anyone, and especially Fred, was to be killed." More to the point, he felt used and "expendable" since he, having been in the apartment earlier on the night, "could have been caught in the raid and probably could have been a victim."

On December 8 someone in the Chicago field office, presumably his "role model" Mitchell, requested a special bonus for O'Neal in recognition for "information of considerable value." On December 11, the request had to be repeated. But, on that same day, dispite the Bureau's material poverty the Director generously authorized "a special payment of $300 over and above authorized levels of payment for uniquely valuable service . . ."

Interesting figure, that three hundred dollars. One wonders how it was arrived at, the biblical thirty pieces of silver adjusted for inflation? In 1982, however, the various agencies involved had to make a somewhat larger settlement (1.85 million) in a suit on behalf of the survivors and families of the deceased.

O'Neal lived for twenty years under an assumed identity in the witness protection program. He surfaced to grant a lengthy on-camera interview-cum-confession, notable for the haunted expression which never left his eyes, to the producers of the P.B.S. series, *Eyes on the Prize*. In 1990, soon after the program aired nationally, he threw himself off a bridge into oncoming traffic.

August 5, 1968

Miraculously, almost unbelievably, one of the barrage of appeals launched by the indefatigable Charles Garry takes. Huey P. Newton is to walk out of the Oakland Courthouse a free man. The waiting crowd is huge, exultant, almost frenzied in the excitement of their moment of triumph.

After the years of unceasing effort, they, the people, had freed their icon, the international symbol of their struggle. A Free Huey is the proof—no, more than that, the very incarnation of the power of the people's will. They surge forward wanting to see, hear, and touch him.

But the people triumphant is in turn almost surrounded by large number of armed, helmeted, sullen policemen with batons in hand. The police, barely controlling their anger and obviously looking for an excuse, press roughly in on the people who, on that of all days, will not be moved.

Accompanied by four Party leaders, the good-looking son of the preacher man stepped out into the bright sunlight, into greater and more complex pressures than he could have imagined, and an immediate danger of a kind he had not faced in prison. Hilliard and Hewitt understood the danger first: if—no, when, the shooting starts they, and especially Huey, will be the first targets.

"Huey, this is bad, man. You gotta talk to the people. Git them to disperse quick. Tell them there's a victory rally at the Park. (Renamed for the martyred "Lil" Bobby Hutton.)

"Is there one planned?"

"Never mind that, we can explain later."

"I'm not going to lie to the people, brother."

"Man, look around you . . . it's gonna be bloodshed, man. These people ain't gonna take no shit today."

"I can't mislead the people. I won't do that."

"We can explain later. . . . I'll explain."

So Newton climbs on a car, removes his shirt and opens his arms as though embracing the people, and thanks them. They say that in that moment his face is transfigured, shining with a radiance "like a prophet." Chanting militant slogans of struggle and victory, the people march away, not to a victorious rally but to an explanation. It is a little anticlimactic. Huey had told his first lie to the people . . . a little white one . . . to avert bloodshed.

■   ■   ■

Freedom, coming at the time it did for the young man, was no easy road. Indeed, it might have been the worst thing that could have happened for him in those circumstances. In prison he had been relatively secure, enjoying the protection of his fame and that of a brotherhood of hard, resolute, and disciplined men. These were the disciples of George Jackson, an inmate of almost mythic reputation, held in near reverence by young black prisoners across the nation.

Outside, the world and Newton's expected role in it, had in three short years changed beyond recognition. The Party had not only become national, but international. He did not know most of the new local leaders across the country or the temper of the rank and file to whom he, in turn, was merely a face on a poster, a name and a myth.

It is undoubtedly this isolation from his constituency, a certain hubris and the rarified atmosphere of pure ideology—readings sent him in prison by supporters—that led to the first tactical mistake of August 29.

But the daily nitty-gritty was more than he could have anticipated: dangerous, unpredictable, confusing, and demanding of attention. A fierce domestic war was in progress. The seven days on either side of his release date will suggest the enormity of what he inherited.

On August 3, two days prior to his release, three Panther offices in Philadelphia had come under police siege. In two of the offices the Panthers resisted, returning the police fire, wounding three policemen, and holding out for hours before surrendering.

Then on August 7, two days after, seventeen-year-old Jonathan Jackson, youngest brother of the prison legend George, walked under arms into the Marin County Courthouse. There, the trial of three of his brother's "radicalized" black inmates is in progress. Jonathan manages to pass weapons to his brother's men, and the four take the judges, prosecutor, and three jurors hostage. In an ensuing shootout under FBI direction, police fire kills young Jackson, two inmates, and the judge.

Newton's first big public appearance is not the victory rally but the next best thing: a political funeral attended by thousands. There he preaches the eulogy for Jonathan Jackson and William J. Christmas, one of the slain inmate revolutionaries. It is possible to discern in the eulogy the rudiments of the principle of revolutionary suicide which is to become a dominant theme of his, and the title of his autobiography.

"They have achieved freedom while we remain slaves. The Black Panther Party will follow the examples of these brave revolutionaries. If the penalty for the quest for freedom is death, then by death we escape to freedom. . . . There is a big, even a revolutionary, difference between thirty million black people and thirty million black people armed to the teeth. We are not alone. . . . We find our comrades wherever in the world the people hear the oppressors' whips. All over the world people are rising up. The high tide of revolution is about to sweep the shores of America. A picture is worth a thousand words, but action is supreme. Our revolutionary comrades Jonathan Jackson and William J. Christmas have made the ultimate sacrifice."

There were other not so supreme sacrifices to be made. The most immediate problem for the Party—after the vexing question of a concrete day-to-day role for an icon who had been off the scene for three years—was the question of security. Huey would be a target, more so even than Martin or Malcolm and the Panthers were determined not to repeat that experience. They checked out the citadel residence of the head of the Hells Angels, but while the fortifications were impressive, police helicopters buzzed them throughout the tour. Finally, with the generous assistance of Burt Schneider, a sympathizer from the Hollywood film colony, they went to the opposite extreme. A penthouse apartment thirty stories above the lake was rented, there to secure the person of the minister by enlisting, as they thought, the round-the-clock security of the wealthy. After all, Charlie Findlay, owner of the Oakland Athletics, would be a neighbor, and "he won't tolerate no helicopter fly overs."

What was not envisioned was the possibility of other neighbors, less disinterested. A surveillance team from the FBI occupied the next apartment even before Newton was in residence. So for two tumultuous years, separated only by a thin wall, the Minister's closest neighbors were the "pigs." Commanding the most sophisticated eavesdropping devices their budget afforded, they would record, for posterity and at the expense of the heavily burdened taxpayers, every executive decision, political strategy, groan of pain, sigh of ecstasy, fart, or belch ensuing from the Minister's residence.

All politics may indeed be local, but there was also the international front to contemplate. And events there were almost unbelievable.

Only three months before he got out of the slammer, solidarity committees from seven European countries—West Germany, France, Denmark, Britain, Sweden, Holland, and Belgium—had called an international conference of solidarity with the Black Panther Party in Munich. A gigantic poster showing his face over the slogan "Free Huey" had smiled down on the proceedings.

Then, too, Eldridge, having quickly worn out his welcome in Cuba, had sought political asylum in Algeria, the soil, as it were, of the Motherland. There, for their doubtless excellent reasons, the revolutionary government had accorded the Black Panther Party the diplomatic status and credentials of a recognized national liberation front. What this meant in the diplomatic protocols of the Third World was quite astonishing. It meant that the Party he and Bobby had founded in the Oakland Poverty Center, now, after a mere four years of operation, had, if not the political *stature*, then at least a diplomatic *status* equal to everybody who was anybody in revolutionary struggle. With, for example, the front for National Liberation of Vietnam which had been in protracted people's war since 1947. Or with the African National Congress of South Africa which had been about black-folks business since 1911. One should never underestimate the power of the Western media, the interests it represents, and the curious effects it can have in the least expected places.

The government of Algeria made available a villa in which to house their diplomatic mission. Theoretically anyway, the erratic Mr. Cleaver would be enjoying the prerogatives of a diplomat, receiving delegations and sending messages in accordance with accepted protocol. And the Party thus recognized could petition for official delegations to such international bodies as the Organization of African Unity or even the United Nations. And Huey P. Newton, the acknowledged leader, even if at present mostly of a inspirational and symbolic kind, was, theoretically speaking, the equal of figures like Ho Chi Minh or Nelson Mandela. That might explain why, on August 29, three weeks after his release, he sent a fraternal communication to the Provisional Government of South Vietnam *and* their Front for National Liberation.

After the proper protocols the Minister informed the Front that:

> *"In the spirit of international revolutionary solidarity the Black Panther Party offers to the National Liberation Front and the Provisional Revolutionary Government of Vietnam an undetermined number of troops to assist you in your fight against American imperialism . . ."*

There is nothing to suggest anything other than that the vast majority of the Party's members were sincerely idealistic black youth, desperate to find some higher vision of their life's meaning and possibility than the stunted circumstances imposed on them by an uncaring society. In defense of that, they were to demonstrate time and again their willingness to do battle when necessary with forces of vastly superior paramilitary training and weaponry.

But that was always—a few provocateurs and Jackanapes aside—only in defense of themselves, their friends, their communities, and their Party. Many had relatives—some drafted, others more willing—in the U.S. Armed Services, which at that time meant, sooner or later, Vietnam. So there was naturally considerable confusion in their ranks on learning of the troop offer three weeks after Huey's coming out.

"Yo, bro, I don't speak no Vietnamese, do you? Is the Brother serious? Or he just messing with the honkies' minds? Perhaps the Minister has been in jail too long, man. Think it's that crazy

Eldridge playing revolutionary diplomat in Algeria? Could be, man."

Whatever its provenance, the offer leapt lightly over the yawning chasm separating ideological theory and fantasy from the concrete limits of brute reality. Cops rampaging through the neighborhood were one thing, but Vietnam? Possibly to fight your own relatives who had no more business there than did you, and very little choice?

But perhaps Nguyen Thi Dinh, Deputy Commander of the Liberation Armed Forces, understood this better than the Minister. Or more likely they both understood the offer to be merely ceremonial, the ritual exchange of fraternal compliments between equals, because Dinh's reply is a masterpiece of the form.

He professed to be deeply moved by the intention *"to send . . . an undetermined number of troops assisting us in our struggle against the U.S. imperialist aggressor."*

"This news was communicated to all cadres and fighters in the field; and all of us are delighted to get more comrades-at-arms, so brave as you, on the very soil of the United States."

There were *"sincere thanks for the warm support."* However, *"so are our thinkings: at present the struggles right in the U.S. or on the South Vietnam battlefields are both making contributions for national liberation and world peace. Therefore your persistent and ever developing struggle is the most active support to our resistance . . ."*

"With profound gratitude we take notice of your enthusiastic proposal; when necessary we shall call for your volunteers to assist us.

Best greetings for unity, militancy and complete victory."

This curious development had an even more inconceivable result: that of placing the venerable Roy Wilkins of the NAACP in full agreement with the militant black youth of the Panther rank and file possibly for the first time ever during that decade.

Wilkins, in an uncharacteristically wry response, had detailed the extent of black poverty and misery at home and wondered at Newton's commitments and priorities, concluding, dismissively, "Newton, an attractive and personable young man, is described . . . as the darling of white revolutionaries. It figures."

Nonetheless, three months later we find the brother still caught up in the language of international diplomacy, and sounding for all the world like a head of state.

In talks with the African National Congress:

"As you know we have offered troops to the Vietnamese people to show our solidarity . . . We have also made it clear that we would send or offer troops to any of our friends who will accept them. . . . We think the ultimate gesture of friendship is to send our comrades to shed blood on your soil in the name of freedom, and against the imperialist enemy. If there is anything else we can do, tell us and we shall consider it."

The young man sentenced to prison in 1968 was an infinitely complex being, holding in precarious balance within himself qualities of mind and emotion so opposed as to be not merely contradictory but impossible. On this all the people who knew him then are agreed.

Stokely Carmichael, even after being falsely denounced by him as a government agent, remembers a sincerity of commitment and a respectfulness, close to humility. David Du Bois' dominant impression is one of "complete honesty" and a "kind of delicacy," this despite recalling seeing him administer a brutal beating. Others will talk about principles so high as to appear a form of innocence. Yet during that same period others will shudder at the memory of a raving egomaniac given to bursts of violence and irrationality.

If an inexperienced youth went in, it was a full-blown legend that emerged from jail in 1970. And he emerged into the cauldron of a low-intensity domestic war; to the adulation, criticism, and challenges of leadership; the high visibility: the pleasures and pressures of American celebrity; to constant threats, plots and rumors of plots; and to an unrelenting campaign of surveillance, destabilization, disinformation, deceit, and the sowing of suspicion. Old friends had been murdered, others jailed; and the motives and loyalties of still others are constantly being called into question. They are denounced and expelled, for Huey, now frenetic, like the Red Queen, the refrain is a constant "off with their heads."

And security? What security? What does not unfold publicly in the omnipresence of the media is being closely monitored by the neighbors. And indeed, when the break with Cleaver finally comes, it is entirely consonant with Party history and practice, coming by way of a transatlantic phone conversation—"the man's technology." And, this highly sensitive political conversation between two prominent "revolutionaries" is broadcast *live over an Oakland radio station!*

From the other side of their common wall his FBI neighbors are able to report gleefully that:

> "It appears that Newton responds violently to any question of his actions or policies or reluctance to do his bidding . . . hastily, without getting the facts or consulting with others. . . . The Bureau feels that this hysterical reaction is triggered by criticism and their criticism is largely result of our counterintelligence projects."

Note:

> "Huey P. Newton has recently exhibited paranoid-like responses. His Hitler-like hysterical reaction, which has very likely been aggravated by our present counterintelligence activity has resulted in

the suspension of loyal Black Panther Party workers. It appears Newton is on the brink of mental collapse and we must intensify our counterintelligence." They done run that boy crazy. Yes, they did.

Huey had once "tried to transform many of the so-called criminal activities going on into the street into something political." Now the street element threatened to transform the political into "something criminal." He withdraws more and more into his penthouse aerie, ruling by decree and fiat, more and more dependent on a goon squad—official term, body guards —to enforce Party discipline, and on large quantities of Courvoisier and cocaine to get him through the days and nights. Crazy Huey.

When not acting out the preemptory imperiousness of a crazed Don Mafioso, he withdraws into yet another incompatible persona, that of the revolutionary intellectual, the theoretician, that bane of every political movement that ever was. Huey did become an otherworldly guru of abstract theoretical systems. But it is almost certainly a mischievous invention that in this persona, he once greeted a gathering in Upper Manhattan with the salutation, "Workers and Peasants of New York . . ." Mystical Huey.

But he officially repudiates Cleaver's crazed New Left adventurism and worship of the gun while trying to reverse the Party's "defection from the Black community." With the help of white philanthropy and contributions—some say extortion—of black businessmen, he launches survival programs. Free school breakfasts, medical care, occasionally clothes and shoes. He tries to found a shoe factory to employ ex-convicts, opens a school, and publicly reembraces the traditional values of the black community. When he speaks of the church, of the condition of the black male and other issues of black life, he is clear, rational, even moving. Sweet Huey.

Then, too, there is the ego-boosting: a triumphant ceremonial visit to the People's Republic of China: pictures with, the urbane Premier Chou En-Lai and with a smiling Samory Machel, President of FRELIMO, and future president of Mozambique, a radiant Huey with children at a nursery of a locomotive parts factory near Peking. Huey as Third World leader. He abandons the Ministry of Defense for the title Supreme Leader, which in turn is abandoned for the more humble and accurate Supreme Servant of the People.

Mike Thelwell remembers:

"It was in 1970—or whatever year the Cambodian invasion was. At an international conference in Kuwait, I saw a graphic illustration of the gulf between the Western media image of the romantic revolutionary as represented by the Panthers and the strikingly different reality of the Third World originals, or for that matter, of the Party "volunteers" for foreign service.

One morning I was puzzled and increasingly apprehensive at repeated congratulations from a succession of strangers for a television speech the previous evening, which I had not made. Even more disturbing was the response to my modest disclaimers.

"But we saw you. You're a Black Panther!"

The confusion resolved itself with the dramatic entrance of a Panther delegation led by Field Marshall Donald Cox—from the international mission in Algeria. ("D.C." and I were both bearded, light-skinned and wearing big Afros and American-style clothes so *ergo* to the local eye . . .) Of course the Field Marshall needed a security detail of about four young Panther "troops." In their paratrooper boots, fatigues and berets, and military bearing they made a stern, impressive appearance. Their revolutionary style as much as their virile, athletic young American physiques elicited many an admiring glance.

That morning's program was a report on the war from the National Liberation Front of Vietnam. My first "real" Viet Cong was not from central casting. In contrast to the Panthers, the Viet Cong representative was a diminutive, middle-aged, painfully thin man in a cheaply made, ill-fitting suit. He looked undernourished, even emaciated, and very frail. A depression in his face where a cheekbone should have been was, I assumed, courtesy of American explosives. Also, the damage to his face seemed to have misaligned his jaw, causing a permanent grin and a lisp. His English was rudimentary. His air of gentle distractedness caused me to wonder whether he were not a mite shell-shocked and sent on a diplomatic mission to recuperate In any event, there was nothing fierce or military in his appearance. Before the war he might have been a village schoolteacher.

The audience listened respectfully to a glowing report. Everything is going precisely according to plan. Oh, yes. The people's victory is assured. Oh, yes. Mainly a matter of time, and not much time at that." The serene assurance of his report is in sharp contrast to the lisping voice, gentle manner and fragile appearance.

A deep American voice begins with the obligatory courtesies of support, but is clearly skeptical. He wonders whether the speaker might have not been briefed on the massive bombing campaign and the forces being massed to invade Cambodia to interdict their supply lines, which was currently being reported in the U.S. press. Surely that will set back the struggle, prolong the war, impose more suffering and bloodshed? I thought I detected in the question an unconscious chauvinism, a very American resentment of the little man's casual dismissal of U.S. military power.

The speaker at first does not understand. He frowns. "My English is not so good. Please?" Then he does, his eyes light up, and the revolutionary actually giggles His tone is consoling.

"Oh, yes, yes. Thank you, please. Thank you, comrade. But please don't to worry. You will see. The imperialists they will have to leave more quick than they go." The head bobs emphatically, again the giggle and final little gesture of dismissal. "Oh, yes. You will see. The imperialists, they will have to run. Yes."

The audience exchange silent looks. Is the guy a little addled?

"What'd you think, man. Revolutionary bravado?" I ask Jim Turner of Cornell.

"I dunno, man. He seemed very sure."

"Yeah, but is it the usual revolutionary bullshit, man?"

After that, we talk with members of the Field Marshall's detail. They are glad to see brothers from home and soon we are deep in conversation.

The troops are young inner city kids. None admit to being under indictment so they, unlike the leadership, don't have to be here, they are volunteers, the "troops."

As we talk, a quite different ironic reality for the picturesque revolutionaries emerges. They turn out to be the most culture-shocked, homesick, displaced young black men I've ever met any-where outside of a prison.

They speak neither French nor Arabic, and typical young Ameri-cans, are not really comfortable with Islamic-Arab culture. Back home, before politics, they followed sports on TV, especially the NBA; shot a little hoop with their homeboys; got down with James Brown or Motown; maybe drank a little wine, smoked some reefer, and styled and grooved with their ladies. Know what I mean?

Now, though, apart from the entire region being Islamic, and more or less fundamentalist and puritan, there was the strict revo-lutionary discipline of the Party to deal with.

"So how you all gettin' on, brothers?" James Turner's voice is gentle with concern and the dam breaks. How much is myth and street legend?

"Tell the truth, man, it's weird. Can't do nothin', bro. They catch you with some herb and it's a life sentence. You can't do no wine, man, for the ko-ran forbid alcohol. An' the ladies, man? They ketch you messing with their daughter? They may drown *her* in the swimming pool, man. Or else bury her *alive* in the desert. Why? Cause the ko-ran forbid the shedding of the blood of family, man. But you? Shoot, they take yo' balls and leave you to bleed to death. Plus you can't speak the language, so how you to git any action? And the TV? Ain't nothing you wanna be watching, that is, if you could even understand the language."

The brother lapsed into a glum silence, his eyes doleful. Then the sad eyes brightened hopefully as an admiring group of young

English women—student radicals all—approached. Finally, a language the brothers could speak.

As we left them to their happier fate, James shook his head sadly. Those are about some very, very unhappy young brothers, Mike."

The troops.

About a week later, I'm walking through Kennedy Airport, returning from the conference. A *New York Times* headline and picture catch my eye. Two G.I.'s are dangling in midair from a helicopter runner in their desperate haste to get out of Cambodia.

Suddenly I again see the ravaged face, grinning, "You will see, please. The imperialists, they will go quicker than they come. Oh, yes!"

August 7, 1974. Oakland

Yet another crisis for Huey and the Party develops when in rapid succession, the Oakland police charge the Supreme Servant with two serious crimes, neither of which can be given even a remotely political spin. He is not able to leave the police station after receiving bail from the charge that he savagely pistol-whipped a middle-aged tailor, before being rearrested on the charge of having shot to death a nineteen-year-old prostitute. It all looks like very sordid street shit, gangster shit. Though he will ultimately be convicted of neither charge (one is withdrawn, the other case is dismissed for lack of witnesses.) He, like Cleaver before him, seeks asylum in Cuba.

In this absence, his Party will undergo yet another metamorphosis, for the times they are a-changing and are no longer there to be seized. Under Elaine Brown it becomes finally an institution with some precedent in American political life: a petty power-brokering, influence peddling, patronage-eating urban political machine. Like the rest of its kind, it is a borderline criminal enterprise, soon to "wither away" like the state under communism.

August 28, 1989. Oakland

In the early-morning hours, not ten blocks away from the center in which Newton and Seales conceived their Party, what the newspapers describe as an unidentified, middle-aged black man is shot and killed by a young crack dealer. Later, the body is identified as that of Huey P. Newton. When apprehended, the shooter says he has never heard of Newton or the Black Panthers. Later reports indicated that Newton's last years had not been happy ones, passed in the misery and degradation of an all-consuming crack habit, poverty, and obscurity. He was, he had often said, prepared to die for the people . . .

Mike Thelwell remembers:

> That first report of the "body of an unidentified black male" was overwhelming in its many sad and precise ironies. These were particularly sharp for me because of an incident in one of my classes the previous year. After class, a student who had never approached me before, asked me to explain a concept which had not been part of the classroom discussion: revolutionary suicide.
>
> I replied that there was no concept to be explained. That the term was an absurdity, more slogan than concept, and that even as slogan it was a sublime self-contradiction, detritus of the political confusion and craziness of the late sixties. Looking both surprised and crestfallen, the young man departed. I watched him leave with mixed feelings. He was black, from a Boston neighborhood trauma-tized by random gun violence among the youth, and he had never before engaged me in any kind of "intellectual" discussion.
>
> But he was back after the next class. This time I explained more fully why the terms were mutually exclusive. Once suicide occurs, I pontificated, we are no longer talking about revolutionaries, but corpses. Corpses do not make revolution, they make fertilizer. A

revolutionary is, by virtue of necessity, inclination, and definition a survivor. Their greatest imperative is to survive: whether prison, torture, battle, exile, or co-optation, but to survive. Any talk of revolutionary suicide is therefore deluded, radical chic nonsense.

The young man looked disappointed. "Prof," he observed quietly, "you haven't read Huey's book, have you?"

"Right. And I'm trying to explain why I don't plan to."

"Well, I wish you would, so we could discuss it."

So, properly chastened, but with considerable resistance, I retrieved my unread copy from the recesses of my basement.

Huey's argument was simplicity itself. And unfortunately for us all, it proceeded over terrain from which we prefer to look away, with his usual grim logic, to a conclusion even grimmer in its implications. It is a discourse of utter hopelessness and desperation, but it is not irrational.

Writing over twenty years ago, Newton described the condition of young black men as endangered. We die, he declared, prematurely at our own hands; by drugs; by inferior health care; by the police and the jails. Or, at a mere leisurely and painful pace, by the attrition of poor educations, stunted prospects and the impoverishment of the spirit. He did not mention homelessness.

Therefore, he reasoned, since the prospect for so many of us is only a short, mean life and a meaningless death, why should we, since not permitted to impose meaning on our lives, not decide to impose at least some meaning on our deaths?

And why not indeed?

Taking arms against the society will be almost certainly suicidal. But that would, at least, not be the random, meaningless, violent deaths visited on so many black men.

(An ugly truth that could not have been more graphically illustrated than by the manner of his death twenty years later, even had it been scripted to that purpose.)

But in these distorted circumstances to elect to "die for the people," although suicidal, would be, in warped contrast, "revolutionary."

Obviously, I thought, this wretchedness did not describe the circumstances of my life. But the situation has grown much worse since Huey wrote this and there must be thousands who would recognize themselves in it. That uncharacteristically insistent young man perhaps? But he, being a college student, must have happier prospects. What was his interest? Hopefully it was only academic. I knew that he had seen too many friends and acquaintances made corpses in his neighborhood streets. And for no acceptable reason.

But we never discussed it. I thought he might come in after the bitter and prophetic ironies of Huey's death. But he never has.

Postscript

The most chilling and saddest stories in Panther Chief of Staff David Hilliard's honest and saddening memoir *A Taste of Glory,* comes not from the history but in the present, a present more awful in its reality and implications than the war stories which preceded it.

The brave old veteran talks about fearing and feeling "humiliated by the kids, the dealers and would-be dealers . . . dressing like millionaire athletes in four-hundred-dollar sports outfits, wearing gold . . . arrogant and violent. Their presence rebukes me. I should be able to talk to them—they are the children of the people the Party organized. Instead, they exhibit only a cool and complete disrespect . . ."

One day the old revolutionary and his family are having a barbecue in the same city park in which he once staged huge rallies. His nephew gets into a petty altercation with another youth, who calls his friends. Suddenly apprehensive, the family rushes to pack up grills, food, blankets. They should have left them and fled.

"Suddenly bullets spray the place . . . the bullets dance for hours it seems, the Uzis popping like firecrackers, the dirt dancing in the open field."

The Chief and his family hug the ground. Then comes an anguished wail. "My baby's been hit" and his eight-year-old niece lies bleeding on the grass.

That should frighten us more than anything the Panthers faced or did. In 1990, the most recent figures available, 4,200 American teenagers were killed by gunfire. That is a number equivalent to the annual rate of American death during the Vietnam War. Half of those dead were Black, though we are not fully 20 percent of the population. Besides that, the 4,200 represents only the fifteen to nineteen age group; the children and young adults are not counted.

This nation, and not only under Reagan, has by heedlessness and neglect, produced a generation more hopeless, lost, abandoned, properly cynical and nihilistic than ever were the Panthers. Except perhaps for a crazed Jackanape or two.

These children standing effectively outside of any stabilizing culture, and more lethally and indiscriminately armed than any previous generation, seem contemptuous of human life, even their own. If ever they look up from this wasteland of self-imposed carnage and conclude that to die for something— anything, even if only revenge—is relative progress, then Newton's principle of revolutionary suicide may make sense to them. Should this happen, this nation may yet look back at the late sixties' with its "confused alarms of conflict and of flight" as a veritable Golden Age of calm and tranquility.

—Ekwueme Michael Thelwell
Pelham, Massachusetts
April 15, 1993

Appendix

The Ten-Point Program

---

1. We want freedom. We want power to determine the destiny of our Black Community.

We believe that black people will not be free until we are able to determine our destiny.

2. We want full employment for our people.

We believe that the federal government is responsible and obligated to give every man employment or a guaranteed income. We believe that if the White American businessmen will not give full employment, then the means of production should be taken from the businessmen and placed in the community so that the people of the community can organize and employ all of its people and give a high standard of living.

3. We want an end to the robbery by the CAPITALIST of our Black Community.

We believe that this racist government has robbed us and

now we are demanding the overdue debt of forty acres and two mules. Forty acres and two mules was promised 100 years ago as restitution for slave labor and mass murder of Black people. We will accept the payment in currency which will be distributed to our many communities. The Germans are now aiding the Jews in Israel for the genocide of the Jewish people. The Germans murdered six million Jews. The American racist has taken part in the slaughter of over fifty million Black people; therefore, we feel that this is a modest demand that we make.

4. We want decent housing fit for shelter of human beings.

We believe that if the White landlords will not give decent housing to our Black community, then the housing and the land should be made into cooperatives so that our community, with government aid, can build and make decent housing for its people.

5. We want education for our people that exposes the true nature of this decadent American society. We want education that teaches us our true history and our role in the present-day society.

We believe in an educational system that will give to our people a knowledge of self. If a man does not have knowledge of himself and his position in society and the world, then he has little chance to relate to anything else.

6. We want all Black men to be exempt from military service.

We believe that Black people should not be forced to fight in the military service to defend a racist government that does not protect us. We will not fight and kill other people of color in the world who, like Black people, are being victimized by the White racist government of America. We will protect ourselves from the force and violence of the racist police and the racist military, by whatever means necessary.

7. We want an immediate end to POLICE BRUTALITY and MURDER of Black people.

We believe we can end police brutality in our Black community by organizing Black self-defense groups that are dedicated to defending our Black community from racist police oppression and brutality. The second Amendment to the Constitution of the United States gives a right to bear arms. We therefore believe that all Black people should arm themselves for self-defense.

8. We want freedom for all Black men held in federal, state, county, and city prisons and jails.

We believe that all Black people should be released from the many jails and prisons because they have not received a fair and impartial trial.

9. We want all Black People when brought to trial to be tried in court by a jury of their peer group or people from their Black communities, as defined by the Constitution of the United States.

We believe that the courts should follow the United States Constitution so that Black people will receive fair trials. The 14th Amendment of the U.S. Constitution gives a man a right to be tried by his peer group. A peer is a person from a similar economic, social, religious, geographical, environmental, historical, and racial background. To do this the court will be forced to select a jury from the Black community from which the Black defendant came. We have been, and are being, tried by all-White juries that have no understanding of the "average reasoning man" of the Black community.

10. We want land, bread, housing, education, clothing, justice, and peace.

When, in the course of human events, it becomes necessary for one people to dissolve the political bands which have connected them with another, and to assume, among the powers of the earth, the separate and equal station to which the laws of nature and nature's God entitle them, a decent respect to the opinions of mankind requires that they should declare the causes which impel them to the separation.

We hold these truths to be self-evident, that all men are created equal; that they are endowed by their Creator with certain unalienable rights; that among these are life, liberty, and the pursuit of happiness. That, to secure these rights, governments are instituted among men, deriving their just powers from the consent of the governed; that, whenever any form of government becomes destructive of these ends, it is the right of the people to alter or to abolish it, and to institute a new government, laying its foundation on such principles, and organizing its powers in such form, as to them shall seem most likely to effect their safety and happiness. Prudence, indeed, will dictate that governments long established should not be changed for light and transient causes; and, accordingly, all experience hath shown that mankind are more disposed to suffer, while evils are sufferable, than to right themselves by abolishing the forms to which they are accustomed. But, when a long train of abuses and usurpations, pursuing invariably the same object, evinces a design to reduce them under absolute despotism, it is their right, it is their duty, to throw off such government, and to provide new guards for their future security.

Index